Cyberbullying

Cyberbullying

Helping Children Navigate Digital
Technology and Social Media

*Stephanie Fredrick, Amanda Nickerson,
Michelle Demaray, and Chunyan Yang*

Copyright © 2025 by John Wiley & Sons, Inc. All rights reserved. All rights reserved, including rights for text and data mining and training of artificial intelligence technologies or similar technologies.

Published by John Wiley & Sons, Inc., Hoboken, New Jersey.

Published simultaneously in Canada.

No part of this publication may be reproduced, stored in a retrieval system, or transmitted in any form or by any means, electronic, mechanical, photocopying, recording, scanning, or otherwise, except as permitted under Section 107 or 108 of the 1976 United States Copyright Act, without either the prior written permission of the Publisher, or authorization through payment of the appropriate per-copy fee to the Copyright Clearance Center, Inc., 222 Rosewood Drive, Danvers, MA 01923, (978) 750-8400, fax (978) 750-4470, or on the web at www.copyright.com. Requests to the Publisher for permission should be addressed to the Permissions Department, John Wiley & Sons, Inc., 111 River Street, Hoboken, NJ 07030, (201) 748-6011, fax (201) 748-6008, or online at http://www.wiley.com/go/permission.

Trademarks: Wiley and the Wiley logo are trademarks or registered trademarks of John Wiley & Sons, Inc. and/or its affiliates in the United States and other countries and may not be used without written permission. All other trademarks are the property of their respective owners. John Wiley & Sons, Inc. is not associated with any product or vendor mentioned in this book.

Limit of Liability/Disclaimer of Warranty: While the publisher and author have used their best efforts in preparing this book, they make no representations or warranties with respect to the accuracy or completeness of the contents of this book and specifically disclaim any implied warranties of merchantability or fitness for a particular purpose. No warranty may be created or extended by sales representatives or written sales materials. The advice and strategies contained herein may not be suitable for your situation. You should consult with a professional where appropriate. Further, readers should be aware that websites listed in this work may have changed or disappeared between when this work was written and when it is read. Neither the publisher nor authors shall be liable for any loss of profit or any other commercial damages, including but not limited to special, incidental, consequential, or other damages.

For general information on our other products and services or for technical support, please contact our Customer Care Department within the United States at (800) 762-2974, outside the United States at (317) 572-3993 or fax (317) 572-4002.

Wiley also publishes its books in a variety of electronic formats. Some content that appears in print may not be available in electronic formats. For more information about Wiley products, visit our website at www.wiley.com.

Library of Congress Control Number: 2024926846

Print ISBN: 9781394276783
ePDF ISBN: 9781394276806
ePub ISBN: 9781394276790

Cover Design: Wiley
Cover Images: © MIA Studio/Shutterstock, © maxim ibragimov/Shutterstock, © Peacefully7/Getty Images

SKY10099165_030125

Contents

Preface *ix*
Acknowledgments *xi*

1 Peer Relationships and Bullying Over the Years *1*
Peer Relationships in Infancy, Toddlerhood, and Early Childhood *2*
Peer Relationships in Middle and Late Childhood *4*
Peer Relationships in Adolescence *5*
Role of Digital Technology in Peer Relationships *8*
Bullying and Cyberbullying *11*
References *15*

2 Digital Media Use: The Early Years *23*
What Is Digital Media and Technology? *24*
Evolution of Digital Media and Technology *24*
Digital Media Use from Infancy to Childhood *28*
Research Methods and Terminology *32*
Effects of Digital Media Use on Child Development *34*
Parent Media Practices and Joint Media Engagement *36*
Summary *39*
References *40*

3 Digital Media Use: The Preteen and Teenage Years *45*
Digital Media Use Among Preteens and Teens *45*
Smartphone Use *48*
Effects of Digital Media Use *49*
Digital Media Use and Youth Mental Health *50*

Digital Media Use and Youth Physical Health 54
Digital Media Use and Youth Academic Performance 56
Benefits of Digital Media Use 58
Summary 59
References 60

4 Cyberbullying and Other Forms of Cyber Aggression 67
Impact of Cyberbullying 73
Why Do Youth Engage in Cyberbullying? 75
Risk and Protective Factors 79
  Risk and Protective Factors for Being Cyberbullied 81
  Risk and Protective Factors for Cyberbullying Others 84
Digital Self-Harm 85
References 88

5 Helping Children Navigate Social and Digital Life 95
Supporting Social-Emotional Competencies and Building Positive Peer Relationships 95
Promoting Safe Media Use 99
Model Responsible Behavior on Social Media 99
Promote Healthy Online Use 100
  Talk About Online Lives 100
  Co-use Media 101
  Engage in Active Mediation 102
  Support Youth to Engage in Bystander Intervention in Online Spaces 104
  Set Limits 105
  Deciding If and When to Give a Child a Smartphone 106
  Setting Rules About Digital Technology Use 107
Monitor Use 109
Resources for Parents and Educators 110
References 112

6 Families Role in Recognizing and Responding to Problematic Online Behaviors 117
Warning Signs 118
Responding to Cyberbullying Involvement 123

Responding to Problematic Social Media Use and Gaming   126
Outside Interventions for Problematic Online Behavior   128
Responding to Digital Self-Harm   130
Summary   130
References   131

7 Schools' Role in Preventing Cyberbullying and Other Forms of Cyber Aggression   135
The Importance of Schools and Family Involvement in Cyberbullying Prevention   136
What Is a Multi-tiered Support System?   137
Social and Emotional Learning and School-wide Digital Citizenship Programs   138
Positive Behavior Intervention Support   147
School-wide and Classroom-wide Mindfulness Programs   150
Restorative Justice Approaches   151
Trauma-Informed Programs   152
Summary   153
References   154

8 School–Family Partnership   159
Communicating with the School   159
Whom Should I Contact at the School If My Child Is Being Cyberbullied?   160
What Information Should I Share?   161
What Should I Expect from the School?   163
The Bullying Is Still Happening: How Can I Best Advocate for My Child?   165
How Can I Work with the School If My Child Is Cyberbullying Others?   167
How Can I Work with the School If My Child Is a Bystander of Cyberbullying?   168
How Educators Can Best Partner with Families?   169
  Engage in Effective Two-Way Communication   169
  Focus on Shared Decision-Making   171
References   174

9 Legal Implications: Problematic Online Behavior and the Law 179
Federal Laws for Harassment *179*
State Laws and School District Policies for Cyberbullying *181*
Civil Law Regarding Cyberbullying *183*
   Davis v. Monroe County Board of Education (1999) 184
   J.S. v. Bethlehem Area School District (2002) 184
   Tinker v. Des Moines Independent School District (1969) 184
When Should School Districts Intervene? *185*
Criminal Cyberbullying Behaviors *186*
  Sexting *187*
    Legal Implications of Sexting *188*
    Responding to Sexting *189*
  Online Predators *190*
Summary *191*
References *192*

10 International Efforts to Address Cyberbullying and Other Forms of Cyber Aggression 195
Global Trends of Cyberbullying *195*
   International Digital Citizenship and Parenting Practices *196*
Laws and Policies on Internet and Device Use Across the Globe *199*
DCE Across the Globe *199*
DCE in Europe *200*
DCE in Asia and the Global South *204*
Summary *209*
References *209*

Subject Index 215

Preface

Raising children and teens is full of joys and challenges – and helping them navigate their worlds of digital technology and social media can be overwhelming for families and other adults. Media headlines tend to focus on the dangers and problems that come with digital technology and social media, which can be hard to balance when it seems like everyone is plugged into a device. What impact does digital media use have on child development? How much use is typical? How can we prevent cyberbullying? When should children get smartphones? How do I work with the school if my child is involved in cyberbullying? These are just some of the questions that we often hear from parents, educators, and others. Our goal with this book is to provide a balanced, research-informed overview of the social aspects of digital technology and cyberbullying for parents and caregivers, as well as other adults working with families and youth (e.g., educators, mental health practitioners). All of us are school psychologists, professors, and parents who have done extensive research on social-emotional development, family and peer relationships, bullying and cyberbullying, and school climate. When the four of us presented our work on cyberbullying at the American Psychological Association annual convention in 2023, Wiley asked if we would be interested in writing a book on this topic. We were excited for the opportunity to provide guidance from our research, as well as from our personal experience. Collectively, we have 10 children (ranging from toddlers to young adults) and have worked with thousands of educators, parents, and youth related to these complex issues! We draw on the research and these experiences to provide guidance on how to teach and promote responsible and safe digital technology/social media so that youth can utilize devices in ways they are meant for – to connect with others, access communities, and be entertained.

In the first part of the book, we provide an overview of peer aggression and bullying behavior. We think this is important to set the stage as there is a lot of overlap between "traditional" forms of bullying (i.e., bullying which occurs in person such as at school) and bullying which occurs online. We then turn our attention to youth engagement in digital technology and social media. We look at the evolution of digital technology over time and how the technological whirlwind of the past three decades has substantially transformed the ways we all live our lives and how we parent. We then focus on cyberbullying and related problematic online behavior, including digital self-harm. We try to answer the question, why do some youth cyberbully others? Chapters 5 and 6 include practical implications for helping youth navigate social and digital life, and how caregivers can recognize and respond to their children's involvement in cyberbullying and related problematic online behavior. Chapters 7 and 8 provide an overview of the school's role in cyberbullying and bullying prevention, and how families can partner with their children's school. Finally, legal implications regarding cyberbullying and international considerations are described in the final two chapters. All implications, guides, and recommendations throughout the book are research-informed. We hope that readers find this information helpful, as it certainly takes a village to raise kids in our digitized world.

Acknowledgments

We would like to express our sincere gratitude to several people who have made this book possible. First and foremost, we would like to thank our families and support networks for their unwavering support of our careers and professional pursuits. This book would not have been possible without their ongoing encouragement, watching kids during evenings and weekends while "mom wrote," and countless number of cooked meals and desserts to keep the research and writing going. It certainly takes a village and we are so appreciative! We also would like to thank our postdoctoral researchers and graduate student team members from the Alberti Center for Bullying Abuse Prevention at University at Buffalo, University of Maryland, and Northern Illinois University: Hannah Rapp, Dylan Harrison, Lucia Sun, Rahnuma E Jannat, Ella Rho, Jingyi Zhang, and Morgan Fellows. Their assistance with gathering research and references, reviewing and editing, and helping to brainstorm scenarios and strategies throughout the book was so helpful. We would also like to thank the thousands of educators, families, and students we have worked with over the years who have taken the time to tell us their stories. Finally, thank you to Wiley, and specifically to Kelly Gomez, for attending our presentation at the American Psychological Association in 2023 and seeing a vision for our collaborative work.

1

Peer Relationships and Bullying Over the Years

Much of this book is focused on cyberbullying and how families, educators, and other adults who care about youth can help them navigate the complex world of digital technology. Before we get into the weeds about the fascinating digital network that connects children and teens with the entire world from the safety of their bedrooms, it is important to look at how youth connect socially with their peers. In this chapter, we look at friendships and other peer relationships, from toddlerhood and kindergarten through the high school years. The importance of these relationships for healthy social and emotional development is highlighted. Challenges and problems within peer relationships are also described, like exclusion, rivalries, jealousy, and in-group/out-group dynamics. We also look at how texting, posting on social media, and online gaming play a role in peer relationships, although much more detail about digital media use is provided in the next two chapters. Different forms of bullying (physical, verbal, relational, and cyberbullying) are introduced, and we explain how bullying is different from other forms of unkindness.

Children learn how to deal with stress from conflict, and how to react to interpersonal hurt, through their experiences in relationships. The very earliest relationships that children have are with their parents. These relationships set the tone for and guide how they may interact with other people in the future. Decades of research have shown that a secure attachment between a child and parent – where the child expects the parent to be there in their time of distress – fulfills needs for love, protection, security, and nurturance, while also providing a model for other close relationships (Ainsworth, 1989; Hazan & Shaver, 1994). The attachment style we develop

Cyberbullying: Helping Children Navigate Digital Technology and Social Media, First Edition. Stephanie Fredrick, et al.
© 2025 John Wiley & Sons, Inc. Published 2025 by John Wiley & Sons, Inc.

based on the parent–child relationship may guide our other relationships later in life. For example, people with secure attachments tend to have honest, close relationships where they express their emotions. People who have developed insecure attachment styles may be clingy or demanding due to fear of abandonment, or they may avoid conflict in relationships. Other insecure attachment styles may include acting in confusing ways (sometimes seeking intimacy and closeness and other times being fearful and distrustful). If you are interested in taking a quick, free test to assess what attachment style may describe you best, see: https://www.psychologytoday.com/us/tests/relationships/relationship-attachment-style-test

As children develop, peer relationships are also important for social and emotional support. Just like healthy relationships with parents, peer relationships also help children to learn and grow in their other-focused skills such as sharing, affection, concern, and responsibility (Hartup, 1989; Pepler & Bierman, 2018). However, like any human relationships, interpersonal hurt and stress can cause unhealthy developments. Researchers tend to study children's peer interactions related to three tendencies (Rubin et al., 2015):

- Moving toward others (for example, prosocial and caring behaviors, such as sharing and helping)
- Moving against others (such as conflict, aggression, and bullying)
- Moving away from others (including avoidance and withdrawal)

Moving toward others can lead to having peers that offer companionship and enjoyment of common interests. All adults living with or working with children should also be aware that peer relationships occur within social networks with different processes such as closeness, norms or values, hierarchies, and power structures (Rubin et al., 2015). We now talk about what children might experience in these relationships across different developmental stages.

Peer Relationships in Infancy, Toddlerhood, and Early Childhood

Children learn through peer interactions from very early on in life. For example, infants and toddlers begin to pay attention to what is of interest to others (also called joint attention), learn to regulate emotions and inhibit impulses, imitate others, develop language skills, and understand cause-and-effect (Hay, 2005). As young children learn to separate from their parents and spend time with other children their age, they learn how to share with others and take turns (Laursen & Hartup, 2002). In the first five years of life, children also develop self-regulation, or the ability to control thoughts, emotions, and behavior, which is important for healthy peer interactions (Ringoot et al., 2022). Examples include being able to wait for a turn on the swing, deal with frustration without a meltdown, or use a quiet voice in a library. Parents are very important in helping children develop these social and emotional skills, and children's social relationships are directly influenced by the relationships they have at home with their parents and siblings (Damon et al., 2008). Showing sensitivity, such as encouraging your child to use their words to express feelings and respecting their needs and interests, leads them to be more self-regulated (Ettekal et al., 2020; Ringoot et al., 2022). Prompting children to pay attention to other children's needs also leads kids to be more likely to share (Laursen & Hartup, 2002).

Dominance and aggression are also common in early childhood, as emotions often feel uncontrollable/overwhelming at this age. Most parents are familiar with the "terrible twos," and the meltdowns that may occur for reasons that may be bewildering to us, such as wanting a hot dog they have already eaten, biting a sibling when they reach for the same toy, and crying and pounding fists on the floor when told they cannot have a shark as a pet. Physically aggressive behaviors, including hitting, pushing, throwing things, pulling hair, and biting, are very common in early childhood, even as early as 6 months of age (Lorber et al., 2019). This aggressive behavior is most likely during toddler years, when they experience strong emotions but do not have the language and self-control to express themselves more effectively (Parlakian, 2016).

Fortunately, as you guide your children to develop the skills to express and manage their emotions, most aggressive behavior decreases, usually between the ages of 3 and 4 (Parlakian, 2016). For example, you might say "I know you are mad but it is not OK to hit" and give them another tool to deal with their anger, such as squeezing a stress ball or taking deep breaths. Then, when the child is calm, give them a chance to rejoin the activity and give them praise. While physical aggression decreases, we also tend to see more relational forms of aggression, such as talking behind others' backs and excluding children from play. Some common examples we see in preschool include saying things like "You can't come to my birthday party" or "We don't want to play with you" (Smith-Bonahue et al., 2015). These behaviors increase from age of 4 to 7, especially among girls (Tremblay, 2022). During this time, continue to encourage caring relationships and help children problem-solve how to better respond to challenging social situations (Smith-Bonahue et al., 2015). For example, saying things like "You got mad that Sophie wasn't doing what you wanted to do," "How do you think she felt when you told her she couldn't play with you and your friends?," and "What else could you say?" helps show that you understand why they might be acting this way and encourages empathy and making other choices.

Peer Relationships in Middle and Late Childhood

By kindergarten and early elementary age, children play with their peers in more complex ways (through sports and games), which helps them to develop communication and negotiation skills (Pepler & Bierman, 2018). It is probably no surprise that children who are cooperative, sociable, and do well in school and sports, tend to be more accepted and less rejected by peers (Rubin et al., 2015). In elementary school, children have a strong need to be accepted and have friends, so children who are rejected or do not have friends are more likely to feel hopeless, withdrawn, and anxious (Ladd, 2006). What is a friend? Researchers define friendship as a voluntary, terminable, nonexclusive relationship that emphasizes equality, reciprocity, and concern for the other as a unique person (Brown, 1981). In other words, we can choose our friends, and children between the ages of 6 and 10 tend to form friendships based on common activities, sharing, and helping (Buhrmester & Furman, 1987).

Being rejected and excluded is common, and managing these experiences is important for healthy social development (Killen et al., 2013). Children who behave aggressively (or are disruptive, threatening, or hurtful) tend to be rejected and excluded by their peers, especially in the younger years (Rubin et al., 2015). On the other hand, children who are withdrawn, shy, and avoidant may be excluded, or left out of groups, or ignored (Rubin et al., 2015). Instead of focusing only on behaviors or characteristics of children who are rejected, it is important for us to realize that people have a natural tendency to categorize others into "in-groups" and "out-groups" (Killen et al., 2013). These categorizations are often related to cultural stereotypes and judgments, as we tend to develop social groups with people who are like us (Damon et al., 2008). Parents generally believe that bullying is related to individual differences such as class, race, sexual orientation, ethnicity, appearance, or ability (Mishna et al., 2020).

As adults, we can guide children in modeling and talking about fairness and equity, values, perspective-taking, and cross-group friendships to create more positive attitudes toward inclusion (Killen et al., 2013). For example, having conversations about things we share in common even with people who look or act different, seeking out diverse experiences and social connections, reading children's books that represent different ethnicities and cultures, and actively trying to recognize and counter our own biases can all help to teach children to be inclusive (Clearinghouse for Military Family Readiness, 2020).

Peer Relationships in Adolescence

As children transition from childhood to adolescence, they tend to shift from relying so much on their parents to spending more time with, trusting, talking with, and supporting their same-aged peers (Laursen & Hartup, 2002; Nickerson & Nagle, 2005). Social acceptance and fitting in becomes very important at this age (DeAngelis, 2023). In upper elementary and middle school, children organize into social groups and cliques, which usually include three to nine people who spend time together and bond over shared activities (Rubin et al., 2015). Interestingly, in early adolescence, friendships are less stable than they were in childhood. This may be because, with all the changes that come with puberty, friendships become more exclusive and may lead to different friend choices (Rubin et al., 2015). Also, teens (especially younger female adolescents) confide more in their friends, which can make the relationships more fragile and prone to betrayal (Benenson & Christakos, 2003). Early adolescence is also when bullying is most common – about 27% of middle schoolers report being bullied while at school compared to about 22% of high schoolers (National Center for Education Statistics, 2022).

Friendships are especially crucial during adolescence, and high-quality friendships have many benefits to social-emotional health.

For example, an increase in friendship quality during adolescence leads to improvements in social competence (Glick & Rose, 2011). Where childhood friendships are often based on common interests and activities, adolescent friendships are more intimate, involving greater concern for other's well-being and a willingness to share private information and discuss sensitive topics (Kobak & Madsen, 2011). Because adolescents are more cognitively developed, have better communication and perspective-taking skills, are more independent, and spend time alone with friends, they are more likely to disclose personal information to friends (Dijkstra & Veenstra, 2011; Rote & Smetana, 2011). Additionally, puberty and sexuality bring about new serious issues requiring intimate conversations, as well as the increased importance of other-sex friendships, and the onset of dating (Furman et al., 1999).

Adolescence is also when male and female friendships have more distinctions. Girls are more likely than boys to disclose to their same-sex friends and to have more positive expectations for the outcomes of disclosing personal feelings (Rose et al., 2012). Despite these positive features of friendships, they can also relate to other potentially problematic outcomes, especially if co-rumination is a part of the friendship (Rubin et al., 2015). Co-rumination, or excessive discussion of problems, can increase feelings of not only closeness, but also depression and anxiety in adolescent girls (Rose et al., 2007). However, co-rumination is less likely to lead to emotional distress for adolescent boys and can even be positive in friendships (Rose et al., 2007). Adolescent girls can experience jealousy when they have to share their close friends with others or when they see a friend succeed in an area where they wish to excel (Parker et al., 2005). Girls with low self-worth are especially likely to become jealous of friends' relationships (Parker et al., 2005). There are also differences in how adolescent girls and boys handle conflicts with friends and siblings. Adolescent boys' conflicts are typically briefer and are more likely to escalate into physical aggression but resolve without explicit effort, whereas girls' conflicts can last longer and sometimes only end when someone formally apologizes (Noakes & Rinaldi, 2006; Raffaelli, 1997).

Perceived popularity also becomes very important at this stage of development (Pouwels et al., 2018). Adolescents are very aware of how they may be seen by others, and they want to be viewed positively (Pouwels et al., 2018). Although popularity used to be thought of as being well-liked, the concept has changed. Children who are tough or dominant, even using aggression to achieve this status, are regarded as "cool" (Rodkin et al., 2006). A shift that takes place as children transition from middle school to high school is that aggression becomes more accepted (Cillessen & Mayeux, 2007). Because not everyone can be at the top of the dominance hierarchy, some adolescents who want to achieve popularity do so through relational aggression (Pouwels et al., 2018). This may involve excluding someone from a clique, telling others to stop talking to someone, spreading rumors, and talking behind someone's back.

In adolescence, hostile and aggressive behaviors targeted toward peers (like bullying and harassment) are strongly associated with having more social status (Faris & Felmlee, 2011; Juvonen & Graham, 2014). In fact, the targets of the bullying may be in the same friend group and may be rivals for high social standing (Faris & Felmlee, 2014). This is reflected in popular media, with movies (e.g., *Mean Girls, Heathers, The Duff*) showing popular students in high school engaging in coercive, mean-spirited tactics to maintain their position in the social hierarchy. Although popularity is something that many adolescents strive for, it is important to realize that it is associated with risks, as they are more likely to engage in aggressive behavior as well as increased alcohol use (Malamut et al., 2021). Parents can help encourage children's self-esteem based on their own accomplishments rather than relying on validation from others, which may be helpful in reducing this kind of mean behavior (Dellasega & Nixon, 2003).

Cliques are also common in adolescence and usually include peers who are similar in achievement, substance use, and behavior (Rubin et al., 2015). Crowds, in contrast, are larger groups that are more reputation-based collectives of those who are seen as similarly stereotyped (e.g., athletes, nerds, gamers; Rubin et al., 2015). Unlike cliques, members of crowds may not necessarily hang out together regularly or engage in shared activities. By late adolescence and in later high school years, these cliques and crowds disintegrate more, as mixed sex groups form and adolescents begin to develop their own personal beliefs and identities (Rubin et al., 2015). Romantic and sexual relationships also emerge in adolescence, although there is a lot of variability (Furman & Rose, 2015) – some are very serious and others do not get involved much at all.

Role of Digital Technology in Peer Relationships

Now that we have discussed the evolving social landscape of youth, let us move on to explore the role that digital technology plays in their relationships. Digital technology – and its constant availability and lack of social cues – has certainly changed how adolescents interact with their peers (Widman et al., 2021). In fact, adolescents communicate with their peers more through digital technology than they do in person (Gomez-Baya et al., 2019). Although much of online behavior mirrors in-person behavior, there are distinct differences in the way online activity may influence an adolescent's development and peer interactions (Nesi et al., 2018).

Some of the features that make online communication appealing to adolescents in terms of presenting oneself and disclosing information are anonymity, asynchronicity, accessibility, and permanence (Nesi et al., 2018; Valkenburg & Peter, 2011). Table 1.1 provides more details of these features, and Chapter 4 discusses how these features sometimes make it easier for individuals to engage in online aggressive behavior or cyberbullying.

Digital technology has particular benefits and risks for many aspects of social development, including identity and intimacy/friendship (Valkenburg & Peter, 2011). Several studies show that online communication (for example, blogging, posting on social media) gives adolescents a sense of mastery and control in what they create and share about themselves, and this use is associated with improved self-esteem (Valkenburg & Peter, 2011). However, 29% of teens report feeling pressure to post content to get positive reactions, and 28% of girls (18% of boys) say social media makes them feel worse about their lives (Vogels & Gelles-Watnick, 2023). Adolescent girls, particularly those struggling with mental health and who are more vulnerable, are more likely to have harmful body images and engage in disordered eating behaviors (Office of the Surgeon General, 2023). This is likely due to comparing themselves to photos and videos (often filtered or altered) on TikTok, Instagram, and Snapchat (Holland & Tiggemann, 2016; Nesi et al., 2023), where it seems that everyone is beautiful, fit, and happy.

With regard to intimacy, "the rich get richer" – in other words, youth with strong social skills and friends can enhance these relationships

Table 1.1 Features of online communication and activity.

Feature	Definition	Outcome
Anonymity	Online communication cannot be attributed to a specific individual	Anonymous online behavior can appear to adolescents as that lacking consequences, leading to impulsive decisions and disinhibited behavior. They may be more willing to disclose personal information and express angry thoughts (often referred to as "keyboard warriors").
Asynchronicity	Lag time between communication (e.g., text messaging, direct messaging) compared to face-to-face communication	Adolescents can edit and adjust their self-presentation in online communication. (It can have a positive effect on self-esteem and allows adolescents to have convenient times to disclose to people of their choosing.)
Accessibility	The ease with which the internet can be used to find, create, or distribute content	Adolescents can seek out like-minded peers online but can also easily interact with unsafe individuals or content.
Permanence	The extent to which content or messages remain accessible following an original interaction or post	Adolescents may put content online without realizing the extent to which their online communication will live on (e.g., even Snapchat and Telegram, two platforms with temporary or "self-destruct" messaging, allow for screenshots). Desire for social connectedness can override caution regarding privacy settings (e.g., posting complaints about others publicly) and can have repercussions for future employment or opportunities.

Source: Adapted from National Academies of Sciences, Engineering, and Medicine (2023); Nesi et al. (2018), and Valkenburg and Peter (2011).

through social media (Valkenburg & Peter, 2011). For adolescents, most close friendships begin in person and are then maintained in both online and in-person settings (Scott et al., 2021). Early adolescents report that digital technology allows them to maintain friendship and intimacy, especially connecting through text messaging to discuss a variety of topics (Mittmann et al., 2022). However, this varies from person to person – another study showed that adolescents who used Instagram frequently experienced the highest levels of closeness with friends, whereas others had less friendship closeness (Pouwels et al., 2021).

Online gaming has also become a popular mainstream activity, particularly for boys, which is a social experience (Mittmann et al., 2022). In fact, 89% of U.S. teens who play video games play with others and 47% have made a friend online because of a video game (Gottfried & Sidoti, 2024). Research has found that support from friends predicts higher levels of active social media use (e.g., posting, liking, commenting; Fredrick et al., 2022). Interacting with existing friends online, particularly through self-disclosure in a safe space, can help improve friendship quality (Valkenburg & Peter, 2011). Most adolescents (80%) also report that social media helps them feel more connected in their friends' lives (Vogels & Gelles-Watnick, 2023).

How are online interactions helpful or harmful for youth who are more socially anxious? Interestingly, some research with young adults (mean age of 19) shows that social anxiety and loneliness do not impede friendship quality where the interactions were primarily online (although they did for in-person friendships; Scott et al., 2021). Some features of the digital environment (asynchronicity, not being visible) may make interactions more gratifying and comfortable for people who are more socially anxious (Scott et al., 2021). Youth with social anxiety, depression, and loneliness may also find communication on social media beneficial because it allows for greater control and practice of social interactions (Chassiakos et al., 2016). Although children with social anxiety may like the ease offered by online interaction, they are also more at risk of being impacted by negative aspects of social media, including bullying, drama, and feeling left out (Nesi et al., 2023). It is problematic for online relationships to completely replace face-to-face interactions – the ideal is for them to complement each other (Scott et al., 2021).

Digital media also creates a unique environment for adolescents to explore their sexual identities (Valkenburg & Peter, 2011; Widman et al., 2021).

Social media can allow LGBTQ+ adolescents access to peers and role models within their community who can provide emotional support and health information (Craig et al., 2021). The anonymity and the lack of physical contact can also make it a safer environment in some ways, although, of course, there are risks as well. In a study of high school students, 90% reported engaging in at least one digital sexual behavior in the previous year, with approximately 72% receiving or sending a sexually explicit message (sext), 62% using social media to flirt or begin a relationship, and 57% looking at pornography online (Widman et al., 2021). Despite this frequent use, less than one-quarter of youth said that they talked to their parents about these issues (Widman et al., 2021).

Of particular concern with regard to digital technology and peer relationships is the focus of this book – cyberbullying. Higher levels of digital technology use relate to cyberbullying (Fredrick et al., in press; Marciano et al., 2020), which is most likely to occur on social media and in online gaming platforms (Chang et al., 2015; Hamm et al., 2015). We now turn to the problems of bullying and cyberbullying.

Bullying and Cyberbullying

Bullying is a topic that has received much attention – it is rare to find a parent who is not concerned that their child may be bullied. Although bullying has been studied in other countries for centuries (see Allanson et al., 2015), it did not become an urgent issue in the United States until the 1999 Columbine school shooting (Cohen & Brooks, 2014). This event caused widespread outrage, concern, and debates about bullying, school violence, and mental health as the perpetrators reportedly suffered from bullying and peer rejection (Koo, 2007). This national attention led school bullying to be viewed as a public health concern, resulting in state laws mandating schools to prevent and address this problem (Nickerson et al., 2013; see Chapter 9 for more information on legislation). Cyberbullying became a mainstream focus after online harassment was connected to multiple teen suicides (Donegan, 2012). One of the most notable was the 2006 suicide of Megan Meier, a 13-year-old from Missouri, whose former friend created a fake account (impersonating a boy) on social media to get information from Megan to later humiliate her by sending increasingly hurtful messages (Pokin, 2007).

These high-profile and tragic events that have been tied to bullying may help explain why the term is so emotionally laden. We now know how serious bullying can be, yet it is often misused to describe other interpersonal difficulties, such as conflict, fighting, and even people acting in mean ways (Englander, 2017). As Elizabeth Englander (2017), founder of the Massachusetts Aggression Reduction Center, cautions, calling everything bullying can take away children's responsibility to navigate some challenging interpersonal situations and can also take away from the harm and distress that victims or targets of bullying experience.

So, how do we know what bullying is? Bullying is considered to have three distinguishing features (Gladden et al., 2014; Olweus, 1993):

- unwanted or intentional aggressive behavior that can inflict harm
- targeted toward someone in a vulnerable position because the person or people doing it are abusing their power (e.g., mental or physical capabilities and popularity)
- behavior is likely to be repeated or ongoing

These three aspects of bullying (unwanted aggression, imbalance of power where the person targeted has difficulty defending, and repeated over time) make it different from other peer problems such as fighting, conflict, and drama. As mentioned earlier in this chapter, social status is very important within peer groups and in school settings. Bullying is a way that people seek out those who may be vulnerable, or who are different, or have fewer friends or lower social status, to exert power over (Bagwell & Schmidt, 2011; Evans & Smokowski, 2016).

Bullying can take many different forms, including physical, verbal, relational (or social/indirect), and cyberbullying. Table 1.2 provides examples of behaviors for each of these forms. Cyberbullying is considered a form of bullying, or a means by which bullying occurs. As discussed more in Chapter 4, however, the three components of bullying can look different in the context of cyberbullying, which can make this challenging to identify and address.

There is no question that it can be challenging for children, parents, teachers, and others to determine what behavior is bullying and what may be other problematic social interactions. It is important to try to do this so that we can respond in ways that are most appropriate and helpful. To make this more concrete, let's consider a few examples of

Table 1.2 Forms of bullying.

Form	Example behaviors
Physical	Hitting, kicking, tripping, pushing, damaging property or possessions
Verbal	Derogatory name-calling, taunting, threats, inappropriate sexual comments
Relational (also called social or indirect)	Excluding someone on purpose, spreading rumors, embarrassing someone publicly, ganging up (telling people not to be friends with someone), manipulating ("do this and I'll like you more")
Cyberbullying	Sending or posting negative, false, or harmful information about someone through digital devices; sharing private and embarrassing information or photos about someone online

Source: Adapted from Stopbullying.gov (2023).

situations and whether they would be considered bullying or other issues, and why.

- Charlie and his friends live near Alex. Sometimes when Charlie and his friends walk past Alex, they ignore him. Other days, they make fun of him and say that he has no friends. Alex leaves home extra early so he does not have to run into them on the way to school.

  This is an example of bullying that is verbal and relational. Charlie and his friends are engaging in unwanted aggression by ignoring, making fun of, and taunting Alex. Because a group of students is taunting an individual, it creates an imbalance of power that leaves Alex vulnerable and makes it harder to defend himself. In addition, the behaviors are repeated over time.

- Tim and Joe are friends but are competitive with each other during gym class. Last week, when Tim did not pass Joe the basketball, Joe pushed Tim, and Tim then punched Joe.

  Despite the concerning nature of this scenario, it does not meet the criteria for bullying. It is a single incident of physical aggression between two friends of relatively equal power.

- Sumaya recently moved to the United States and is still learning English. Other students say she is stupid, ignore her, and deliberately leave her out of group activities. This has been going on all year.

This is an example of both verbal and relational bullying, as there is mean name-calling as well as intentional exclusion. There is a power imbalance because Sumaya is new to the school and does not yet speak English fluently, and there is a group of students exploiting this. The bullying has been ongoing throughout the school year.

- Selena finds out her friend Jessica talked about her behind her back to another friend, and this makes her very upset. After speaking with her about it, Jessica stops.

While this example may share some similarities with other instances of bullying, it is missing a few key characteristics. There is no known power imbalance between Selena and Jessica. The talking behind her back happened once and Jessica stops when Selena asks her to. If the behavior was repeated, continuing after being asked to stop, this could escalate to bullying.

- Some girls create an anonymous Instagram account and post unflattering pictures of Sarah, along with lies about her having sexually transmitted infections.

This is an example of cyberbullying, as the perpetrators in this example are posting cruel rumors and gossip about Sarah. The harmful actions are clearly intentional and willful.

Clearly, there are some nuances in deciding what behaviors are bullying or cyberbullying behavior versus other problematic interpersonal interactions. As parents and educators, we want to help guide our children in the best way possible through these issues, but our responses will be different depending on the situation. For example, if a child and their friend have a fight or conflict, we may help the child see how their behavior contributed to the conflict and problem-solve with them a way to repair the harm, such as through an apology, talking it over, taking some space and distance, or other strategies. If the child is being bullied, thus in a vulnerable position where someone has abused their power to hurt them, we would not ask what they did to contribute to the situation and/or encourage them to repair harm. We would still problem-solve how to best handle the situation, but we would not put the child in that vulnerable position and instead advocate that they get the support and resources needed to be free from this harm and to start the healing process. Later chapters in this book will describe in detail how families and schools can prevent and respond to cyberbullying, but first, we focus on children's use of digital media.

References

Ainsworth, M. D. S. (1989). Attachments beyond infancy. *American Psychologist*, 44(4), 709–716. https://doi.org/10.1037/0003-066X.44.4.709.

Allanson, P. B., Lester, R. R., & Notar, C. E. (2015). A history of bullying. *International Journal of Education and Social Science*, 2(12), 31–36. https://ijessnet.com/wp-content/uploads/2022/10/5-16.pdf.

Bagwell, C. L., & Schmidt, M. E. (2011). *Friendships in childhood and adolescence*. New York: Guilford Press.

Benenson, J. F., & Christakos, A. (2003). The greater fragility of females' versus males' closest same-sex friendships. *Child Development*, 74(4), 1123–1129. https://doi.org/10.1111/1467-8624.00596.

Brown, B. B. (1981). A life-span approach to friendship: Age-related dimensions of an ageless relationship. *Research in the Interweave of Social Roles*, 2, 23–50. https://psycnet.apa.org/record/1982-30138-001.

Buhrmester, D., & Furman, W. (1987). The development of companionship and intimacy. *Child Development*, 58(4), 1101–1113. https://www.jstor.org/stable/1130550.

Chang, F. C., Chiu, C. H., Miao, N. F., Chen, P. H., Lee, C. M., Huang, T. F., & Pan, Y. C. (2015). Online gaming and risks predict cyberbullying perpetration and victimization in adolescents. *International Journal of Public Health*, 60(2), 257–266. https://doi.org/10.1007/s00038-014-0643-x.

Chassiakos, Y. L. R., Radesky, J., Christakis, D., Moreno, M. A., & Cross, C. (2016). Children and adolescents and digital media. *Pediatrics*, 138(5), e20162593. https://doi.org/10.1542/peds.2016-2593.

Cillessen, A. H. N., & Mayeux, L. (2007). Expectations and perceptions at school transitions: The role of peer status and aggression. *Journal of School Psychology*, 45(5), 567–586. http://dx.doi.org/10.1016/j.jsp.2007.05.004.

Clearinghouse for Military Family Readiness. (2020, August 7). *Teaching children about respecting differences*. Pennsylvania State University. https://thrive.psu.edu/blog/teaching-children-about-respecting-differences/.

Cohen, J., & Brooks, R. (2014). *Confronting school bullying: Kids, culture, and the making of a social problem*. Lynne Rienner.

Craig, S. L., Eaton, A. D., McInroy, L. B., Leung, V. W. Y., & Krishnan, S. (2021). Can social media participation enhance LGBTQ+ youth well-being? Development of the social media benefits scale. *Social Media + Society*, 7(1), 2056305121988931. https://doi.org/10.1177/2056305121988931.

Damon, W., Lerner, R. M., Kuhn, D., Siegler, R. S., & Eisenberg, N. (2008). *Child and adolescent development: An advanced course*. John Wiley & Sons.

DeAngelis, T. (2023, January 13). *How to help kids navigate friendships and peer relationships*. American Psychological Association. https://www.apa.org/topics/parenting/navigating-friendships.

Dellasega, C., & Nixon, C. (2003). *Girl wars: 12 strategies that will end female bullying*. Simon & Schuster.

Dijkstra, J. K., & Veenstra, R. (2011). Peer relations. In B. Brown & M. Prinstein (Eds.), *Encyclopedia of adolescence* (2nd ed., pp. 255–259). Academic Press.

Donegan, R. (2012). Bullying and cyberbullying: History, statistics, law, prevention and analysis. *The Elon Journal*, *3*(1), 33–42. https://www.academia.edu/download/52286760/2012_DoneganRichard_Bullying-and-Cyberbullying_Articulo.pdf.

Englander, E. K. (2017). Understanding bullying behavior: What educators should know and can do. *American Educator*, *40*(4), 24. https://eric.ed.gov/?id=EJ1123847.

Englander, E., Donnerstein, E., Kowalski, R., Lin, C. A., & Parti, K. (2017). Defining cyberbullying. *Pediatrics*, *140*(Supplement 2), S148–S151. https://doi.org/10.1542/peds.2016-1758u.

Ettekal, I., Eiden, R., Nickerson, A. B., Molnar, D. S., & Schuetze, P. (2020). Developmental cascades to children's conduct problems: The role of socioeconomic adversity, maternal sensitivity, depression and substance use, and children's conscience. *Development and Psychopathology*, *32*(1), 85–103. http://doi.org/10.1017/S095457941800144X.

Evans, C. B. R., & Smokowski, P. R. (2016). Theoretical explanations for bullying in school: How ecological processes propagate perpetration and victimization. *Child and Adolescent Social Work Journal*, *33*, 365–375. http://doi.org/10.1007/s10560-015-0432-2.

Faris, R., & Felmlee, D. (2011). Status struggles: Network centrality and gender segregation in same-and cross-gender aggression. *American Sociological Review*, *76*(1), 48–73. http://doi.org/10.1177/0003122410396196.

Faris, R., & Felmlee, D. (2014). Casualties of social combat: School networks of peer victimization and their consequences. *American Sociological Review*, *79*(2), 228–257. http://doi.org/10.1177/0003122414524573.

Fredrick, S. S., Ettekal, I., Domoff, S., & Nickerson, A. B. (2024). Patterns of child and adolescent digital media use: Associations with school support, engagement, and cyber victimization. *Psychology of Popular Media.* Advance online publication. https://doi.org/10.1037/ppm0000570.

Fredrick, S., Nickerson, A. B., & Livingston, J. (2022). Adolescent social media use: Pitfalls and promises in relation to cybervictimization, friend support, and depression. *Journal of Youth and Adolescence, 51,* 361–376. https://doi.org/10.1007/s10964-021-01561-6.

Furman, W., Brown, B., & Feiring, C. (Eds.). (1999). *Contemporary perspectives on adolescent romantic relationships.* New York: Cambridge University Press.

Furman, W., & Rose, A. J. (2015). Friendships, romantic relationships, and peer relationships. In M. E. Lamb & R. M. Lerner (Eds.), *Handbook of child psychology and developmental science: Socioemotional processes* (7th ed., pp. 932–974). John Wiley & Sons, Inc. https://doi.org/10.1002/9781118963418.childpsy322.

Gladden, R. M., Vivolo-Kantor, A. M., Hamburger, M. E., & Lumpkin, C. D. (2014). *Bullying surveillance among youth: Uniform definitions for public health and recommended data elements, version 1.0.* Atlanta, GA: National Center for Injury Prevention and Control, Centers for Disease Control and Prevention and U.S. Department of Education.

Glick, G. C., & Rose, A. J. (2011). Prospective associations between friendship adjustment and social strategies: Friendship as a context for building social skills. *Developmental Psychology, 47*(4), 1117. https://doi.org/10.1037/a0023277.

Gomez-Baya, D., Rubio-Gonzalez, A., & Gaspar de Matos, M. (2019). Online communication, peer relationships and school victimisation: A one-year longitudinal study during middle adolescence. *International Journal of Adolescence and Youth, 24*(2), 199–211. https://doi.org/10.1080/02673843.2018.1509793.

Gottfried, J., & Sidoti, O. (2024). *Teens and video games today.* Pew Research Center. https://www.pewresearch.org/internet/2024/05/09/teens-and-video-games-today/.

Hamm, M. P., Newton, A. S., Chisholm, A., Shulhan, J., Milne, A., Sundar, P., Ennis, H., Scott, S., & Hartling, L. (2015). Prevalence and effect of cyberbullying on children and young people: A scoping review of social media studies. *JAMA Pediatrics, 169*(8), 770–777. https://doi.org/10.1001/jamapediatrics.2015.0944.

Hartup, W. W. (1989). Social relationships and their developmental significance. *American Psychologist, 44*(2), 120–126. https://doi.org/10.1037/0003-066X.44.2.120.

Hay, D. F. (2005). Early peer relations and their impact on children's development. *Encyclopedia on Early Childhood Development*, *1*(1), 1–6. www.child-encyclopedia.com/pdf/expert/peer-relations/according-experts/early-peer-relations-and-their-impact-childrens-development.

Hazan, C., & Shaver, P. R. (1994). Attachment as an organizational framework for research on close relationships. *Psychological Inquiry*, *5*(1), 1–22. https://doi.org/10.1207/s15327965pli0501_1.

Holland, G., & Tiggemann, M. (2016). A systematic review of the impact of the use of social networking sites on body image and disordered eating outcomes. *Body Image*, *17*, 100–110. https://doi.org/10.1016/j.bodyim.2016.02.008.

Juvonen, J., & Graham, S. (2014). Bullying in schools: The power of bullies and the plight of victims. *The Annual Review of Psychology*, *65*, 159–185. http://doi.org/10.1146/annurev-psych-010213-115030.

Killen, M., Mulvey, K. L., & Hitti, A. (2013). Social exclusion in childhood: A developmental intergroup perspective. *Child Development*, *84*(3), 772–790. https://doi.org/10.1111/cdev.12012.

Kobak R., & Madsen, S. (2011). Attachment. In B. Brown & M. Prinstein (Eds.), *Encyclopedia of adolescence* (Vol. 2, pp. 18–24). New York: Academic Press.

Koo, H. (2007). A time line of the evolution of school bullying in differing social contexts. *Asia Pacific Education Review*, *8*(1), 107–116. https://files.eric.ed.gov/fulltext/EJ768971.pdf.

Ladd, G. W. (2006). Peer rejection, aggressive or withdrawn behavior, and psychological maladjustment from ages 5 to 12: An examination of four predictive models. *Child Development*, *77*(4), 822–846. https://doi.org/10.1111/j.1467-8624.2006.00905.x.

Laursen, B., & Hartup, W. W. (2002). The origins of reciprocity and social exchange in friendships. *New Directions in Child and Adolescent Development*, *95*, 27–40. https://doi.org/10.1002/cd.35.

Lorber, M. F., Del Vecchio, T., Slep, A. M., & Scholer, S. J. (2019). Normative trends in physically aggressive behavior: Age-aggression curves from 6 to 24 months. *The Journal of Pediatrics*, *206*, 197–203. https://doi.org/10.1016/j.jpeds.2018.10.025.

Malamut, S. T., Van den Berg, Y. H., Lansu, T. A., & Cillessen, A. H. (2021). Bidirectional associations between popularity, popularity goal, and aggression, alcohol use and prosocial behaviors in adolescence: A 3-year prospective longitudinal study. *Journal of Youth and Adolescence*, *50*, 298–313. http://doi.org/10.1007/s10964-020-01308-9.

Marciano, L., Schulz, P. J., & Camerini, A. (2020). Cyberbullying perpetration and victimization in youth: A meta-analysis of longitudinal studies. *Journal of Computer-Mediated Communication, 25*(2), 163–181. https://doi.org/10.1093/jcmc/zmz031.

Mishna, F., Sanders, J. E., McNeil, S., Fearing, G., & Kalenteridis, K. (2020). "If somebody is different": A critical analysis of parent, teacher and student perspectives on bullying and cyberbullying. *Children and Youth Services Review, 118*, 105366. https://doi.org/10.1016/j.childyouth.2020.105366.

Mittmann, G., Woodcock, K., Dörfler, S., Krammer, I., Pollak, I., & Schrank, B. (2022). "TikTOK is my life and snapchat is my ventricle": A mixed-methods study on the role of online communication tools for friendships in early adolescents. *The Journal of Early Adolescence, 42*(2), 172–203. https://doi.org/10.1177/02724316211020.

National Academies of Sciences, Engineering, and Medicine. (2023). *Social media and adolescent health*. Washington, DC: The National Academies Press. https://doi.org/10.17226/27396.

National Center for Education Statistics. (2022). *Measuring student safety: New data on bullying rates in school*. Institute for Education Statistics. https://nces.ed.gov/blogs/nces/post/measuring-student-safety-new-data-on-bullying-rates-at-school.

Nesi, J., Choukas-Bradley, S., & Prinstein, M. J. (2018). Transformation of adolescent peer relations in the social media context: Part 1–A theoretical framework and application to dyadic peer relationships. *Clinical Child and Family Psychology Review, 21*, 267–294. https://doi.org/10.1007/s10567-018-0261-x.

Nesi, J., Mann, S., & Robb, M. B. (2023). *Teens and mental health: How girls really feel about social media*. San Francisco, CA: Common Sense Media.

Nickerson, A. B., Cornell, D. G., Smith, D., & Furlong, M. (2013). School antibullying efforts: Advice for policymakers. *Journal of School Violence, 12*(3), 268–282. http://dx.doi.org/10.1080/15388220.2013.787366.

Nickerson, A. B., & Nagle, R. J. (2005). Parent and peer attachment in late childhood and early adolescence. *Journal of Early Adolescence, 25*(2), 223–249. https://doi.org/10.1177/0272431604274174.

Noakes, M. A., & Rinaldi, C. M. (2006). Age and gender differences in peer conflict. *Journal of Youth and Adolescence, 35*, 881–891. https://doi.org/10.1007/s10964-006-9088-8.

Office of the Surgeon General. (2023). *Social media and youth mental health: The U.S. Surgeon General's Advisory*. U.S. Department of Health and Human Services. https://www.hhs.gov/sites/default/files/sg-youth-mental-health-social-media-advisory.pdf.

Olweus, D. (1993). *Bullying at school: What we know and what we can do*. Blackwell Publishing.

Parker, J. G., Low, C. M., Walker, A. R., & Gamm, B. K. (2005). Friendship jealousy in young adolescents: Individual differences and links to sex, self-esteem, aggression, and social adjustment. *Developmental Psychology, 41*(1), 235. https://doi.org/10.1037/0012-1649.41.1.235.

Parlakian, R. (2016). *Aggressive behavior in toddlers*. Zero to Three. https://www.zerotothree.org/resource/aggressive-behavior-in-toddlers/.

Pepler, D. J., & Bierman, K. L. (2018). *With a little help from my friends: The importance of peer relationships for social-emotional development*. Edna Bennett Pierce Prevention Research Center, Pennsylvania State University. https://prevention.psu.edu/wp-content/uploads/2022/05/rwjf450248-PeerRelationships-1.pdf.

Pokin, S. (2007). *Megan's story*. Megan Meier Foundation. https://www.meganmeierfoundation.org/megans-story.

Pouwels, J. L., Lansu, T. A., & Cillessen, A. H. (2018). A developmental perspective on popularity and the group process of bullying. *Aggression and Violent Behavior, 43*, 64–70. https://doi.org/10.1016/j.avb.2018.10.003.

Pouwels, J. L., Valkenburg, P. M., Beyens, I., van Driel, I. I., & Keijsers, L. (2021). Social media use and friendship closeness in adolescents' daily lives: An experience sampling study. *Developmental Psychology, 57*(2), 309. https://doi.org/10.1037/dev0001148.

Raffaelli, M. (1997). Young adolescents' conflicts with siblings and friends. *Journal of Youth and Adolescence, 26*(5), 539–558. https://doi.org/10.1023/A:1024529921987.

Ringoot, A. P., Jansen, P. W., Kok, R., van IJzendoorn, M. H., Verlinden, M., Verhulst, F. C., Bakermans-Kranenburg, M., & Tiemeier, H. (2022). Parenting, young children's behavioral self-regulation and the quality of their peer relationships. *Social Development, 31*(3), 715–732. https://doi.org/10.1111/sode.12573.

Rodkin, P. C., Farmer, T. W., Pearl, R., & Acker, R. V. (2006). They're cool: Social status and peer group supports for aggressive boys and girls. *Social Development, 15*(2), 175–204. https://www.doi.org/10.1046/j.1467-9507.2006.00336.x.

Rose, A. J., Carlson, W., & Waller, E. M. (2007). Prospective associations of co-rumination with friendship and emotional adjustment: Considering the socioemotional trade-offs of co-rumination. *Developmental Psychology, 43*(4), 1019–1031. http://doi.org/10.1037/0012-1649.43.4.1019.

Rose, A. J., Schwartz-Mette, R. A., Smith, R. L., Asher, S. R., Swenson, L. P., Carlson, W., & Waller, E. M. (2012). How girls and boys expect disclosure about problems will make them feel: Implications for friendships. *Child Development, 83*(3), 844–863. http://doi.org/10.1111/j.1467-8624.2012.01734.x.

Rote, W. M., & Smetana, J. G. (2011). Social cognition. In B. Brown & M. Prinstein (Eds.), *Encyclopedia of adolescence* (Vol. 1, pp. 333–341). New York: Academic Press.

Rubin, K. H., Bukowski, W. M., & Bowker, J. C. (2015). Children in peer groups. In M. H. Bornstein, T. Leventhal, & R. M. Lerner (Eds.), *Handbook of child psychology and developmental science: Ecological settings and processes* (7th ed., pp. 175–222). John Wiley & Sons, Inc.

Scott, R. A., Stuart, J., & Barber, B. L. (2021). Contemporary friendships and social vulnerability among youth: Understanding the role of online and offline contexts of interaction in friendship quality. *Journal of Social and Personal Relationships, 38*(12), 3451–3471. https://doi.org/10.1177/02654075211029384.

Smith-Bonahue, T., Smith-Adcock, S., & Ehrentraut, J. H. (2015). "I won't be your friend if you don't!": Preventing and responding to relational aggression in preschool classrooms. *Young Children, 70*(1), 76. https://www.naeyc.org/resources/pubs/yc/nov2015/preventing-relational-aggression.

Stopbullying.gov. (2023). *What is bullying*. https://www.stopbullying.gov/bullying/what-is-bullying.

Tremblay, R. E. (2022). The development and prevention of physical aggression. *Encyclopedia on early childhood development* (3rd ed., revised). https://www.child-encyclopedia.com/aggression/according-experts/development-and-prevention-physical-aggression.

Valkenburg, P. M., & Peter, J. (2011). Online communication among adolescents: An integrated model of its attraction, opportunities, and risks. *Journal of Adolescent Health, 48*(2), 121–127. https://doi.org/10.1016/j.jadohealth.2010.08.020.

Vogels, E. A., & Gelles-Watnick, R. (2023, April 24). *Teens and social media: Key findings from Pew Research Center surveys*. Pew Research Center.

https://www.pewresearch.org/short-reads/2023/04/24/teens-and-social-media-key-findings-from-pew-research-center-surveys/.

Widman, L., Javidi, H., Maheux, A. J., Evans, R., Nesi, J., & Choukas-Bradley, S. (2021). Sexual communication in the digital age: Adolescent sexual communication with parents and friends about sexting, pornography, and starting relationships online. *Sexuality & Culture, 25*(6), 2092–2109. https://doi.org/10.1007/s12119-021-09866-1.

2

Digital Media Use: The Early Years

Have you ever paused to reflect on the technological whirlwind of the past 30 years? It is quite impressive if you stop to consider the evolution of digital technology and notice how much our lives have changed over the past three decades due to technology:

- The creation of pocket-sized powerhouses such as the iPod evolving into smartphones and smart watches
- Social networking sites such as Facebook and Instagram transforming how we connect and socialize
- The revolution of video games from consoles in the living room to massively multiplayer online games
- Chalkboards and textbooks being swapped for smart boards and Chrome books in the classroom

This chapter provides an overview of digital media and technology, including what it is, how it has evolved, and how we have changed our perceptions over time. We then describe digital media use during childhood, specifically from infancy through age 8 (see Chapter 3 for digital media use during preteen and teenage years). We examine how often children use digital media, their interests in different types of digital media, and how trends have changed over time. An overview of research on the effects of digital media use is provided, with a focus on how screen media use is associated with child development, including cognitive development (e.g., language, memory), social-emotional skills (e.g., behavior problems, social skills), and physical health. First, let us dive into what digital media and technology is.

Cyberbullying: Helping Children Navigate Digital Technology and Social Media,
First Edition. Stephanie Fredrick, et al.
© 2025 John Wiley & Sons, Inc. Published 2025 by John Wiley & Sons, Inc.

What Is Digital Media and Technology?

What do we mean when we say, "digital media" or "digital technology"? The term "media" comes from the Latin word *Medias,* which means "the middle" or "medium." In other words, media is a means of communication that provides information or entertainment from one person to another (or to large groups of people). Within the media industry, media is thought of as *traditional* and *digital* (or new) forms of media (McCormack, 2022). Traditional forms of media do not require the use of the internet and include print (newspapers, books, magazines, billboards, etc.) and broadcast (television, film, and radio) media; these forms of media have been around for decades. Digital media, however, uses the internet and electronic devices and includes any media that is transmitted as digital data, such as streaming videos, reading online articles, going on social networking sites, emailing, texting, or playing video games. Digital media can also include traditional media, which has been digitized (e.g., electronic books or magazines). Digital media is often more interactive (e.g., allowing users to post or comment, click on links), while traditional media only allows for one-way communication and sometimes at a certain time (e.g., watching the news or TV show at the scheduled airtime). Digital technology can be thought of as tools that "contain" the media (i.e., information and/or entertainment; Irwin, 2016).

For this book, we define digital media as the use of any electronic/digital tools, including a television, computer or laptop, cell phone or smartphone, tablet, gaming console, and wearable technology (e.g., glasses, watches), to communicate, consume, or create content/information and/or be entertained. Throughout the book, we will refer to different types of digital media, such as social media, gaming, watching television and videos, and others. We have provided definitions of each of these types of digital media in Table 2.1.

Evolution of Digital Media and Technology

When did digital media become ubiquitous in our lives? To better understand how digital media impacts youth today, let us first explore the evolution of digital media and technology, especially over the past few decades. The rise of the internet and ownership of personal computers

Evolution of Digital Media and Technology | 25

Table 2.1 Definitions of digital media.

Type of digital media	Definition	Examples
E-reading	Reading on a mobile device, including an e-reader, mobile phone, or tablet.	Reading a book on Kindle or Kindle app
Online videos	Watching videos, typically on mobile devices (e.g., smartphone, tablet).	YouTube, TikTok
Mobile media	Media that is consumed through mobile devices (e.g., smartphones, tablets, smart watches), which can connect to the internet and download apps.	Watching a YouTube video on an iPhone, reading a text from a smart watch
Social media	Sites or platforms that allow users to interact with others through the sharing of content (photos and videos), liking or responding to other people's content (liking it and commenting), or through direct messaging (DM). Social media platforms can be accessed with any device with internet access (e.g., smartphone, computer, and tablet).	Facebook, Snapchat, Instagram, Discord, Reddit, TikTok, Twitter, WhatsApp
Screen media	Any activity that requires looking at a visual screen. It does not include listening to music, podcasts, or audiobooks.	Watching television or videos, playing video games, being on social media, texting, reading on a device, using virtual reality, completing work on a laptop
Television	Content watched on a TV set, which includes "live tv," or through streaming platforms, such as Netflix.	Any show (e.g., Bluey) that is watched on a TV set
Video games	Playing any game on a video game console (e.g., Xbox, PlayStation, Switch), a handheld console (e.g., Gameboy, Nintendo DS), a computer, or a mobile device (e.g., smartphone, tablet). This can include both single-player games (e.g., Astro's Playroom, Legend of Zelda) or multiplayer games (e.g., League of Legends). Many video games allow for either single-player or multiplayer modes.	Roblox, Fortnite, League of Legends

Source: Definitions adapted from *The Common Sense Census: Media Use by Kids Age Zero To Eight*, by Rideout and Robb (2020).

began in the 1990s (the internet became publicly available in 1990) and by the year 2000, 50% of U.S. households had a personal computer and access to the internet from their own homes (Ortiz-Ospina, 2019). However, this was often limited to a single room in their house, such as their living room or a computer room. This "post-Internet Era" occurred from about 1990 to 2006, when teens were able to instant message (IM) with their friends, read and contribute to message boards, and (gasp!) talk to strangers in chat rooms.

Video games became common in households in the mid- to late-1980s and 1990s. Nintendo came out with home consoles in 1985 and Game Boy, founded in 1989, was the first mainstream handheld console (SEGA also released the Genesis system in 1989 and became rivals with Nintendo). A rise in fighter games throughout the 1990s (e.g., Street Fighter, Mortal Kombat) and parent concerns regarding youth exposure to violent content led to the creation of the Entertainment Software Rating Board (rating games "E" for everyone or "M" for mature). In 1994, games began to come pre-installed on cell phones (i.e., Snake, Tetris). Gaming consoles and playing games on computers continued to rise in popularity among youth throughout the next decade (1995–2005), and by 2009 many young people were playing online games on social media platforms (e.g., Farmville on Facebook) and smartphones (Joseph, 2023; The Strong National Museum of Play, n.d.). Today, most youth play video games on a gaming console or a smartphone (Gottfried & Sidoti, 2024).

Cell phones became popular in the 1990s, as they became smaller (the first cell phone invented in 1973 was over 2 pounds!) and more affordable (McNamee & Yu, 2023). By 2004, 45% of teens (ages 12 to 17) owned a cell phone, with most teens (59%) getting their first cell phone when they turned 16 (Lenhart, 2009). Cell phones at this time typically had basic plans with limited minutes and an extra cost (e.g., 10 cents) to text (27% of teens used text messaging daily in 2006; Lenhart, 2009). By 2008 (in just four years!), over half (51%) of 12-year-olds owned a cell phone (see Chapter 3 for more on smartphone ownership and usage among teens). Apple launched the iPhone in 2007, and the first Android smartphone became available in 2008. This marked the beginning of the mobile era and changed the media landscape substantially for children, adolescents, and adults.

In the 1990s, blogs became a popular early form of social networking. MySpace, initially launched in 2003, was one of the first online social networking sites and quickly rose in popularity – in 2006, it became the most visited website in the United States (even surpassing Google). MySpace was the first social media platform to become popular among youth. Many preteens and teenagers used this platform when it was popular (between 2003 and 2009), and parents began to get concerned about the amount of time youth were spending on their computers to talk to their friends (Neary, 2006). Other, more user-friendly, social networking sites swiftly surpassed MySpace in popularity, including Facebook (founded in 2004) and Twitter (founded in 2006). Over the next two decades, we saw an explosion of social media platforms, including Instagram (founded in 2010), Snapchat (founded in 2011), and TikTok (founded in 2016). Although not as popular among teens, Facebook remains (as of April 2024) the most popular social media platform, with more than 3 billion monthly active users (Dixon, 2024). The rise of TikTok was astounding as it gained, on average, 20 million new users per month during its first two years (2016–2018) and continued to rise in popularity throughout the pandemic (Ortiz-Ospina 2019). Young people (aged 10- to 19 years) make up 25% of TikTok's user base, with many adults concerned about the app's popularity among preteens aged 14 and under (Ceci, 2024; Zhong & Frenkel, 2020).

Access to and use of digital media and technology have risen at unprecedented rates over the past three decades, first among households and then among individuals. The ways in which we all live our lives have changed rapidly – and with rapid change often comes fear and panic. In fact, there is a long history of older generations considering anything "new and different" to corrupt society, often misjudging young people for engaging in new trends and pop culture. This dates back to the mid-19th century when people panicked over the rise of chess-playing (Thompson, 2014). On 2 July 1859 (over 160 years ago), the following was written in *Scientific American*:

> "… a pernicious excitement to learn and play chess has spread all over the country, and numerous clubs for practicing this game have been formed in cities and villages. Why should we regret this? it may be asked. We answer, chess is a mere amusement of a very inferior character, which robs the mind of valuable time that might be devoted to nobler acquirements, while at the same time it affords no benefit whatever to the body." (p. 9)

We have seen other similar trends over the years related to activities/interests including Dungeons and Dragons, video arcade games, comic books, Harry Potter, and the list goes on (see Pyle and Cunningham (2014) for an interesting historical perspective on these trends). Panic over the latest trends often comes in waves until older generations become comfortable and the fear subsides. As parents, educators, or other adults working with youth, it is easy to panic about things youth are doing that we do not understand or did not have access to as kids. It is *incredibly* challenging to figure out how to help kids navigate things we do not understand. The rapid pace of technology has left many parents feeling that they cannot keep up and have little control over the presence of media in their children's lives (Radesky & Rosenblum, 2022). Most parents (66%) feel that parenting is harder than it was 20 years ago, with many saying digital technology and social media are the reasons it is more challenging (Auxier et al., 2020). It is also likely that parents 20 years ago felt that parenting was harder than when they were kids. Although the purpose of this book is to discuss the negative effects of digital media (i.e., cyberbullying and related online problematic behavior), excessive fear or panic about digital media use may shut down opportunities to engage in conversations with our kids about healthy digital media use to prevent some of these negative effects. We hope readers will keep this in mind as we focus on cyberbullying in Chapters 4 to 10. Next, let us turn to digital media use during childhood.

Digital Media Use from Infancy to Childhood

Without a doubt, digital media and technology are ever-present elements of young children's lives. Most children have used a mobile device (e.g., smartphone or tablet) before 12 months of age (Kabali et al., 2015). Common Sense Media, a nonprofit organization based in the United States that provides resources for families and educators on digital media, conducts large-scale surveys asking parents to report on their child's (aged 8 or younger) digital media use. Their most recent national data are from February/March 2020 right before the COVID-19 pandemic. On average, parents reported that their children (aged 8 and younger) were on screen media 2 hours and 24 minutes a day (see Figure 2.1 for average times by age), which has stayed fairly consistent since Common Sense Media began

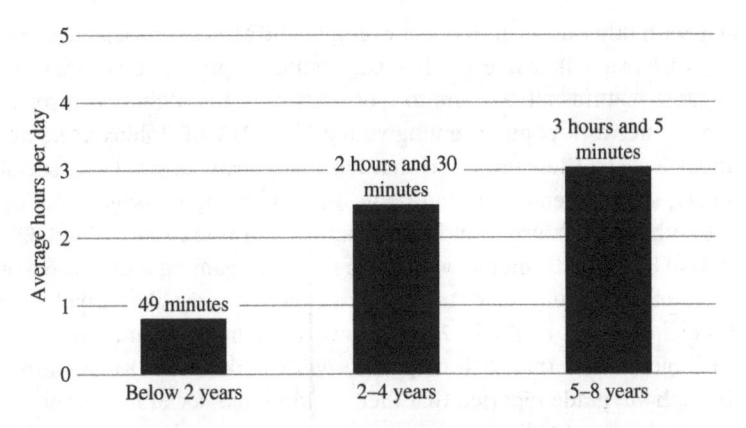

Figure 2.1 Average time spent on screen media per day by age. *Source*: Adapted from *The Common Sense Census: Media Use by Kids Age Zero To Eight*, by Rideout and Robb (2020).

Chart data:
- Below 2 years: 49 minutes
- 2–4 years: 2 hours and 30 minutes
- 5–8 years: 3 hours and 5 minutes

collecting data in 2011 (parents reported their child engaged with screen media for 2 hours and 16 minutes per day in 2011). It is important to keep in mind that these are averages and there is a lot of variation in screen media use from child to child. Almost a quarter (23%) of the sample did not use any screen media and a quarter (24%) used screen media for more than four hours (Rideout & Robb, 2020). Screen media use is higher among children from families who have a low income, have less education, and whose parents spend more time on devices (Levine et al., 2019; Radesky & Christakis, 2016).

Watching television and videos (e.g., watching YouTube videos or shows on streaming platforms such as Netflix) accounts for almost three-quarters (73%) of screen media use, with those under 2 years averaging 45 minutes a day and children aged 2 to 8 years averaging about two hours a day. Many children watch TV/videos or play games on mobile devices such as a tablet or smartphone, and over half (61%) of 5- to 8-year-olds own a tablet (12% own a smartphone). Children aged 5 to 8 years spend an average of 40 minutes a day playing video games, with boys averaging more than twice the time as girls (31 minutes versus 14 minutes a day; Rideout & Robb, 2020). The amount of time children spend on gaming remained steady from 2011 to 2020; however, gaming in this age group has become more social in that children can play with other users online. For example, the Minecraft social features allow users to talk to one another using public or private server chats, or in-game features allow users to type texts on signs. Roblox is a social gaming network popular among young kids (21% of Roblox users are under 9 years; Clement, 2024) that has many features similar to social media, such as sending friend requests, exchanging messages, trading with other Roblox users, and voice chatting (for users 13+). About 32% of 5- to 8-year-olds interact with others through gaming and only 6% of children aged 8 and under use social media platforms like Snapchat or TikTok (Rideout & Robb, 2020). However, a more recent survey by EdChoice found that 29% of parents with children in Kindergarten through 4th grade reported that their children use social media very or extremely often (Aldis, 2023).

YouTube use is common among younger kids, with most parents (80%) indicating that their child (11 or younger) watched videos on YouTube (Auxier et al., 2020). As part of their 2020 survey on young children's media use, Common Sense Media collected and analyzed more than 1,600 YouTube videos children had viewed (Radesky et al., 2020). Although most of the videos were considered age-appropriate, 27% contained inappropriate content, which included physical violence (e.g., guns, car crashes), interpersonal violence (e.g., bullying), scary elements (e.g., familiar characters made to look frightening), bad language, sexual content (e.g., characters mimicking sexual positions), substance use, and stereotypes (e.g., inappropriate accents or impressions). About 25% of the videos were educational (e.g., teaching moral or social-emotional concepts, how to draw), and 24% featured positive role models or diverse representation (e.g., multicultural stories from PBS Kids; Radesky et al., 2020).

Young children are also likely to see negative content through advertisements, which appear in 85% of all videos as sidebar ads (displayed on the right hand of the screen; could be easily confused as video recommendations), banner ads (shown on the bottom of the screen; occasionally covered video content), or ads played before the video starts. Most ads contain information not meant for children (e.g., ads for mattresses, vacation sites, insurance), and 20% of the ads contained violent themes (e.g., violent video games), sexual content, drugs or alcohol, or politics (Radesky et al., 2020). However, these mostly occurred in the videos meant for preteens and teens (but were being viewed by children aged 8 and under). Keep in mind that ads change depending on an individual's viewing history and information collected by Google (Radesky et al., 2020).

According to Pew Research Center, the majority of parents indicate they are somewhat or very concerned that their child spends too much time in front of screens, and they are concerned about the use of smartphones on children's development (Auxier et al., 2020). Although cyberbullying does not typically occur during early childhood, these early years are crucial for developing skills that set the stage for current and future healthy relationships (as discussed in Chapter 1). The American Academy of Pediatrics (AAP) and the American Academy of Child and Adolescent Psychiatry (AACAP) have established recommendations for families on digital media use, which can be found in Table 2.2. However, we know that digital media use varies considerably from child to child, and not all children and families are able to follow these recommendations. Does digital media use really interfere with

Table 2.2 Digital media recommendations by age.

Age range	Digital media recommendations
Toddlers under 18 months	• Video chatting with an adult
Toddlers 18 to 24 months	• Watching *only* educational programming (i.e., shows or games that teach academic skills, such as counting or identifying shapes, or social-emotional skills such as how to manage strong feelings) with a caregiver

Children aged 2 to 5	• Watching limited noneducational screen time
	  ▪ One hour per weekday
	  ▪ Three hours per weekend day

Children older than 5 years	• No specific amount of screen time recommended • Parents should ensure media use is not displacing other important activities (e.g., sleep, physical activity, and time with friends and family) • Talk to child(ren) about healthy and appropriate media use

Source: Recommendations from the American Academy of Pediatrics (AAP; 2022) and the American Academy of Child and Adolescent Psychiatry (AACAP; 2024).

healthy child development? Fortunately, there has been quite a bit of empirical research dedicated to answering this question.

Research Methods and Terminology

In this chapter, we focus on summarizing research studies that have explored how screen media use affects children's development, including areas such as language, memory, and behavior. We focus on systematic reviews and meta-analyses, which are comprehensive summaries of prior studies on a single topic. Meta-analyses go one step further than systematic reviews and use statistical techniques to combine numerical results from prior studies. Systematic reviews and meta-analyses are helpful in identifying the limitations of prior studies and giving ideas for future research. For example, one limitation is that many screen time studies have used "cross-sectional" designs. This means that the researchers measured screen media use and other variables of interest (e.g., ability to focus), at the same time point, among a group of children. A longitudinal study design measures variables repeatedly over time in the same group of children and allows researchers to measure how children change and develop over time. Refer to Table 2.3 for specific examples from these study designs.

Cross-sectional and longitudinal studies are considered observational studies because researchers collect participants' information without changing the participant's environment, such as asking them to complete a task or do something different in their daily lives. Unlike observational studies, experimental studies look at how changing one variable affects other variables. For example, a researcher might ask families to stop all screen use for two weeks and then compare their children's behavior or mood with kids who kept using screens as usual. In randomized control trials (RCTs), participants are randomly assigned to different groups to see how a specific change (such as less screen time) affects them. RCTs are considered the most reliable type of study because they help ensure that the results are not influenced by other factors, since participants are randomly assigned to either the treatment or the control group. However, it is often difficult to do RCTs with screen time as it is hard to control how much screen time children get in real life. Because of this, there are only a few RCTs looking into the effects of screen media.

Table 2.3 Research methods and terminology.

Method/terminology	Example	Design features
Cross-sectional study	A researcher goes to a middle school on the first day of school and gives a survey to students from all different grades. The survey asks students to report on their screen time use and attention span.	• Single data collection point • Data are collected on two or more variables • Developmental trends assumed by comparing data between student grades and ages
Longitudinal study	A researcher visits a middle school on the first day of school each year for several years and surveys the same group of students each time. The survey measures their screen time use and attention span. This study tracks how changes in screen time and attention span develop over time for the same group of students.	• Multiple data collection points • Data collected from the same participants over time • Developmental trends assumed by comparing data from the same group of children at different time points
Experimental study or RCT	A researcher randomly assigns participants into two groups. One group is asked to reduce their screen time for two weeks (treatment group), while the other group continues their usual screen time (control group). The researcher gives a survey on depression symptoms to participants in both the treatment and control group before the start of the study and at the conclusion of the two week period. The researcher compares the depression symptoms of the two groups to see if the reduction in screen time had an impact on depression symptoms.	• Participants are randomly assigned to a treatment group or a control group. • In the treatment group, researchers control one specific factor to see how it affects the participants. • One or more outcomes are measured in both groups and compared.

(Continued)

Table 2.3 (Continued)

Method/terminology	Example	Design features
Systematic review	A researcher collects numerous studies on a specific topic, such as how screen time affects child development. They first check the quality of each study to ensure reliability. Then, they organize and summarize the findings by grouping them into themes, such as "screen time and sleep" or "screen time and social interactions."	• Summarizes findings of multiple studies • Highlights different or even conflicting study results to give a clearer overall view of the topic • Relies on a researcher's expertise to make sense of different study results
Meta-analysis	A researcher collects studies, all asking the same research question (e.g., what effect does screen time have on children's sleep?). The researcher then looks at factors that might influence the results, such as the age or gender of the participants, their (dis)ability status, or how strict their parents are about screen time. The researcher aims to get a clearer overall picture of how screen time affects sleep and which factors might make a difference.	• Statistically describes effects and trends from many studies by using only numerical data • Provides more reliable results than looking at a single study • Includes a larger participant sample since a number of participants from several studies are combined

Effects of Digital Media Use on Child Development

Children younger than 2 years have very limited ability to learn from content on screens without a physical adult there to guide them (Radesky & Christakis, 2016). Longitudinal studies have found that excessive TV watching in early childhood is associated with impairments in cognitive and language development, memory, sleep, attention, and reading skills (Hinkley et al., 2014; Pagani et al., 2010; Schmidt et al., 2009; Zimmerman & Christakis, 2005). Even exposure to televisions in the background is associated with less focused play, poorer parent–child interactions, and fewer words spoken by a parent (Nichols, 2022). After 2 years of age, children are more likely to benefit from watching educational shows (e.g., Sesame Street, Daniel Tiger, Bluey), particularly if shows are discussed with a caregiver or parent, or playing educational games (e.g., PBS Kids, Khan Academy Kids; Radesky & Christakis, 2016). A systematic review and meta-analysis (including 24 cross-sectional and 17 longitudinal studies) found that screen media use (e.g., TV watching, background television, computer use, mobile use, and/or video games) was associated with lower language skills in young children; however, educational programs and co-viewing (i.e., a parent or caregiver viewing media together with their child) was associated with more language skills (Madigan et al., 2020). One randomized control trial found that replacing programming, which showed aggressive behavior (e.g., Power Rangers), with educational or prosocial programming (e.g., Dora the Explorer, Sesame Street) was associated with greater social competence skills and reduced externalizing (i.e., angry, aggressive, oppositional) behavior among preschool children, particularly for boys from low-income households (Christakis et al., 2013).

Although prior research has focused on effects of watching television, one meta-analysis examined the effects of smartphone and tablet use in early childhood (Mallawaarachchi et al., 2022). This study did not find a significant association between smartphone/tablet use and psychosocial (e.g., behavior problems, social skills) and cognitive development, though there was a small but significant association between device use and poorer sleep quality. However, a recent longitudinal study conducted during the COVID-19 pandemic (2020 to 2022) found that higher levels of tablet use at 3.5 years were associated with higher levels of anger and frustration one year later, which was then associated with more tablet use one year later (Fitzpatrick et al., 2024). Prior research has found a relation between media use and lower executive functioning (i.e., ability to focus and shift attention, memory, inhibitory control), such as between watching television and executive functioning among preschoolers (Nathanson et al., 2014); however, a recent meta-analysis (which included findings across 15 cross-sectional and longitudinal studies) found no association between overall screen time use and executive functioning for children aged 0 to 6 (Bustamante et al., 2023). Another meta-analysis found that screen time was weakly but significantly associated with both more externalizing (e.g., aggressive, inattentive) and internalizing (e.g., anxiety, depression) behavior of children aged 12 years and younger, and this was especially true for boys and externalizing behavior (Eirich et al., 2022). Regarding physical health, Fang et al.'s (2019) meta-analysis found an increased risk for overweight/obesity among children who engaged in screen time (especially watching television and computer use) for more than two hours per day.

Previous research mostly looked at how the amount of screen time affects children, without considering what they were doing on screens. Mallawaarachchi et al. (2024) conducted a systematic review and meta-analysis that explored the impact of different aspects of screen use (like content, type of use, and co-use with parents) on cognitive and psychosocial outcomes in children aged 6 years and younger. They reviewed 100 studies, including cross-sectional, longitudinal, and RCTs. Their findings indicated that more program viewing (e.g., watching television and videos) and background television were linked to poorer cognitive outcomes, while program viewing, exposure to age-inappropriate content, and caregiver screen use were associated with poorer psychosocial outcomes. Although the study found these associations, the effects were small and similar small-to-medium effects were observed in other meta-analyses on screen time and various child outcomes (Bustamante et al., 2023; Eirich et al., 2022; Madigan et al., 2020). Interestingly, gaming or app use was not significantly associated with cognitive or psychosocial outcomes and one study even found improved executive functioning skills (i.e., delay gratification, working memory) after playing with an educational app compared to watching a cartoon (Huber et al., 2018).

Parent Media Practices and Joint Media Engagement

Have you ever used screens to soothe your child during moments of distress? While this may seem like a quick fix, recent long-term studies reveal a concerning trend: using devices to calm children can lead to increased emotional reactivity (e.g., big emotions) and difficulties in managing anger and frustration over time (Konok et al., 2024), particularly for boys (Radesky et al., 2023). Though not the focus of this chapter, these findings highlight the importance of parent media practices on young children's development and media habits. Parents report it is challenging to attend to both their own mobile devices and the requests of their children (Radesky et al., 2016). When parents use devices when they are with their children, there are fewer verbal exchanges and even harsher parent responses (Radesky et al., 2014, 2015). This is understandable, as parents often have to multitask, making it frustrating (for both the parent and the child!) when a parent is trying to respond to an email, while their child is asking for snacks, playtime, and attention.

Joint media engagement involves viewing, playing, and/or using media with others (Takeuchi & Stevens, 2011), and for the purpose of this chapter, we focus on joint media engagement between children and their parents or caregivers. Media activities involving joint media engagement are important and common aspects of digital media use for younger users (Ewin et al., 2021). Co-viewing is watching a television show or video with your child (or watching your child play a video game). Co-viewing can sometimes involve parent–child interactions and discussion, such as asking your child about the content they are viewing or connecting content to the child's prior experiences. Co-using or co-playing involves using or playing video or mobile games with your child (see Table 2.4).

Table 2.4 Examples of joint media engagement.

Term	Definition	Example
Passive co-viewing	Watching a TV show or video with your child, or watching your child play a video game or a game on a mobile device.	Daisy is 5-year-old and watches an episode of Bluey on the television every day she gets home from school. Her mom sits next to her on the couch and watches with her, occasionally checking and scrolling on her iPhone.
Active co-viewing	Watching a TV show or video with your child, or watching your child play a game while interacting and engaging in discussion regarding the content.	Every Saturday morning, 2-year-old Jaxon plays on the Daniel Tiger's Grr-ific Feelings app on his dad's iPad. Jaxon's dad sits next to him and engages in the activities with Jaxon (e.g., singing along to songs, counting to 4), models deep breathing, and asks Jaxon to identify the feelings of characters in the app.
Co-using/ co-playing	Using media with your child or playing video/mobile games with your child.	Rylee, an 8-year-old, has been spending a lot of time on Roblox on her tablet playing Adopt Me! Rylee's mom is not familiar with the game, so Rylee shows her how to play. Rylee's mom creates a Roblox account and now she plays the game with Rylee on her own computer.

2 Digital Media Use: The Early Years

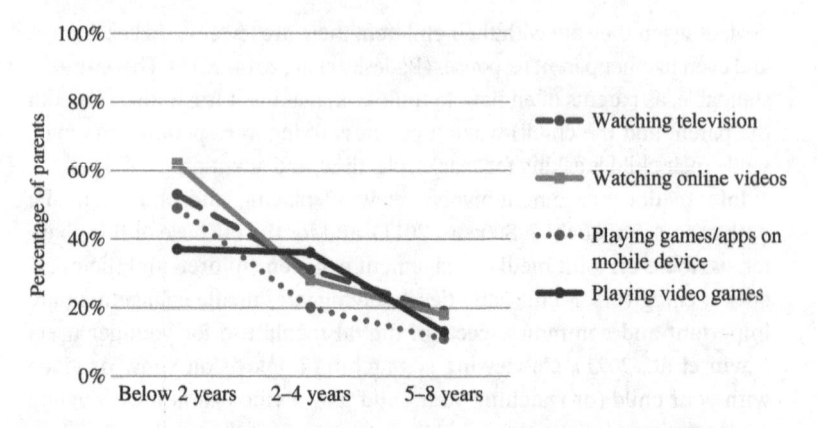

Figure 2.2 Percentage of parents reporting co-using or co-viewing with children aged 8 and under. *Source*: Adapted from *The Common Sense Census: Media Use by Kids Age Zero to Eight* (Table 41, p. 41), by Rideout and Robb (2020).

Many parents report co-viewing television (84%), online videos (74%), playing games (63%), or playing video games (62%) with their children aged 8 and under (Radesky et al., 2020), although it is not clear to what extent parents engage in discussion while co-viewing with their children. Co-viewing also declines with increasing child age (see Figure 2.2), which is typical as children begin to be more independent and parents may feel less heed to co-view programs with them. However, given some of the positive effects of joint media engagement (discussed next), it may be worthwhile to co-view and co-use media with children even as they get older.

It can be challenging to co-view or co-play on smaller mobile devices (e.g., tablet and smartphone), unless the parent is playing on their own device (as described in the co-playing example in Table 2.4). In Mallawaarachchi et al.'s (2024) meta-analysis previously described, co-using media with parents and siblings was associated with improved cognitive outcomes for children aged 6 and under. Another systematic review reported that joint media engagement was associated with reduced parent–child conflict and sharing of quality experiences, although findings were inconsistent regarding other positive outcomes of shared media activities, including language and parental warmth (Ewin et al., 2021). It is important to note that joint or shared media engagement is different from active mediation of your child's media. Active mediation may include setting rules and limits surrounding technology and/or media use (e.g., no devices while eating dinner or in the bedroom, setting up parental controls, or privacy settings on devices or apps), following your child's social media accounts, and/or asking your child about their device use. Although these strategies may be important, especially for younger users, they are different than actively playing or using media with your child. More information on co-using media and active parental mediation can be found in Chapter 5.

Summary

The advancement of digital media and technology rose at unprecedented rates in the past three decades, rapidly changing the ways in which we communicate, get information, entertain ourselves, and parent. Such rapid changes can understandably raise anxiety in those of us raising and/or working with youth. On average, children (up to 8 years old) are spending over two hours a day on screen media. Watching television and videos, and playing online games are the most popular ways young children engage with digital media. Although social media use is limited at this age, more and more children are utilizing online games to interact with others (e.g., Roblox). As we will discuss in Chapter 5, if young children are engaging in social gaming, we recommend close monitoring, keeping all accounts private and/or turning off social features.

Overall, research shows that excessive screen time, especially for passive activities such as watching television, is linked to poorer cognitive and social outcomes. However, educational content tends to have positive effects. The impact of screen time on development is generally small, and other factors like genetics and opportunities to engage in nonscreen activities play a significant role. Parental media practices also matter. Using screens to calm children or using devices in their presence can lead to negative outcomes, whereas co-viewing and co-playing with a child (i.e., joint media engagement) is associated with positive outcomes, such as cognitive skills. We know that adolescents use digital media in drastically different ways compared to children and the next chapter will review digital media use among preteens and teenagers.

References

Aldis, A. (2023, October). *New survey explores parent concerns on social media usage and absenteeism.* https://www.edchoice.org/engage/new-survey-explores-parent-concerns-on-social-media-usage-and-absenteeism/.

American Academy of Child & Adolescent Psychiatry. (2024, May). *Screen time and children.* https://www.aacap.org/AACAP/Families_and_Youth/Facts_for_Families/FFF-Guide/Children-And-Watching-TV-054.aspx.

American Academy of Pediatrics. (2022, July). *Beyond screen time: A parent's guide to media use.* https://www.healthychildren.org/English/family-life/Media/Pages/healthy-digital-media-use-habits-for-babies-toddlers-preschoolers.aspx.

Auxier, B., Anderson, M., Perrin, A., & Turner, E. (2020). *Parenting children in the age of screens.* Pew Research Center. https://www.pewresearch.org/internet/2020/07/28/parenting-children-in-the-age-of-screens/.

Bustamante, J. C., Fernández-Castilla, B., & Alcaraz-Iborra, M. (2023). Relation between executive functions and screen time exposure in under 6 year-olds: A meta-analysis. *Computers in Human Behavior, 145*, 107739. https://doi.org/10.1016/j.chb.2023.107739.

Ceci, L. (2024, May). *TikTok: Distribution of global audiences 2024, by age and gender.* https://www.statista.com/statistics/1299771/tiktok-global-user-age-distribution/.

Christakis, D. A., Garrison, M. M., Herrenkohl, T., Haggerty, K., Rivara, F. P., Zhou, C., & Liekweg, K. (2013). Modifying media content for preschool children: A randomized controlled trial. *Pediatrics, 131*(3), 431–438. https://doi.org/10.1542/peds.2012-1493.

Clement, J. (2024, February). *Roblox user distribution worldwide 2023, by age group.* https://www.statista.com/statistics/1190869/roblox-games-users-global-distribution-age/.

Dixon, S. J. (2024, July). *Most popular social networks worldwide as of April 2024, by number of monthly active users.* https://www.statista.com/statistics/272014/global-social-networks-ranked-by-number-of-users/.

Eirich, R., McArthur, B. A., Anhorn, C., McGuinness, C., Christakis, D. A., & Madigan, S. (2022). Association of screen time with internalizing and externalizing behavior problems in children 12 years or younger: A systematic review and meta-analysis. *JAMA Psychiatry, 79*(5), 393–405. https://doi.org/10.1001/jamapsychiatry.2022.0155.

Ewin, C. A., Reupert, A. E., McLean, L. A., & Ewin, C. J. (2021). The impact of joint media engagement on parent–child interactions: A systematic review. *Human Behavior & Emerging Technologies, 3*(2), 230–254. https://doi.org/10.1002/hbe2.203.

Fang, K., Mu, M., Liu, K., & He, Y. (2019). Screen time and childhood overweight/obesity: A systematic review and meta-analysis. *Child: Care, Health, and Development, 45*(5), 744–753. https://doi.org/10.1111/cch.12701.

Fitzpatrick, C., Pan, P. M., Lemieux, A., Harvey, E., Rocha, F. A., & Garon-Carrier, G. (2024). Early-childhood tablet use and outburst of anger. *JAMA Pediatrics, 178*(10), 1035–1040. https://doi.org/10.1001/jamapediatrics.2024.2511.

Gottfried, J., & Sidoti, O. (2024). *Teens and video games today.* Pew Research Center. https://www.pewresearch.org/internet/2024/05/09/teens-and-video-games-acknowledgments.

Hinkley, T., Verbestel, V., Ahrens, W., Lissner, L., Molnár, D., Moreno, L. A., Pigeot, I., Pohlabeln, H., Reisch, L. A., Russo, P., Veidebaum, T., Tornaritis, M., Williams, G., Henauw, S. D., Bourdeaudhuij, I. D. (2014). Early childhood electronic media use as a predictor of poorer well-being: a prospective cohort study. *JAMA Pediatrics, 168*(5), 485–492. https://doi.org/10.1001/jamapediatrics.2014.94.

Huber, B., Yeates, M., Meyer, D., Fleckhammer, L., & Kaufman, J. (2018). The effects of screen media content on young children's executive functioning. *Journal of Experimental Child Psychology, 170,* 72–85. https://doi.org/10.1016/j.jecp.2018.01.006.

Irwin, S. O. (2016). *Digital media: Human-technology connection.* Lexington Books/Fortress Academic.

Joseph, C. (2023, December). *The history and evolution of video games.* Medium. https://medium.com/@collins.joseph/the-history-and-evolution-of-video-games-323f7d689615.

Kabali, H. K., Irigoyen, M. M., Nunez-Davis, R., Budacki, J. G., Mohanti, S. H., Leister, K. P., & Bonner, R. L. (2015). Exposure and use of mobile media devices by young children. *Pediatrics, 136*(6), 1044–1050. https://doi.org/10.1542/peds.2015-2151.

Konok, V., Binet, M.-A., Korom, Á., Pogány, Á., Miklósi, Á., & Fitzpatrick, C. (2024). Cure for tantrums? Longitudinal associations between parental digital emotion regulation and children's self-regulatory skills. *Frontiers* in *Child and Adolescent Psychiatry, 3,* 1276154. https://doi.org/10.3389/frcha.2024.1276154.

Lenhart, A. (2009, August). *Teens and mobile phones over the past five years: Pew internet looks back.* https://www.pewresearch.org/internet/2009/08/19/teens-and-mobile-phones-over-the-past-five-years-pew-internet-looks-back/.

Levine, L. E., Waite, B. M., Bowman, L. L., & Kachinsky, K. (2019). Mobile media use by infants and toddlers. *Computers in Human Behavior, 94,* 92–99. https://doi.org/10.1016/j.chb.2018.12.045.

Madigan, S., McArthur, B. A., Anhorn, C., Eirich, R., & Christakis, D. A. (2020). Associations between screen use and child language skills: A systematic review and meta-analysis. *JAMA Pediatrics, 174*(7), 665–675. https://doi.org/10.1001/jamapediatrics.2020.0327.

Mallawaarachchi, S. R., Anglim, J., Hooley, M., & Horwood, S. (2022). Associations of smartphone and tablet use in early childhood with psychosocial, cognitive, and sleep factors: A systematic review and meta-analysis. *Early Childhood Research Quarterly, 60,* 13–33. https://doi.org/10.1016/j.ecresq.2021.12.008.

Mallawaarachchi, S., Burley, J., Mavilidi, M., Howard, S. J., Straker, L. M., Kervin, L., Staton, S., Hayes, N., Machell, A., Torjinski, M., Brady, B., Thomas, G., Horwood, S., White, S., Zabatiero, J., Rivera, C., & Cliff, D. P. (2024). Early childhood screen use contexts and cognitive and psychosocial outcomes: A systematic review and meta-analysis. *JAMA Pediatrics, 178*(10), 1017–1026. https://doi.org/10.1001/jamapediatrics.2024.2620.

McCormack, E. (2022). *Traditional media vs. digital media: How the PR landscape has changed.* https://www.touchdownpr.com/traditional-media-vs-digital-media/.

McNamee, K., & Yu, M. (2023, April). *50 years ago, Martin Cooper made the first cellphone call.* https://www.npr.org/2023/04/03/1167815751/50-years-ago-martin-cooper-made-the-first-cell-phone-call.

Nathanson, A., Aladé, F., Sharp, M. L., Rasmussen, E. E., & Christy, K. (2014). The relation between television exposure and executive function among preschoolers. *Developmental Psychology, 50*(5), 1497–1506. https://doi.org/10.1037/a0035714.

Neary, L. (2006, February). *Teens create their own space online.* National Public Radio. https://www.npr.org/transcripts/5182960.

Nichols, D. L. (2022). The context of background TV exposure and children's executive functioning. *Pediatric Research, 92*, 1168–1174. https://doi.org/10.1038/s41390-021-01916-6.

Ortiz-Ospina, E. (2019, September). *The rise of social media.* https://ourworldindata.org/rise-of-social-media.

Pagani, L. S., Fitzpatrick, C., Barnett, T. A., & Dubow, E. (2010). Prospective associations between early childhood television exposure and academic, psychosocial, and physical well-being by middle childhood. *Archives of Pediatrics & Adolescent Medicine, 164*(5), 425–431. https://doi.org/10.1001/archpediatrics.2010.50.

Pyle, K. C., & Cunningham, S. (2014). *Bad for you: Exposing the war on fun!* Henry Holt and Company.

Radesky, J. S., Kaciroti, N., Weeks, H. M., Schaller, A., & Miller, A. L. (2023). Longitudinal associations between use of mobile devices for calming and emotional reactivity and executive functioning in children aged 3 to 5 years. *JAMA Pediatrics, 177*(1), 62–70. https://doi.org/10.1001/jamapediatrics.2022.4793.

Radesky, J. S., Kistin, C., Eisenberg, S., Gross, J., Block, G., Zuckerman, B., & Silverstein, M. (2016). Parent perspectives on their mobile technology use: The excitement and exhaustion of parenting while connected. *Journal of Developmental & Behavioral Pediatrics, 37*(9), 694–701. https://doi.org/10.1097/DBP.0000000000000357.

Radesky, J. S., Kistin, C. J., Zuckerman, B., Nitzberg, K., Gross, J., Kaplan-Sanoff, M., Augustyn, M., & Silverstein, M. (2014). Patterns of mobile device use by caregivers and children during meals in fast food restaurants. *Pediatrics, 133*(4), e843–e849. https://doi.org/10.1542/peds.2013-3703.

Radesky, J. S., Miller, A. L., Rosenblum, K. L., Appugliese, D., Kaciroti, N., & Lumeng, J. C. (2015). Maternal mobile device use during a structured parent–child interaction task. *Academic Pediatrics, 15*(2), 283–244. https://doi.org/10.1016/j.acap.2014.10.001.

Radesky, J. S., & Rosenblum, K. (2022). A relationship-based framework for early childhood media use. In *Contemporary issues in perinatal education: Knowledge into practice* (pp. 188–197). Routledge. https://doi.org/10.4324/9781003223771-29.

Radesky, J. S., Schaller, A., Yeo, S. L., Weeks, H. M., & Robb, M. B. (2020). *Young kids and YouTube: How ads, toys, and games dominate viewing.* San Francisco, CA: Common Sense Media.

Rideout, V., & Robb, M. B. (2020). *The common sense census: Media use by kids age zero to eight.* San Francisco, CA: Common Sense Media.

Schmidt, M. E., Rich, M., Rifas-Shiman, S. L., Oken, E., & Taveras, E. (2009). Television viewing in infancy and child cognition at 3 years of age in a US cohort. *Pediatrics, 123*(3), 370–375. https://doi.org/10.1542/peds.2008-3221.

The Strong National Museum of Play. (n.d.). *Video game history timeline.* https://www.museumofplay.org/video-game-history-timeline/.

Takeuchi, L., & Stevens, R. (2011). *The new coviewing: Designing for learning through joint media engagement.* New York: The Joan Ganz Cooney Center at Sesame Workshop.

Thompson, C. (2014, May). *Why chess will destroy your mind.* Medium. https://medium.com/message/why-chess-will-destroy-your-mind-78ad1034521f.

Zimmerman, F. J., & Christakis, D. A. (2005). Children's television viewing and cognitive outcomes. *Archives of Pediatrics & Adolescent Medicine, 159*(7), 619–625. https://doi.org/10.1001/archpedi.159.7.619.

Zhong, R., & Frenkel, S. (2020, September). *A third of TikTok's U.S. users may be 14 or under, raising safety questions. New York Times.* https://www.nytimes.com/2020/08/14/technology/tiktok-underage-users-ftc.html.

3

Digital Media Use: The Preteen and Teenage Years

The preteen (9- to 12 years) and teenage (13- to 18 years) years are a time of development when smartphone use increases, and youth are more autonomous (with parents being less likely to monitor and co-use digital technology as described in Chapter 2). Most preteens and teens use digital media to talk with their friends and classmates (e.g., Snapchat), engage with others who share the same hobbies or interests (e.g., YouTube, Reddit, online gaming), explore their own social identities (e.g., TikTok, Instagram), and/or seek community. This chapter explores the changes and trends in how preteens and teens have used digital media over the years. Times have certainly changed since the days when the school librarian would introduce the internet solely as a "learning tool." You may be wondering how digital media, or the constant connection between teens and the rest of the world, impacts their social lives and choices, emotional well-being, and schoolwork. This chapter provides a summary of research on all these important topics, as they are crucial to understand as we work together to prevent cyberbullying and related problematic online behavior.

Digital Media Use Among Preteens and Teens

As described in Chapter 2, digital media is the use of any electronic/digital tools, including a television, computer or laptop, cell phone or smartphone, tablet, gaming console, and wearable technology (e.g., glasses, watches), to communicate, consume or create content/information, and/or

Cyberbullying: Helping Children Navigate Digital Technology and Social Media, First Edition. Stephanie Fredrick, et al.
© 2025 John Wiley & Sons, Inc. Published 2025 by John Wiley & Sons, Inc.

be entertained. Researchers used to be most interested in measuring the amount of time (e.g., minutes, hours) individuals were on screens. To some extent, we are still interested in this question; however, with adolescents and adults being on screens almost constantly, researchers are trying to better understand what that use involves.

If someone asked you how often you use digital technology (e.g., your smartphone) throughout your day, what would you say? It is a hard question to answer! When preteens and teens are asked this question, 9- to 12-year-olds report they are on digital media an average of 5½ hours per day and 13- to 18-year-olds about 8½ hours per day (Rideout et al., 2022). This does not necessarily mean that they are sitting with a screen in front of them for 5½ (or 8½) hours, as they often use multiple screens at once. For example, if Elisa reported that she spends one hour watching television and two hours on social media per day, one of her social media hours could be while she was watching television (Rideout et al., 2022), which is referred to as "media multi-tasking" (Pagano et al., 2023). Close to half (46%) of teens say they use the internet almost constantly (Vogels et al., 2022) and most teens have multiple devices for going online – including smartphones (95% report owning a smartphone), desktop or laptop computer (90%), gaming console (83% overall – 91% of boys and 75% of girls), and tablet (65%; Anderson et al., 2023). Having a home computer or tablet is less common in lower-income households (Anderson et al., 2023).

Organizations such as Pew Research Center and Common Sense Media have conducted large national surveys of preteens and teens to examine ways that young people use digital media. These surveys have found that the most popular way teens like to spend time online/on their devices is by watching videos, with 93% of teens indicating they use YouTube and about 16% reporting watching YouTube almost constantly (Anderson et al., 2023). The second and third most popular ways to spend time online are on social media or online gaming. Teens report spending over two hours per day on social media (Rideout et al., 2022). Popular apps and platforms for girls include TikTok, Instagram, and Snapchat and for boys YouTube, Twitch, and Reddit (see Figure 3.1), although most teens (both boys and girls) are on YouTube and TikTok every day (Vogels et al., 2022). TikTok is particularly hard for adolescents to resist, and they tend to spend the longest amount of time on this app. Teens describe TikTok as "easy" and "irresistible" – they may go on to watch a quick video and then will unintentionally watch

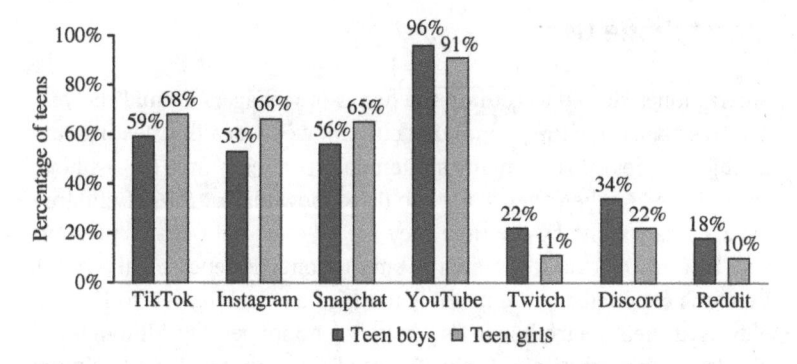

[Figure: Bar chart showing percentage of teen boys and teen girls using various social media platforms]

- TikTok: Teen boys 59%, Teen girls 68%
- Instagram: Teen boys 53%, Teen girls 66%
- Snapchat: Teen boys 56%, Teen girls 65%
- YouTube: Teen boys 96%, Teen girls 91%
- Twitch: Teen boys 22%, Teen girls 11%
- Discord: Teen boys 34%, Teen girls 22%
- Reddit: Teen boys 18%, Teen girls 10%

Figure 3.1 Percentage of teen boys and girls who report using social media platforms. *Source*: Adapted from *Teens, Social Media and Technology 2023*, by Anderson et al. (2023).

videos for a few hours. This is often a result of algorithms knowing them so well and playing videos that are engaging to them. Use of Facebook among teens has dropped significantly – from 71% in 2014–2015 to 33% in 2023, while reported use of Instagram (from 52% to 59%) and Snapchat (from 41% to 50%) has remained steady over the past decade (Anderson et al., 2023).

All these numbers and percentages represent the *average times* among adolescents who participated in these large surveys. It is important to keep in mind that digital media use can look drastically different from one individual to the next and that time spent online or on devices is just one aspect of digital media use (Popat & Tarrant, 2023; Radesky et al., 2023). For example, one person may spend an hour messaging and joking with friends, while another person might be reading or scrolling through hate-fueled and/or violent content on social media. Researchers have defined two main types of social media use: passive and active use. Passive social media use is defined as browsing, scrolling, and reading others' posts and comments. Active social media use involves interacting with others through posting, commenting, messaging, and liking others' content. The type of use (active vs. passive), the content they are viewing, and the interactions (or noninteractions) they are having with others is arguably much more important than simply the amount of time they are spending online (Popat & Tarrant, 2023).

Smartphone Use

Smartphones started to get into the hands of teenagers around the year 2007 (as opposed to flip phones that only allowed for calling, texting, and taking pictures). While many millennials got their first (flip) phone around age 16 when they started to drive, now almost 50% of children have a smartphone by the time they are 11-years-old (43% of preteens and 88% to 95% of teens own a smartphone; Rideout et al., 2022). Research conducted by Common Sense Media found that 11- to 17-year-olds used their smartphones for about 4½ hours per day, although use per day varied drastically (only 10% used smartphones for 10 or more hours per day; Radesky et al., 2023). More than four hours may seem like a long time to be on your phone; however, keep in mind that youth (and adults) often use smartphones as background noise while they are doing work or other tasks (e.g., listening to music or streaming videos while doing homework).

Common Sense Media also found that preteens and teens in their sample checked their phones about 51 times per day (range 2 to 498 times per day), with younger teens checking their phones less frequently compared to older teens. On a typical day, teens receive about 237 notifications, although they only see or engage with about 46 notifications a day (Radesky et al., 2023). That is certainly a lot for a young person to juggle. Addictive feeds using algorithms can also be challenging for youth (and adults) to understand and navigate. Social media and other online platforms (e.g., search engine results, news feeds) utilize personalized algorithms (based on personal data such as your age and viewing history) to prioritize content (e.g., videos, advertisements) seen by the viewer. For example, if an individual posts and views a lot of TikTok dance challenges, they will see more of them on their feed. Algorithms can be helpful in that they allow for a personalized and engaging online experience; however, they can also be harmful and addictive. Videos or other content with harmful (e.g., violent, sexual) content can sometimes be accidentally (or intentionally) clicked on, which may lead to a snowball effect of suggesting these kinds of videos. These feeds can also be addictive, which is why teenagers are saying that TikTok videos are hard to stop watching as TikTok is constantly recommending short videos that are personalized for them.

Recognizing these challenges for youth, states have begun to create policies and bills aimed at reducing or preventing aspects of smartphone use that can be harmful to youth. For example, New York just passed the Stop Addictive Feeds Exploitation (SAFE) For Kids Act, which prevents social media companies from using addictive feeds and places time limitations on notifications (i.e., not allowing push notifications between midnight and 6 a.m.) unless approved by a parent. Maryland recently passed the Maryland Age-Appropriate Design Code Act, which bans platforms from using addictive features, such as auto-playing media and spamming users with notifications. This is very likely just the beginning of states across the country developing bans aimed at creating safer online spaces for youth.

Effects of Digital Media Use

We have seen a steady increase in time spent on digital media over the past several years, especially with social media and online gaming. From 2015 to 2019, media use for teens grew by 11%, but from 2019 to 2021, media use grew by 17% for both preteens and teens (Rideout et al., 2022). These trends are likely to continue. So how does all this time spent on digital media impact preteens and teens? Researchers, policymakers, and the general public are concerned about its effects on physical health, mental health, and schoolwork. Despite the recent attention to this topic, the answer to this question is complicated!

Earlier in this chapter, we discussed the challenges in measuring the amount of time youth are spending online or on their devices, as it is constant throughout the day. As challenging as it is to *measure* media use, it is even harder to measure to what extent media use affects mental health, physical health, and academic achievement. As discussed in Chapter 2, longitudinal designs, where researchers measure media use and other variables of interest (e.g., symptoms of depression and sleep quality) over time, are needed to determine if digital media use causes changes (as opposed to things like depression or poor sleep causing people to use media more). Most research studies on the effects of digital media use have been cross-sectional (i.e., studies that measure media use and other variables of interest at a single point in time), which makes it almost impossible to determine the causal relationship between media use and youth well-being. Finally, most research has focused on the amount of time spent on digital media use without examining content and interactions. Spending seven hours per day on digital media could look like a mix of watching videos for school, playing interactive games with friends, and sharing memes with family – but it also could include passively scrolling through feeds of violent, hateful, or unrealistically idealized images and being unable to stop even when feeling down. Below is a summary of recent empirical research on the impact of digital media use on adolescents' mental health (e.g., anxiety, depression), physical health (e.g., sleep), risky behavior (e.g., sexual behavior, substance use), and schoolwork. As described in Chapter 2, we focus on findings from systematic reviews and meta-analyses, as these studies provide us with rich information on available empirical research conducted to date.

Digital Media Use and Youth Mental Health

The area that has probably received the most attention from researchers, policymakers, practitioners, and teenagers themselves is the effects of digital media use, especially social media use, on adolescent mental health. In the past decade, we have seen escalating mental health problems, such as depression and anxiety, among adolescents. In December 2021, the U.S. Surgeon General issued an advisory on protecting youth mental health and in 2023 issued another advisory on social media use and youth mental health. It is not surprising that researchers and others have proposed that rising mental health concerns among young people are due to increased use of social media (Haidt, 2024; Twenge, 2020). What does the research say on the effects of digital media use on youth mental health?

When looking at the association between mental health and the amount of time an individual spends online or on devices, the relationship is small (Ivie et al., 2020; Orben & Przybylski, 2019; Tang et al., 2021). One systematic review of longitudinal studies found a small association between higher amounts of total screen time and subsequent depression symptoms, and mobile phone and computer/internet use (compared to watching television, playing video games, and using social media) was more strongly associated with depression symptoms

(Tang et al., 2021). A longitudinal study conducted with German adolescents found that time spent on the internet and social media was not associated with life satisfaction or depression over a period of nine years (from 2008 to 2016; Schemer et al., 2021). However, another longitudinal study, which included 6,596 U.S. adolescents (12- to 15-year-olds), found that use of social media for more than three hours per day was associated with depression and anxiety after accounting for effects of prior mental health problems (Riehm et al., 2019). This means that, for individuals who were on social media for more than three hours per day, social media use uniquely contributed to mental health problems. Overall, it seems that screen time, and specifically social media use, may be connected to worse mental health for some youth. However, these effects are small and for many teens may be nonexistent. This is why it is important to consider:

- what digital media is being used for,
- what emotions are driving social media use, and
- how much negative content is being consumed.

Some research has highlighted the importance of age and gender when considering social media use effects and mental health. Orben et al. (2022) found that older adolescents (16- to 21-year-olds) in the United Kingdom who reported no social media use or excessive social media use (four or more hours a day) reported lower life satisfaction compared to those who reported social media in more moderate amounts (approximately one to three hours a day). However, for younger adolescents, those who reported higher levels of social media use also reported lower life satisfaction. In this case, the outcome measured (i.e., life satisfaction) was not as extreme as clinical levels of depression, anxiety, or hopelessness, but rather focused on whether adolescents felt happy or satisfied with their lives. They also found that social media use predicted decreases in life satisfaction one year later for 11- to 13-year-old adolescent girls and 14- to 15-year-old boys, indicating there may be "sensitive periods" for negative effects of social media.

Theories have been developed to explain the association between digital media use and mental health, such as:

- The *Goldilocks Hypothesis* suggests that very little to no media use or excessive use may be harmful in a society where using media is the norm (Przybylski & Weinstein, 2017). This theory was supported in Orben et al.'s (2022) finding that moderate levels of social media use (one to three hours per day) was related to higher levels of life satisfaction for older adolescents (but not for younger adolescents).

- The *Differential Susceptibility to Media Effects Model* (DSMM) says that certain individuals may be more susceptible to the effects of digital media use (Valkenburg & Peter, 2013), based on their age, gender, or tendencies to engage in social comparison. For example, one longitudinal study of Dutch adolescents found that for some adolescents, engagement with social media was associated with increased life satisfaction, whereas for others, increased social media activities were associated with decreased life satisfaction (Boer et al., 2022).

Studies that capture more nuanced media use, such as problematic use, exposure to harmful content, or negative social interactions (e.g., cyberbullying), have reported more consistent negative impacts on mental health. For example, in Boer et al.'s (2022) longitudinal study, time spent on social media was no longer related to life satisfaction after accounting for social media use problems (e.g., exhibiting feelings of withdrawal when not on social media and feeling preoccupied with social media use). A meta-analysis and systematic review found that negative social media-related behaviors (e.g., experiencing cyberbullying, viewing or generating content related to self-harm, problematic social media use) and *not* frequency of social media use were associated with self-injurious thoughts and behaviors (Nesi et al., 2021). Social media use is considered problematic when an individual shows addiction-like tendencies (e.g., they are not able to control their use despite attempts to stop or reduce use), engages in excessive use, and/or engages in ways that have significant detrimental impacts on their life (see Chapter 6 for more information on problematic use). Problematic social media use is associated with depression, anxiety, low self-esteem, life satisfaction, loneliness, and depression (Huang, 2020; Shannon et al., 2022; Wu et al., 2024).

As mentioned before, it is important to look at the what (i.e., content) and why of digital media use to determine its impact on youth mental health. Common Sense Media conducted research in which they asked teens to download an app on their phone, which tracked their phone activity for nine days, in addition to filling out surveys about their media use. They found aspects of problematic content, including:

- Use of apps on smartphones with mature (17+) or adult-only (18+) ratings, such as porn (Pornhub), fantasy sports or betting apps (Yahoo Fantasy Sports, Daily Fantasy, and Sleeper Fantasy Football), Telegram, Reddit, Parler, 4chan, casino games, or violent games (e.g., Call of Duty; Radesky et al., 2023). Approximately 73% of youth have been exposed to pornography and slightly over half are younger than 13 (Robb & Mann, 2023).
- Use of social media platforms for appearance-related purposes (e.g., following or viewing beautify accounts featuring make-up or fashion). Adolescent girls who follow these types of accounts report more negative body image compared to girls who use platforms primarily for communication (e.g., chatting or messaging with friends), and this is especially true for adolescent girls when compared to young adults (Markey & Daniels 2022; Markey et al., 2024).
- Use of apps to message, video chat, or send photos to strangers. Many adolescent girls who use Instagram, Snapchat, and TikTok report that they have been contacted by strangers on these platforms in ways that make them uncomfortable (Nesi et al., 2023).
- Exposure to harmful suicide-related content (e.g., graphic content or content that glorifies or promotes self-harm) on Instagram, TikTok, and Snapchat, although teens also report being exposed to these messages "in person" just as frequently (Nesi et al., 2023).
- Exposure to hate-based content online (cyberhate), with approximately 64% of teens being exposed to hate-fueled content (Rideout & Robb, 2018). Exposure to cyberhate is especially frequent for youth with minoritized identities, as adolescent girls of color report exposure to racist content or language on TikTok or Instagram at least monthly. LGBTQ+ adolescents are almost twice as likely as non-LGBTQ+ adolescents to encounter hate speech (e.g., posting rude, mean, or offensive comments or pictures) related to their sexual or gender identity (Nesi et al., 2023).

Exposure to hate-field content, especially if the content is targeting the person's identity, is distressing and associated with negative mental health outcomes (e.g., depression, anxiety), as well as political violence and delinquency (Fulantelli et al., 2022). To address some of the concerns related to exposure to harmful content and being contacted by strangers, Instagram recently announced that accounts for users under the age of 16 will be private and they would need parent approval to make their account public, which means that they can only be messaged or tagged by people they follow (Allyn, 2024). Further, content involving self-harm, eating disorders, and nudity is now blocked for teen users under the age of 18 (Kerr, 2024).

Digital Media Use and Youth Physical Health

In addition to mental health, there have been efforts to understand the effects of digital media use on adolescents' physical health, particularly related to sleep. Over half of teens (59%) use their phones after midnight on school nights (Radesky et al., 2023), especially YouTube, social media, gaming, and reading. Teens report that TikTok is commonly used during this time, but it can be hard to fall asleep, as it is so stimulating. One meta-analysis of 23 longitudinal studies found that traditional media use (e.g., watching television or videos), social media use, prolonged use, and dysfunctional use led to sleep problems (Pagano et al., 2023) with small-to-moderate effects. Other systematic reviews have found similar (i.e., small to moderate) associations between problematic smartphone use and sleep (Mac Cárthaigh et al., 2020).

Digital media use may impact sleep for a variety of different reasons, including:

- a desire to use media that delays the time to fall asleep (called sleep displacement theory);
- notifications that interrupt sleep (e.g., 70% of adolescents are sent at least one text message between 10 p.m. and 6 a.m.; Troxel et al., 2015);
- exposure to bright light or blue screen light close to bedtime suppressing the release of melatonin;
- consuming content that creates cognitive arousal (i.e., an abundance of thoughts before bedtime; Bauducco et al., 2024).

Research has found that sleep disruption (e.g., receiving messages in the middle of the night) and sleep displacement (e.g., using media instead of going to sleep) have stronger effects on sleep (delaying sleep more than an hour per night) compared to exposure to bright or blue light and cognitive arousal (which delays sleep less than 10 minutes per night; Bauducco et al. [2024]). However, each individual adolescent is different and certain vulnerability factors may impact associations between media use and sleep. For example, adolescents with more positive perceptions of risk-taking are more likely to continue to play video games and go to bed later despite knowing they have to get up early for school (Reynolds et al., 2015). Adolescents who are more vulnerable to social norms or pressures and a fear of missing out (FOMO) may also stay up late so that they do not miss group chats, messages, or posts from friends, or could watch videos or television they know will be talked about the next day at school (Bauducco et al., 2024).

In addition to sleep, researchers have also focused on the impact of digital media use and other health indicators, such as weight (typically measured with measurements of body mass index [BMI]), physical activity, and diet). Systematic reviews and meta-analyses have found moderate evidence that higher levels of screen time, such as watching television, is associated with higher BMI and less healthy diet (e.g., higher intake of energy-dense foods and/or lower intake of less healthy food groups; Carson et al., 2016; Stiglic & Viner, 2019). Studies have shown that participants who cut down on the amount of time they watch television were more likely to reduce their BMI than participants who did not cut down on TV watching time (Tremblay et al., 2011).

A major limitation to this research is that most studies focus on watching television rather than using other digital devices (e.g., smartphone use, social media, computer use, video games). We also need more studies to learn if certain types of use (e.g., exposure to certain content, addictive use) impact physical health. Cross-sectional studies have found that additive phone use is associated with maladaptive eating habits (Domoff et al., 2020b). Youth who use their smartphones for excessive gaming are also more likely to have higher BMI (Brodersen et al., 2023). A meta-analysis of cross-sectional studies found small-to-moderate correlations between social media use and engagement in risky behaviors, including substance use and risky sexual behaviors, and effects were larger for risky sexual behaviors among younger adolescents (mean age 12- to 15-years-old) compared to older adolescents (mean age 18-years-old; Vannucci et al., 2020). Exposure to certain online content is likely important in explaining the link between digital media and youth engagement in unsafe or risky behavior. For example, cross-sectional studies have found that alcohol-related social media engagement (e.g., viewing or interacting with alcohol-related content) is associated with alcohol use and related problems among young adults (Curtis et al., 2018), and exposure to sexually explicit material is associated with engagement in risky sexual behaviors, such as having sexual intercourse without a condom (Smith et al., 2016).

Digital Media Use and Youth Academic Performance

One area that has received less attention in the literature is how digital media use impacts adolescents' academic achievement and schoolwork. In their systematic review and meta-analysis of cross-sectional studies, Adelantado-Renau et al. (2019) found that watching television and playing video games were associated with poorer academic performance. In a longitudinal study, watching more than two hours of television at 8 to 9 years was associated with a 12-point loss on a reading achievement test three to four years later, and using a computer for more than one hour was associated with a 12-point decrease in math, although no association was found between playing video games and performance on reading and math achievement tests (Mundy et al., 2020). Other meta-analyses have indicated a significant, but small, relationship between social media use and lower academic performance (Appel et al., 2020; Huang, 2018; Gordon & Ohannessian, 2024; Marker et al., 2018). Teenagers who report heavy or constant social media use (e.g., > five hours per day) report feeling less connected to and more negative about their school (Foerster & Röösli, 2017; Sampasa-Kanyinga et al., 2019, 2022), and have lower academic performance (Sampasa-Kanyinga et al., 2019, 2022; Tang & Patrick, 2020) compared to peers with infrequent or moderate use. Addictive phone use (i.e., experiencing tolerance, withdrawal, and/or significant impairments related to phone use) is also associated with poorer academic performance (Domoff et al., 2020). However, almost all empirical studies in this area have been cross-sectional and research is needed, which examines the extent to which media use impacts academic performance over time.

Several theories have been developed to explain why students' digital media use may relate to their academic performance, such as:

- Time displacement refers to social media use reducing the amount of time for learning, studying, and other school-related pursuits or activities (Przybylski & Weinstein, 2017; Reinhardt et al., 2023).
- The gap hypothesis (Kumpulainen & Sefton-Green, 2012; Prensky, 2001) indicates that students who use digital media outside of school may become disengaged with school if their real interests or digital talents are not taught or used sufficiently at school. Students who prefer digital learning but do not get the opportunity to engage digitally at school become less engaged with school over time (Hietajärvi et al., 2020).
- Adolescents also enjoy having media in the background when they work on schoolwork (e.g., texting, using social media, playing TikTok videos while doing homework); however, one-quarter to one-third of teenagers report that this negatively impacts the quality of their work (Rideout & Robb, 2018).

Most middle and high school students (97%) use their smartphones while they are at school (for about 43 minutes per day; Radesky et al., 2023). While at school, students tend to go on social media, watch videos on YouTube, and play online games. Schools have a variety of cell phone policies (and enforcement of policies also tends to vary from school to school). Policies can vary from banning cell phones completely (e.g., requiring students to place their phones in a locked pouch), allowing phone use only at certain times of the day (e.g., during lunch, in between classes), banning specific sites, and/or allowing teachers to create classroom-specific phone expectations. Unfortunately, very little research has been conducted in the United States on these policies (such as cell phone bans), and how they relate to educational outcomes for students. In our discussions with teachers and school administrators, the use of cell phones at school is not only causing major disruptions to learning, but also giving rise to other problematic behavior at school, such as physical fighting (e.g., students using phones to schedule fights), cyberbullying, gambling, and buying drugs.

There is a growing movement for states and school districts to ban cell phones in middle and high schools (Gecker, 2024). As of August 2024, four states have laws that ban or restrict cell phones in schools (Florida,

Indiana, Louisiana, and South Carolina), and other states have laws that either limit or encourage districts to limit cell phone use during school (Alabama, Connecticut, Ohio; Rock, 2024). Although policies can be helpful, it is ultimately up to school administration and teachers to come up with strategies to enact and enforce these policies, and creating a state- or school-wide ban may not be so simple. When teachers integrate technology, students view this positively, and they are more likely to be engaged (Bond & Bedenlier, 2019; Schindler et al., 2017; Ventouris et al., 2021). Ultimately, this is a growing issue that needs more research to ultimately inform best practices and policies for smartphone use during school.

Benefits of Digital Media Use

Just as digital media use can be harmful for some teens, it can also be healthy and even beneficial. There is great potential in using digital media to promote youth's physical and mental health. For example, playing active video games (e.g., Dance, Dance Revolution) and mobile phone games lead to improved physical activity and better eating habits (i.e., increased fruit and vegetable consumption; Oh et al., 2022). Adolescent girls also report finding helpful information and resources about mental health on TikTok, Instagram, Snapchat, and YouTube (Nesi et al., 2023), and research has found that TikTok is a promising platform to expose young users to evidence-based mental health resources (Motta et al., 2024). In addition, social media platforms are continuing to focus on mental health. For example, Meta recently created a new policy that allows for expert resources to be shared when teens search for terms related to suicide, self-harm, or eating disorders (and harmful content related to this content will be blocked).

The use of social media and gaming communities allows youth to seek social support, strengthen peer relationships, find community, and engage in identity development. This is especially important for youth from marginalized or minoritized backgrounds where they may not feel supported or included in their homes, schools, or neighborhoods. LGBTQ+ adolescents are more likely than their non-LGBTQ+ peers to say that they frequently use social media (TikTok, Instagram) to connect with others who share similar identities or interests (Nesi et al., 2023).

Although exposure to racist content is absolutely an issue, approximately 70% of adolescent girls of color who use TikTok and Instagram also report they see positive or identity-affirming content related to race at least monthly (Nesi et al., 2023). As discussed in Chapter 1, teens report that utilizing digital technology allows them to maintain and even strengthen friendships, and social media helps them stay connected with their friends. In some cases, digital technology allows youth to engage in self-disclosure in a safe space (e.g., direct messaging with friends) and be their authentic selves. We hope that readers will keep this in mind as we turn our focus for the remainder of the book to a negative aspect of digital media use: cyberbullying.

Summary

Preteens and teens are spending a lot of time doing many different things on digital media across various devices. The unfortunate reality is that research findings are often inconclusive. More research is needed about digital media use content, context, and reasons for using media instead of simply focusing on time spent behind screens to truly unpack how media use is affecting youth. Knowing these limitations in the research, stating that digital media use, and especially social media use, is bad for all youth is overstating and oversimplifying what we know so far on this complex relationship between digital media use and adolescent development. Having said that, we are hearing from youth that it is difficult to stop using technology. Youth are primarily utilizing their smartphones to communicate with their friends and peers and yet the design of apps (e.g., addictive algorithms) makes it challenging to put their phones down (Radesky et al., 2023). This may especially be the case for adolescents who may have certain vulnerability factors, such as positive perceptions of risk-taking (e.g., deciding that staying up late is more rewarding than the consequence of being tired in the morning), or anxiety regarding social exclusion if they miss out on a group chat or trending video. Further, research has consistently found that social media use may be more harmful to younger adolescents compared to older adolescents, and especially for young adolescent girls. This is a critical finding since more than half of preteens (9- to 12-year-olds) are utilizing social media (approximately 20 minutes per day; Rideout et al., 2022), including TikTok, Snapchat, Discord, Instagram, and Facebook on their smartphones (Radesky et al., 2023), despite social media apps only allowing accounts for those aged 13 years or older. Fortunately, social media platforms are making strides to create safer online spaces for teens, including blocking harmful content from teens' accounts and requiring parent permission to make teens' accounts public. These are important steps forward for youth to continue to utilize digital media in safe and responsible ways.

References

Adelantado-Renau, M., Moliner-Urdiales, D., Cavero-Redondo, I., Beltran-Valls, M. R., Martínez-Vizcaíno, V., & Álvarez-Bueno, C. (2019). Association between screen media use and academic performance among children and adolescents: A systematic review and meta-analysis. *JAMA Pediatrics*, *173*(11), 1058–1067. https://doi.org/doi:10.1001/jamapediatrics.2019.3176.

Allyn, B. (2024, September). *Instagram makes all teen accounts private, in a highly scrutinized push for child safety*. National Public Radio. https://www.npr.org/2024/09/17/g-s1-23181/instagram-teen-accounts-private-meta-child-safety.

Anderson, M., Faverio, M., & Gottfried, J. (2023). *Teens, social media, and technology 2023*. Washington, DC: Pew Research Center. https://www.pewresearch.org/internet/2023/12/11/teens-social-media-and-technology-2023/.

Appel, M., Marker, C., & Gnambs, T. (2020). Are social media ruining our lives? A review of meta-analytic evidence. *Review of General Psychology*, *24*(1), 60–74. https://doi.org/10.1177/1089268019880891.

Bauducco, S., Pillion, M., Bartel, K., Reynolds, C., Kahn, M., & Gradisar, M. (2024). A bidirectional model of sleep and technology use: A theoretical review of how much, for whom, and which mechanisms. *Sleep Medicine Reviews*, *76*, 101933. https://doi.org/10.1016/j.smrv.2024.101933.

Boer, M., Stevens, G., Finkenauer, C., & Eijnden, R. (2022). The complex association between social media use intensity and adolescent wellbeing: A longitudinal investigation of five factors that may affect the association. *Computers in Human Behavior*, *128*, 107084. https://doi.org/10.1016/j.chb.2021.107084.

Bond, M., & Bedenlier, S. (2019). Facilitating student engagement through educational technology: Towards a conceptual framework. *Journal of Interactive Media in Education, 2019*(1), 1–14. https://doi.org/10.5334/jime.528.

Brodersen, K., Hammami, N., & Katapally, T. R. (2023). Is excessive smartphone use associated with weight status and self-rated health among youth? A smart platform study. *BMC Public Health, 23*, 234. https://doi.org/10.1186/s12889-023-15037-8.

Carson, V., Hunter, S., Kuzik, N., Gray, C. E., Poitras, V. J., Chaput, J., Saunders, T. J., Katzmarzyk, P. T., Okely, A. D., Gorber, S. C., Kho, M. E., Sampson, M., Lee, H., & Tremblay, M. S. (2016). Systematic review of sedentary behaviour and health indicators in school-aged children and youth: An update. *Applied Physiology, Nutrition, and Metabolism, 41*(6 Suppl. 3), 240–265. https://doi.org/10.1139/apnm-2015-0630.

Curtis, B. L., Lookatch, S. J., Ramo, D. E., McKay, J. R., Feinn, R. S., & Kranzler, H. R. (2018). Meta-analysis of the association of alcohol-related social media use with alcohol consumption and alcohol-related problems in adolescents and young adults. *Alcoholism: Clinical and Experimental Research, 42*(5), 978–986. https://doi.org/10.1111/acer.13642.

Domoff, S. E., Foley, R. P., & Ferkel, R. (2020a). Addictive phone use and academic performance in adolescents. *Human Behavior & Emerging Technologies, 2*(1), 33–38. https://doi.org/10.1002/hbe2.171.

Domoff, S. E., Sutherland, E. Q., Yokum, S., & Gearhardt, A. N. (2020b). Adolescents' addictive phone use: Associations with eating behaviors and adiposity. *International Journal of Environmental Research and Public Health, 17*(8), 2861. https://doi.org/10.3390/ijerph17082861.

Foerster, M., & Röösli, M. (2017). A latent class analysis on adolescents' media use and associations with health-related quality of life. *Computers in Human Behavior, 71*, 266–274. https://doi.org/10.1016/j.chb.2017.02.015.

Fulantelli, G., Taibi, D., Scifo, L., Schwarze, V., & Eimler, S. C. (2022). Cyberbullying and cyberhate as two interlinked instances of cyber-aggression in adolescence: A systematic review. *Frontiers in Psychology, 13*, 909299. https://doi.org/10.3389/fpsyg.2022.909299.

Gecker, J. (2024, February). *Kids are using phones in class, even when it's against the rules. Should schools ban them all day?* The Associated Press.

Gordon, M. S., & Ohannessian, C. M. (2024). Social media use and early adolescents' academic achievement: Variations by parent–adolescent communication and gender. *Youth & Society, 56*(4), 651–672. https://doi.org/10.1177/0044118X231180317.

Haidt, J. (2023). *The anxious generation: How the great rewiring of childhood is causing an epidemic of mental illness.* Penguin Press.

Hietajärvi, L., Lonka, K., Hakkarainen, K., Alho, K., & Salmela-Aro, K. (2020). Are schools alienating digitally engaged students: Longitudinal relations between digital engagement and school engagement. *Frontline Learning Research, 9*(1), 33–55. https://doi.org/10.14786/flr.v8i1.437.

Huang, C. (2020). A meta-analysis of the problematic social media use and mental health. *International Journal of Social Psychiatry, 68*(1), 12–33. https://doi.org/10.1177/0020764020978434.

Huang, C. (2018). Social network site use and academic achievement: A meta-analysis. *Computers & Education, 119*, 76–83. https://doi.org/10.1016/j.compedu.2017.12.010.

Ivie, E. J., Pettitt, A., Moses, L. J., & Allen, N. B. (2020). A meta-analysis of the association between adolescent social media use and depressive symptoms. *Journal of Affective Disorders, 275*, 165–174. https://doi.org/10.1016/j.jad.2020.06.014.

Kerr, D. (2024, January). *Under growing pressure, meta vows to make it harder for teens to see harmful content.* National Public Radio. https://www.npr.org/2024/01/09/1223583540/meta-harmful-content-instagram-harder-teens-facebook.

Kumpulainen, K., & Sefton-Green, J. (2012). What is connected learning and how to research it? *International Journal of Learning and Media, 4*(1), 9–24. http://doi.org/10.1162/IJLM.

Mac Cárthaigh, S., Griffin, C., & Perry, J. (2020). The relationship between sleep and problematic smartphone use among adolescents: A systematic review. *Developmental Review, 55*, 100897. https://doi.org/10.1016/j.dr.2020.100897.

Marker, C., Gnambs, T., & Appel, M. (2018). Active on Facebook and failing at school? Meta-analytic findings on the relationship between online social networking activities and academic achievement. *Educational Psychology Review, 30*, 651–677. https://doi.org/10.1007/s10648-017-9430-6.

Markey, C. H., August, K. J., Gillen, M. M., & Rosenbaum, D. L. (2024). An examination of youths' social media use and body image: Considering TikTok, Snapchat, and Instagram. *Journal of Media Psychology: Theories,*

Methods, and Applications. Advance online publication. https://dx.doi.org/10.1027/1864-1105/a000420.

Markey, C. H., & Daniels, E. (2022). An examination of preadolescent girls' social media use and body image: Type of engagement may matter most. *Body Image, 42*, 145–149. https://doi.org/10.1016/j.bodyim.2022.05.005.

Motta, M., Liu, Y., & Yarnell, A. (2024). "Influencing the influencers:" A field experimental approach to promoting effective mental health communication on TikTok. *Scientific Reports, 14*, 5864. https://doi.org/10.1038/s41598-024-56578-1.

Mundy, L. K., Canterford, L., Hoq, M., Olds, T., Moreno-Betancur, M., Sawyer, S., Kosola, S., & Patton, G. C. (2020). Electronic media use and academic performance in late childhood: A longitudinal study. *PLoS One, 15*(9), e0237908. https://doi.org/10.1371/journal.pone.0237908.

Nesi, J., Burke, T. A., Bettis, A. H., Kudinova, A. Y., Thompson, E. C., MacPherson, H. A., Fox, K. A., Lawrence, H. R., Thomas, S. A., Wolff, J. C., Altemus, M. K., Soriano, S., & Liu, R. T. (2021). Social media use and self-injurious thoughts and behaviors: A systematic review and meta-analysis. *Clinical Psychology Review, 87*, 102038. https://doi.org/10.1016/j.cpr.2021.102038.

Nesi, J., Mann, S., & Robb, M. B. (2023). *Teens and mental health: How girls really feel about social media.* San Francisco, CA: Common Sense.

Oh, C., Carducci, B., Vaivada, T., & Zulfiqar, B. A. (2022). Interventions to promote physical activity and healthy digital media use in children and adolescents: A systematic review. *Pediatrics, 149*, e2021053852I. https://doi.org/10.1542/peds.2021-053852I.

Orben, A., & Przybylski, A. K. (2019). The association between adolescent well-being and digital technology use. *Nature Human Behavior, 3*, 173–182. https://doi.org/10.1038/s41562-018-0506-1.

Orben, A., Przybylski, A. K., Blakemore, S., & Kievit, R. (2022). Windows of developmental sensitivity to social media. *Nature Communications, 13*, 1649. https://doi.org/10.1038/s41467-022-29296-3.

Pagano, M., Bacaro, V., & Crocetti, E. (2023). "Using digital media or sleeping ... that is the question." A meta-analysis on digital media use and unhealthy sleep in adolescence. *Computers in Human Behavior, 146*, 107813. https://doi.org/10.1016/j.chb.2023.107813.

Prensky, M. (2001). Digital natives, digital immigrants. *On the Horizon, 9*(5), 1–6. https://doi.org/10.1108/10748120110424816.

Przybylski, A. K., & Weinstein, N. (2017). A large-scale test of the Goldilocks hypothesis: Quantifying the relations between digital-screen use and the mental well-being of adolescents. *Psychological Science, 28*(2), 204–215. https://doi.org/10.1177/0956797616678438.

Popat, A., & Tarrant, C. (2023). Exploring adolescents' perspectives on social media and mental health and well-being: A qualitative literature review. *Clinical Child Psychology and Psychiatry, 28*(1), 323–337. https://doi.org/10.1177/13591045221092884.

Radesky, J., Weeks, H. M., Schaller, A., Robb, M., Mann, S., & Lenhart, A. (2023). *Constant companion: A week in the life of a young person's smartphone use*. San Francisco, CA: Common Sense.

Reinhardt, A., Willhelm, C., & Mayen, S. (2023). Time for digital media but no time for school? An investigation of displacement effects among adolescents of gen X, Y, and Z. *Psychology of Popular Media, 13*(4), 633–642. https://psycnet.apa.org/doi/10.1037/ppm0000479.

Reynolds, C. M., Gradisar, M., Kar, K., Perry, A., Wolfe, J., & Short, M. A. (2015). Adolescents who perceive fewer consequences of risk-taking choose to switch off games later at night. *Acta Paediatrica, 104*, e222–e227. https://doi.org/10.1111/apa.12935.

Rideout, V., Peebles, A., Mann, S., & Robb, M. B. (2022). *Common sense census: Media use by tweens and teens, 2021*. San Francisco, CA: Common Sense Media.

Rideout, V., & Robb, M. B. (2018). *Social media, social life: Teens reveal their experiences*. San Francisco, CA: Common Sense Media.

Riehm, K. E., Feder, K. A., Tormohlen, K. N., Crum, R. M., Young, A. S., Green, K. M., Pacek, L. R., La Flair, L. N., & Mojtabai, R. (2019). Associations between time spent using social media and internalizing and externalizing problems among U.S. youth. *JAMA Psychiatry, 76*(12), 1266–1273. https://doi.org/10.1001/jamapsychiatry.2019.2325.

Robb, M. B., & Mann, S. (2023). *Teens and pornography*. San Francisco, CA: Common Sense Media.

Rock, A. (2024, August 23). Which states have banned cell phones in schools? Campus Safety. https://www.campussafetymagazine.com/insights/which-states-have-banned-cell-phones-in-schools/161286/.

Sampasa-Kanyinga, H., Chaput, J., & Hamilton, H. (2019). Social media use, school connectedness, and academic performance among adolescents. *The Journal of Primary Prevention, 40*, 189–211. https://doi.org/10.1007/s10935-019-00543-6.

References | 65

Schindler, L. A., Burkholder, G. J., Morad, O. A., & Marsh, C. (2017). Computer-based technology and student engagement: A critical review of the literature. *International Journal of Educational Technology in Higher Education, 14*, 25. https://doi.org/10.1186/s41239-017-0063-0.

Sampasa-Kanyinga, H., Hamilton, H. A., Goldfield, G. S., & Chaput, J. (2022). Problem technology use, academic performance, and school connectedness among adolescents. *International Journal of Environmental Research and Public Health, 19*(4), 2337. https://doi.org/10.3390/ijerph19042337.

Schemer, C., Masur, P. K., Geib, S., Müller, P., & Schäfer, S. (2021). The impact of internet and social media use on well-being: A longitudinal analysis of adolescents across nine years. *Journal of Computer-Mediated Communication, 26*(1), 1–21. https://doi.org/10.1093/jcmc/zmaa014.

Shannon, H., Bush, K., Villeneuve, P. J., Hellemans, K., & Guimond, S. (2022). Problematic social media use in adolescents and young adults: Systematic review and meta-analysis. *JMIR Mental Health, 9*(4), e33450. https://doi.org/10.2196/33450.

Smith, L. W., Liu, B., Degenhardt, L., Richters, J., Patton, G., Wand, H., Cross, D., Hocking, J. S., Skinner, S. R., Cooper, S., Lumby, C., Kaldor, J. M., & Guy, R. (2016). Is sexual content in new media linked to sexual risk behaviour in young people? A systematic review and meta-analysis. *Sexual Health, 13*(6), 501–515. https://doi.org/10.1071/SH16037.

Stiglic, N., & Viner, R. M. (2019). Effects of screentime on the health and well-being of children and adolescents: A systematic review of reviews. *BMJ Open, 9*, e023191. https://doi.org/10.1136/bmjopen-2018-023191.

Tang, S., & Patrick, M. E. (2020). A latent class analysis of adolescents' technology and interactive social media use: Associations with academics and substance use. *Human Behavior and Emerging Technologies, 2*(1), 50–60. https://doi.org/10.1002/hbe2.154.

Tang, S., Werner-Seidler, A., Torok, M., Mackinnon, A. J., & Christensen, H. (2021). The relationship between screen time and mental health in young people: A systematic review of longitudinal studies. *Clinical Psychology Review, 86*, 102021. https://doi.org/10.1016/j.cpr.2021.102021.

Tremblay, M. S., LeBlanc, A. G., Kho, M. E., Saunders, T. J., Larouche, R., Colley, R. C., Goldfield, G., & Gorber, S. C. (2011). Systematic review of sedentary behaviour and health indicators in school-aged children and youth. *Journal of Behavioral Nutrition and Physical Activity, 8*, 98. https://doi.org/10.1186/1479-5868-8-98.

Troxel, W. M., Hunter, G., & Scharf, D. (2015). Say "GDNT": Frequency of adolescent texting at night. *Sleep Health, 1*(4), 300–303. https://doi.org/10.1016/j.sleh.2015.09.006.

Twenge, J. M. (2020). Why increases in adolescent depression may be linked to the technological environment. *Current Opinion in Psychology, 32*, 89–94. https://doi.org/10.1016/j.copsyc.2019.06.036.

U. S. Public Health Service, U.S. Surgeon General's Advisory. (2021). *Protecting youth mental health*. Author. https://www.hhs.gov/sites/default/files/surgeon-general-youth-mental-health-advisory.pdf.

U. S. Public Health Service, U.S. Surgeon General's Advisory. (2023). *Social media and youth mental health*. Author. https://www.hhs.gov/sites/default/files/sg-youth-mental-health-social-media-advisory.pdf.

Valkenburg, P. M., & Peter, J. (2013). The differential susceptibility to media effects model. *Journal of Communication, 63*(2), 221–243. https://doi.org/10.1111/jcom.12024.

Vannucci, A., Simpson, E. G., Gagnon, S., & Ohannessian, C. M. (2020). Social media use and risky behaviors in adolescents: A meta-analysis. *Journal of Adolescence, 79*, 258–274. https://doi.org/10.1016/j.adolescence.2020.01.014.

Ventouris, A., Panourgia, C., & Hodge, S. (2021). Teachers' perceptions of the impact of technology on children and young people's emotions and behaviours. *International Journal of Educational Research Open, 2*, 100081. https://doi.org/10.1016/j.ijedro.2021.100081.

Vogels, E. A., Gelles-Watnick, R., & Massarat, N. (2022). *Teens, social media, and technology*. Pew Research Center. https://www.pewresearch.org/internet/2022/08/10/teens-social-media-and-technology-2022/.

Wu, W., Huang, L., & Yang, F. (2024). Social anxiety and problematic social media use: A systematic review and meta-analysis. *Addictive Behaviors, 153*, 107995. https://doi.org/10.1016/j.addbeh.2024.107995.

4

Cyberbullying and Other Forms of Cyber Aggression

As discussed in Chapters 2 and 3, youth are engaging in digital media, especially social media and gaming, at unprecedented rates. Understandably, the increased use of technology has led to growing concerns about youth's involvement in cyberbullying and witnessing online aggression. Additionally, many adults fear that youth are normalizing or becoming indifferent toward inappropriate behaviors, including cyberbullying, in the digital world where adult censorship is often minimal. This chapter provides a more detailed overview of cyberbullying, including different forms of cyberbullying, its impact, and the individuals most at risk for engaging in cyberbullying and being a target. We also discuss relationships, personality characteristics, and other factors that help to safeguard children from cyberbullying, and we will learn about factors that protect children's mental health and well-being if they are experiencing cyberbullying. These factors are also discussed in more detail in the next three chapters.

Chapter 1 provided an overview of traditional forms of bullying and discussed the three main characteristics of traditional bullying that make it distinct from peer conflict or other aggressive behavior. These characteristics include (1) aggressive behavior intended to harm the victim(s), (2) a power imbalance between the aggressor and the victim(s) that makes it challenging or impossible for the victim(s) to defend themselves, and (3) repetition of the harmful behavior (Gladden et al., 2014; Olweus, 1993). Yet, researchers, educators, and others have struggled to agree on a definition of cyberbullying. In particular, there are questions about what these three characteristics of traditional bullying look

Cyberbullying: Helping Children Navigate Digital Technology and Social Media,
First Edition. Stephanie Fredrick, et al.
© 2025 John Wiley & Sons, Inc. Published 2025 by John Wiley & Sons, Inc.

like – and whether they are relevant – in a digital world. For example, is a behavior considered repetitive if a harmful post was viewed or posted multiple times over a long period by different people on Instagram? A power imbalance can also look quite different within a digital space. A child who does not hold power within a school context (e.g., is not liked by their peers or classmates) may feel more confident engaging in aggressive behaviors online toward peers who otherwise hold more power. This may be why hurtful or humiliating videos or photos get shared so widely, as youth may feel more comfortable or confident commenting, liking, or even re-sharing content to gain attention, but they would never join in on bullying in person. As discussed later in this chapter, digital technology can sometimes create a "disinhibition effect," where people feel less restrained online and communicate in ways they would not if they were face-to-face with someone (Joinson, 1998; Udris, 2014). However, it is important to note that in most cases, an individual's online behavior mirrors their offline behavior. Youth who are involved in one form of bullying (e.g., physical or relational) are much more likely to be involved in another form (e.g., cyber).

Peter and Petermann (2018) defined cyberbullying as, "using information and communication technologies (ICT) to repeatedly and intentionally harm, harass, hurt and/or embarrass a target" (p. 359). More recently, Sameer Hinduja and Justin Patchin (co-creators of the Cyberbullying Research Center: https://cyberbullying.org) created a definition of cyberbullying that focuses on the distress of the involved target or victim. They define cyberbullying as "... willful and repeated harm inflicted through the use of computers, cell phones, and other electronic devices" (Hinduja & Patchin, 2023, p. 10). We reintroduce the power imbalance component to the definition and define cyberbullying as the use of a digital device (e.g., mobile phone, tablet, gaming console) to inflict purposeful and repeated aggressive behaviors involving a power imbalance and causing distress for the victim or target (Nickerson et al., 2024; Patchin & Hinduja, 2006). When we talk to youth and educators, they are often able to identify these three characteristics of bullying and cyberbullying (i.e., intentional distress to the target, power imbalance, and repetition), likely due to increased bullying awareness and school-based prevention programming. However, it can often be challenging in real situations to determine whether behavior constitutes as cyberbullying. As mentioned in Chapter 1, we often hear youth and educators overidentifying all mean or unkind behavior as bullying and the same goes for cyberbullying. Let us consider a few examples of situations and whether they would be considered cyberbullying or other issues, and why.

- Ava films Alexa losing a fight in the cafeteria and posts it on TikTok. People send the video to their friends and everyone laughs.

    Although this situation began in school and ended up online, the willful spreading of the video with the intention of teasing and mocking Alexa occurred via social media. This is an example of cyberbullying.
- Gabe posts about a controversial political topic on Instagram. Sam comments that this is an ignorant viewpoint. The two begin arguing about the topic in the comments.

    This is an example of conflict rather than cyberbullying. Both participants are participating equally in the conflict. This scenario could escalate to cyberbullying if Gabe or Sam makes it more personally attacking, or encourages others to engage and harass the other person or their viewpoint.
- Emma shared personal information with her friend, Asha, via text, and made her promise not to send it to or tell anyone. Asha accidentally opened her phone with the message open and their other friend saw it.

    This would not be considered cyberbullying. Although the outcome of the event may mirror a cyberbullying incident (e.g., Emma's personal information is shared without her consent), Asha did not intentionally act with malice.
- Kristen is having a birthday party this weekend. She invited all the girls in the drama club, except Lauren. She told the other girls it was because Lauren was annoying. She creates a chat group with all the other girls talking about the party and tells them not to invite Lauren to their parties either.

    This scenario is an example of cyberbullying, although the unkind behavior began before the group chat was formed. This is a scenario that we often like to include in our work with youth, as they are often mixed on whether this constitutes as cyberbullying or not. Youth often say, "but we can't invite everyone to our birthday party!" And yes, we agree you cannot invite all your peers to your birthday party. Kristen not inviting Lauren to her birthday party does not mean

Kristen is engaging in bullying behavior. However, Kristen telling her friends that Lauren is annoying is unkind behavior and when she tells them not to invite her to other parties via the group chat, this crosses the line into cyberbullying (i.e., social exclusion). The power imbalance in this scenario is Kristen's social influence and she is utilizing digital media to exert this power to socially alienate Lauren.

According to a recent survey of 13- to 17-year-olds from the Cyberbullying Research Center, the most common forms of cyberbullying include:

- posting mean or hurtful comments,
- excluding someone from group chats,
- spreading rumors online, and
- embarrassing or humiliating someone online (Patchin & Hinduja, 2024).

See Table 4.1 for descriptions and examples of common forms of cyberbullying (e.g., trolling, tagging). Cyberbullying occurs through social media (e.g., Snapchat, Instagram, TikTok), text messages, online forums, and online gaming communities; it is most likely to occur in online gaming and on social media (Kowalski et al., 2019).

Social media apps that allow users to post content or comments anonymously (e.g., Yik Yak, Sidechat, Fizz, Whisper, NGL) or allow content to be viewed temporarily (e.g., Snapchat) increase the risk for harmful content, including cyberbullying (Ansary, 2020). Fizz, Sidechat, and Yik Yak are all location-based and allow users to post anonymously to other users within the same geographic location. Fizz and Sidechat are more popular among college students as they require users to have a university email to create an account. Whisper, however, is not university or location-based and anyone can see or post on this app. Due to widespread reports of cyberbullying, harassment, and other risky behavior (e.g., buying and selling drugs), there have been recent attempts to ban anonymous apps on college campuses. For example, the University of North Carolina (UNC) system drew media attention when the UNC president, Peter Hans, made an announcement at a UNC System Board of Governors meeting that he plans to move forward with a ban on anonymous apps, including Yik Yak, Sidechat, Fizz, and Whisper, across 17 schools in the UNC System. The apps could neither be downloaded on university- or state-owned devices nor be accessed from the campus Wi-Fi network. Students could still access the apps from personally

Table 4.1 Forms of cyberbullying.

Behavior	Definition	Example
Online harassment or cyberstalking	Sending repeated threatening messages or posts to someone to incite anxiety and fear	Julie broke up with her boyfriend, Juan. He created a new Instagram account in someone else's name and sent her repeated threatening messages. Each time she tried to block him, he would create a new account.
Exclusion	Purposely leaving someone out of a group chat or tagging someone in a group picture or post so they can see they were not invited	A group of friends from Stacy's class regularly interacts on Instagram group where they discuss school events, make plans for outings, and exchange memes. Stacy is deliberately removed from the group following a minor argument with the most popular girl in that circle. They intend to make her feel alienated, so they plan an outing, take pictures, and share them on their Instagram profiles, ensuring that Stacy can see and feel left out.
Photoshopping or tagging	Altering photos of someone or tagging someone in photos with the intention of being cruel	Using an AI face swap app, Julie's ex-boyfriend altered her photo by adding her face to a fake body-revealing girl's image. He then uploaded that photo and tagged her with a caption, which alluded to promiscuous behavior.
Denigration	Posting gossip, rumors, or other untrue statements about someone	Audrey told some of her classmates that Adrianna had sex with Greg in a group chat. Information spread fast at school. Adrianna was upset because this was not true.
Impersonation/ identity theft	Pretending to be someone else with the sole purpose of being cruel	Nora was a new girl who was targeted by a group of students in her class. They created a fake Instagram account using her name and pictures and used this profile to post racist and inappropriate content and comment harshly on other students' posts. Two months later, Nora received a call from her school's principal regarding a complaint from a student about offensive remarks she allegedly made in one of his posts. It was then that she first became aware of the issue.

(Continued)

Table 4.1 (Continued)

Behavior	Definition	Example
Trickery/outing (doxing)	Tricking someone into sharing sensitive information and then sharing it publicly	Brian asks his girlfriend Sophia to share nude photos while they are messaging. The next day at school, Sophia's friend Milli shows her that the screenshots of their chat went viral, with many of her classmates sharing those screenshots with inappropriate captions.
Flaming or trolling	Sending hostile or vulgar messages to provoke someone	Sam received a lot of praise from his teachers as he scored the highest in his math and science classes. A few of his classmates became jealous and sent him a barrage of hostile and derogatory messages, including insults and encouragement to self-harm. They mocked him about his appearance and spread rumors about his sexuality.
Cyberflashing	Sending someone nonconsensual explicit images or videos	Carl sends follow request on Instagram to all newly enrolled junior girls at his school. When they decline or do not respond to his request, he sends them explicit images of himself to harass them.
Happy slapping	Filming someone without their consent and posting the video online	Harry starts filming a TikTok video of Gwen and Daisy fighting during gym class. He posted the video on TikTok without Gwen and Daisy knowing and it went viral.
Digital self-harm	Posting or sharing harmful content about oneself	Nancy has a fake Instagram account under a pseudonym. She sends herself hurtful messages saying awful things about herself in the NGL app, where the sender's name remains anonymous. She then uploads those as her Instagram stories saying that she is unlovable and hated by everyone.

owned devices and different networks. It is important to keep in mind that even for apps that do not allow anonymous posting, it is common for users to create fake accounts, affording more opportunities for cyberbullying.

It is challenging to accurately capture how frequently youth are experiencing cyberbullying, as research surveys often utilize different descriptions of cyberbullying (with some capturing all three characteristics of bullying and others only capturing one or two characteristics). However, research and other national surveys have found that cyberbullying tends to peak among middle school and early high school students. In a national survey representative of the U.S. population from the Cyberbullying Research Center, 54.6% of teenagers (aged 13 to 17) said they have experienced cyberbullying at some point in their lives (Patchin & Hinduja, 2024). These findings are similar to other national surveys, such as the Pew Research Center (Vogels, 2022), which found that 46% of adolescents in their sample reported experiencing cyberbullying at some point in their lives. The prevalence tends to be lower when asking youth to report on their experiences within a certain timeframe, such as within the past 30 days or within the past school year. In another national survey administered to high school students by the Centers for Disease Control and Prevention (CDC, 2024), 21% of girls and 12% of boys reported they had been electronically bullied in the previous year and Cyberbullying Research Center reported that 26.5% adolescents indicated they had been victims within the past month (Patchin & Hinduja, 2024). Cyberbullying has steadily increased in the past seven years (16.7% in 2016 to 26.5% in 2023). This is perhaps not surprising as digital technology use has continued to grow exponentially among preteens and teens.

Impact of Cyberbullying

Youth and adults are more aware than ever before regarding the harmful impact that bullying has on youth, likely due to increased bullying awareness over the past few decades, particularly in schools. Research has consistently demonstrated that cyberbullying has many negative outcomes, and experiencing cyberbullying is just as harmful, and in some cases more harmful, as experiencing bullying "in person," such as at school (Ansary, 2020; Vaillancourt et al., 2017). Being cyberbullied can make a child feel incredible distress, as it can feel hopeless to try and get a picture or video taken down once it is circulating or not understand why you have been excluded from group chats. It can feel isolating especially if a child does not feel that they can get help from their parents, teachers, or peers.

A child who experiences cyberbullying repeatedly and over time is more likely to report negative outcomes (e.g., depression) compared to a child who experiences cyberbullying occasionally. In research, this is called a "dose-response effect" (Vaillancourt et al., 2017), which means that the outcome (in this case, the child's mental health, physical health, and/or academic performance) is based on how often they are cyberbullied (i.e., levels of distress increase as victimization increases).

Youth who are cyberbullied can experience a wide range of concerns including the following:

- anxiety, depression, low self-esteem, loneliness, social isolation, and suicidal ideation and attempts (Fredrick & Demaray, 2018; Farrington et al., 2023; Fisher et al., 2016; Rose & Tynes, 2015)
- somatic complaints, sleep problems, poor physical health, and risky sexual behavior (Farrington et al., 2023; Fisher et al., 2016)
- school-related problems, including school refusal, skipping class, less engagement at school, and lower test scores and grades (Gardella et al., 2017)
- substance use (e.g., alcohol, cannabis, tobacco) and abuse (e.g., binge drinking)
- problematic internet or device use, and problematic gaming (Lui et al., 2021; Neumayer et al., 2023)

It is important to note that these adverse outcomes, such as social anxiety or sleeping problems, can be experienced by youth immediately or within a few months after being cyberbullied and they can also persist over time. In fact, youth who experience cyberbullying as a child or adolescent are more likely to experience stress, anxiety, low self-esteem, and social problems as adults (Fredrick et al., 2021; Nicolai et al., 2018; Pabian & Vandebosch, 2019).

Although the impact of cyberbullying others has not received nearly as much attention from researchers compared to being cyberbullied, youth who cyberbully others are also likely to experience a wide range of negative outcomes. These outcomes can include:

- bullying others "in person" and aggression and violence later in life (Katzer et al., 2009)
- apathy toward others and feeling justification for their aggressive behavior (Falla et al., 2021, 2023)

- feelings of stress, anxiety, depression, and suicidal ideation (Barlett et al., 2024; Farrington et al., 2023; Zych et al., 2015)
- substance use, sleep problems, and poor physical health (Bartlett et al., 2024)

Youth who cyberbully others *and* are cyberbullied (which researchers call being a "bully-victim") experience more adverse outcomes compared to youth involved only as either the victim or aggressor (Bayraktar et al., 2014). Further, youth who are involved in *both* traditional ("in person") forms of bullying and bullying online also report poorer outcomes (Mitchell et al., 2016). Unfortunately, we often hear from youth that bullying that starts online often extends to the school day (or vice versa, bullying which occurs in person will often continue online).

Why Do Youth Engage in Cyberbullying?

It can be challenging for parents and other adults to understand why some youth are cruel in online spaces. What is the point of being so cruel to your peers and classmates? Although this is a very complex question, researchers have focused on a combination of factors that may help us to understand why youth engage in such unkind behavior online. These factors include specific features of digital technology or online spaces (e.g., anonymity), youth brain development, and other risk factors specific to individual youth and their environment (such as personality traits, social skills, and peer groups), which are described in further detail in the next sections.

Disinhibition refers to behaving in ways an individual typically would not behave due to concerns about judgment from others or with self-representation (Joinson, 1998; Udris, 2014). The concept of disinhibition has been used to explain why people's behavior is different in a digital context compared to a face-to-face environment (e.g., sharing information publicly online or behaving aggressively online). Online disinhibition can be relatively harmless (e.g., some individuals may feel more comfortable complimenting others online) or it can be toxic. Toxic disinhibition is when people feel more comfortable behaving in ways that are harmful to others through digital technology than they would in person, such as being rude, making threats, or sharing hate-based content. Perhaps not surprisingly, researchers have found that adolescents who report higher levels of toxic disinhibition (e.g., they indicate they feel more comfortable creating or sharing harmful information online compared to in person) are more likely to be involved with cyberbullying and online hate (Charaschanya & Blauw, 2017; Udris, 2014; Wachs & Wright, 2018; Wachs et al., 2019). Chapter 1 discussed features of online communication that are appealing to children and adolescents, including the ability to be anonymous, to adjust self-presentation through asynchronous communication, accessibility of information and social interaction, and permanence of content. These features overlap with features of online disinhibition, which can be found in Table 4.2.

Another reason why youth may be motivated to cyberbully others is that youth often do not report cyberbullying (to adults or others), which is related to the minimization of authority as described in Table 4.2. There are many reasons youth may not report cyberbullying:

- Fear of retaliation from the bully or others for reporting cyberbullying
- Short time duration of posts on certain platforms, such as Snapchat, makes it challenging to document posts (e.g., Snapchat provides the user with a notification if an individual took a screenshot of their post) and report the evidence
- Fear of parents or other adults taking their devices away to "protect" them from further harassment
- Beliefs that adult involvement will not help or even make the situation worse (e.g., if the bully gets "in trouble" they could retaliate)
- Not realizing the behavior is cyberbullying or believe they should be able to handle it on their own

Finally, it is important to realize that youth brains are not yet fully developed. That is, the part of the brain responsible for impulse control, judgment, and reflective thinking is not fully developed until young adulthood (i.e., mid- to late-20s; Ansary, 2020; Pharo et al., 2011). Adolescents are particularly vulnerable in situations that affect their mood, which is why they engage in more risk-taking and recklessness compared to adults (Steinberg, 2005). As discussed in Chapter 1, adolescence is a time in which youth are placing more importance on social status and their relationship with their peers. They will respond

Table 4.2 Features of online disinhibition and associations with cyberbullying.

Online disinhibition feature	Definition	Association with cyberbullying
Anonymity	Perception that an individual can hide or change their identity	Adolescents may feel safer engaging in cyberbullying because they feel more confident they will not get caught. Being anonymous also makes it easier for individuals to detach themselves from their behavior. Adolescents often create multiple social media accounts under pseudonyms to remain anonymous and avoid consequences.
Invisibility	Perception that an individual cannot be seen by others	Feeling "invisible" overlaps with feeling anonymous; adolescents may feel invisible on social platforms with large audiences. For example, they may be more likely to join in on cyberbullying by re-sharing or liking harmful posts as they may be one of many who are contributing to the sharing of posts.
Asynchronicity	Lag time between communication (e.g., text messages, direct messages, commenting on posts)	For in-person interactions, immediate social cues (e.g., facial expressions, body language, tone of voice) help us to gauge the impact of our words. Adolescents may not grasp the impact of their harmful words/content online as they often do not see the victim's response (e.g., facial expression) or the response is delayed.

(Continued)

Table 4.2 (Continued)

Online disinhibition feature	Definition	Association with cyberbullying
Self-absorption	Becoming overly focused on an individual's own thoughts and feelings	Adolescents may become overly absorbed in their own feelings or emotions about a situation (e.g., jealously, frustration, anger) and may struggle to see things from another person's point of view, especially if they cannot see the other people and their social cues. This may also lead to adolescents justifying their harmful behavior. In fact, it is common for those who bully others to believe that the victim deserved to be bullied.
Disconnected from reality	Perception that online environment or online interactions are not connected to reality or to "real life"	An adolescent's digital world may allow them to feel a sense of detachment from "real life." This can be exacerbated by the ability to be anonymous, invisible, and to interact with others in asynchronous ways. These features may make it difficult for adolescents to understand the impact and permanency of their actions online.
Minimization of Authority	Perception that there is no authority or adult supervision online	There tends to be minimal adult supervision in online spaces and low reporting rates of cyberbullying. Youth prefer apps or platforms on which adults (e.g., their parents) are not active or they will create fake accounts that are not followed by their parents.

Source: Information adapted from Cheung et al. (2016) and Suler (2004).

in heightened ways to being rejected by their peers because peer relationships are so important during this developmental period. They also engage in behaviors that gain peer attention and more social status (e.g., re-sharing a harmful post to get likes on social media). There are psychological drives or reasons for engaging in bullying behaviors, like wanting power or control, having poor social skills, and displacing hurt from parents or others. In addition to these psychological drives, there may be greater social pressure or even gratification for bullying in online spaces due to the wide audience and the perceived lack of consequences. Overall, the combination of low adult supervision, the perception that cyberbullying will not be reported, the potential lack of repercussions for such behavior, and heightened vulnerability to peer-related issues are all potent contributors to cyberbullying others (Ansary, 2020; Kowalski et al., 2019; Zych et al., 2019). These are all general factors to consider when thinking about why youth may cyberbully others. However, some children and adolescents may have certain experiences, perceptions, or personality traits that make them more or less likely to be involved in cyberbullying, and these factors are discussed next.

Risk and Protective Factors

What makes some children less likely to be involved in cyberbullying? Protective factors are characteristics that reduce the likelihood of something harmful happening or the impact of that harmful event (Substance Abuse and Mental Health Services Administration, n.d.). Thus, protective factors are things that reduce youth's likelihood of becoming involved in cyberbullying. For example, we know that children who have good communication skills, can read social cues, and are able to regulate their emotions are less likely to be cyberbullied. These skills would all be considered protective factors. For youth who have been cyberbullied, protective factors can reduce the negative impact of cyberbullying. If Jasmine is being cyberbullied but has friends who support her and stick up for her, Jasmine is less likely to experience mental health problems (such as depression) because of being cyberbullied. In this case, having supportive friends is a protective factor for Jasmine.

Alternatively, risk factors are the opposite of protective factors. A risk factor *increases* the likelihood that a child will be involved in cyberbullying and they may amplify the negative impact of cyberbullying. Children who are constantly utilizing technology and have difficulty regulating their emotions are more likely to be involved in cyberbullying. If Jasmine did not have a group of peers to support her when she was being cyberbullied and felt isolated, she would be much more likely to experience depression. In this case, social isolation would be considered a risk factor for Jasmine.

Risk and protective factors can be within an individual child (e.g., their personality traits, skills, or behavior), their family and peers (e.g., the child's relationship with their parents and friends), and the larger community (e.g., schools, neighborhoods). The concept of these different "layers" (e.g., individual, family, peers, school, neighborhood, larger society; see Figure 4.1) that impact children's learning and development was initially conceptualized by Uri Bronfenbrenner, who developed the well-known Ecological Systems Theory (Bronfenbrenner, 1979). We can take this same framework and apply it to risk and protective factors for cyberbullying across these different layers.

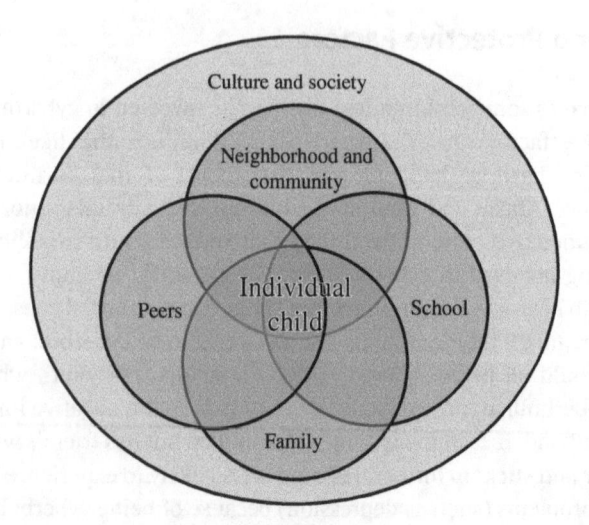

Figure 4.1 Factors that impact youth development.

Risk and Protective Factors for Being Cyberbullied

Researchers have found that some of the most beneficial protective factors for being cyberbullied are having social-emotional skills, such as having high self-esteem, social competence (i.e., understanding social cues, having good communication skills, and building positive relationships with others), and being able to manage strong emotions and stress (e.g., emotional regulation or management; Zych et al., 2019). For example, a child who sees rage bait content online (i.e., content meant to provoke a big reaction, such as using sensational headlines or provocative statements on controversial topics) and can continue scrolling or put down their device is much less likely to be cyberbullied compared to a child who engages with this type of content. Perhaps not surprising, children and adolescents who spend less time online are less likely to experience cyberbullying (Fredrick et al., 2024; Zych et al., 2019). Adolescents who say they are online almost constantly are more likely to have been harassed online compared to those who report being online less often (53% vs. 40%; Vogels, 2022) and are also more likely to have experienced multiple forms of cyberbullying (37% vs. 21%). Of course, children can be cyberbullied without being online as peers can still post harmful content about them. Digital citizenship skills such as making safe decisions, being respectful, and thinking critically while using digital devices (Fredrick et al., 2023) are also related to less online harassment (Jones & Mitchell, 2016).

Children who have low self-esteem or feel inadequate, make quick decisions (without thinking things through first), and struggle to recognize social cues and empathize with others are more likely to be cyberbullied. Further, youth who experience mental health challenges, such as anxiety, depression, and suicidal ideation, and those who spend more time using digital media are more likely to be cyberbullied (Zych et al., 2019). As mentioned earlier in this chapter, how youth interact online is often very similar to their offline or "in person" behavior. Children and adolescents who are bullied in person (e.g., at school) are more likely to be bullied online. Finally, there is an increasingly disproportionate impact of bullying on youth who have minoritized identities (based on race, ethnicity, gender, sexual orientation, disability, and religious beliefs). Bias-based cyberbullying is a form of cyberbullying in which the aggressor specifically targets an individual's social identity (e.g., gender, sexual orientation, race, ethnicity, religious beliefs, and disability). Unfortunately, this form of cyberbullying is on the rise. For example, cyberbullying has increased among Asian American youth (13.9% in 2016 to 23.5% in 2022). Teens (ages 13 to 17 years) report being harassed online due to their race or ethnicity (22%), gender (20%), religion (18%), sexual orientation (13%), or disability (7%; ADL's Center for Technology and Society, 2023). Bias-based bullying and cyberbullying have a damaging impact and are associated with more negative mental and physical health outcomes compared to bullying and cyberbullying, which do not target an individual's identity (Mulvey et al., 2018).

As previously mentioned, characteristics of the child's family, peers, schools, and community can also serve as risk or protective factors. Parental warmth and feeling supported by parents and caregivers are strong protective factors (Zych et al., 2019), as is support from peers. As shown in the example above of Jasmine, having close and supportive friends is important to reduce feelings of social isolation, especially when cyberbullying is involved. In some cases, it can even be helpful for youth if their friends have also been cyberbullied. This may help them to realize that it is not their fault, they are not alone in this experience, and they can commiserate together with their friends (Schacter & Juvonen, 2018). Children and adolescents who enjoy school and view their school and neighborhood as safe and positive places are less likely to be cyberbullied. In contrast, children are more likely to be cyberbullied when they have negative relationships with their parents and siblings and have parents who utilize parenting styles that lack warmth and support (e.g., use of strict rules and punishment or are overly permissive as was discussed in Chapter 1). Due to stressors involved with financial challenges, youth from low-income and/or single-parent households are also more likely to be cyberbullied. Children who have experienced trauma, such as physical or sexual abuse, are also more likely to be cyberbullied (Zych et al., 2019). See Table 4.3 for more information on the risk and protective factors of being cyberbullied.

Table 4.3 Risk and protective factors for being cyberbullied.

	Protective factors	Risk factors
Child	• High self-esteem • Interacts well with others • Can regulate big emotions and feelings • Has coping strategies for managing stressful situations • Empathetic toward others • Uses technology responsibly and has digital citizenship skills	• Identifies with minoritized background, such as sexual orientation or gender identity • Low self-esteem • Makes quick decisions without thinking things through • Difficulty recognizing social cues, such as tone of voice and body language, and understanding the perspective of others • Mental health problems, such as depression, anxiety, or suicidal thinking • Excessively uses technology or uses technology in inappropriate ways (e.g., utilizes apps meant for 18+)
Family	• Feels support and warmth from parents • Open and ongoing communication with parents, especially regarding technology use • Parental guidance and restrictions on device use appropriate with the child's developmental level	• Negative or high-conflict family environment • Low parental supervision and monitoring of device use or overly monitors or restricts device use • Low-income or single-parent household • Trauma from family or others, such as physical or sexual abuse
Peers	• High-quality peer relationships and friendships (characterized by high support and low conflict) • Friends who defend them in bullying and cyberbullying situations • Friends who have also been bullied or cyberbullied	• Feeling like they have no friends (i.e., social isolation) • Conflicts arise frequently in relationships with peers

(Continued)

Table 4.3 (Continued)

	Protective factors	Risk factors
School	• Views school as a safe and positive place • Positive relationships with teachers and other adults at school • Can identify at least one adult at school they feel comfortable talking to about stressful situations	• Views school as unsafe • Attends school where bullying and related aggressive behavior happens frequently • Does not feel supported by teachers at school
Community	• Views neighborhood as a safe and positive place • Can identify at least one safe and supportive adult in their community (e.g., church, coach, or other leader involved in extracurricular activity, neighbor)	• Feels unsafe in their neighborhood • Violent behavior happens frequently in their neighborhood or extracurricular activities

Risk and Protective Factors for Cyberbullying Others

Many of the risk and protective factors mentioned previously for being cyberbullied are also risk and protective factors for cyberbullying others. For example, youth who can regulate big emotions (especially anger or frustration), communicate and interact well with others both in person and online, and utilize technology responsibly are less likely to cyberbully others (Kowalski et al., 2019; Zych et al., 2019). However, it is important to note some age differences in these skills. Although children who bully others are more likely to have poor social skills, adolescents who bully others can often understand social nuances and navigate social situations well (Cook et al., 2010). In fact, as discussed in Chapter 1, adolescents often utilize their social skills or popularity to bully others through rumor spreading or damaging others' relationships. Youth who have digital citizenship skills, especially those who say they use the internet to improve their school, community, or help their friends (a term called "online civic engagement"), are less likely to cyberbully others (Jones & Mitchell, 2016). For example, an adolescent who uses Instagram and Snapchat to raise awareness about environmental issues and reduce waste at their school would be engaging in online civic engagement.

In contrast, being impulsive, lacking empathy, and justifying harmful behavior are all risk factors for cyberbullying others. Youth who are aggressive or bullying others "in person" are much more likely to also be aggressive and bully others online. In their review of research, Zych et al. (2019) found that the strongest protective factors were low technology use and peer-related factors, such as feeling accepted by their peers and having a supportive friend group. Feeling rejected by peers, having peers who engage in delinquent behavior, and belonging to a peer group that normalizes bullying are all strong risk factors (Chen et al., 2017). At the family level, a positive parent/child relationship, a warm home environment, and parental supervision of technology are protective. Finally, perceptions of a positive school climate and satisfaction with school are also protective. See Table 4.4 for more information on risk and protective factors for cyberbullying others.

Digital Self-Harm

About 5% to 10% of youth report engaging in digital self-harm, which consists of posting or sharing harmful content about oneself (Patchin & Hinduja, 2017). Typically, these behaviors align with the traditional characteristics of cyberbullying (repetition of intentional harmful behavior in online spaces or through digital technology), except that the aggressor and the target are the same person. For example, someone could create another account on Instagram (either an anonymous account or in a different name) and use that account to post harmful content on their own (real) profile. Although this is a relatively new trend, it first became well known following the suicide of 14-year-old Hannah Smith in 2013 in England. She had been cyberbullied on the social media platform Ask. fm; however, when this case was investigated, it turned out that she was the one posting the negative comments.

Certain youth may be more at risk for engaging in digital self-harm, including youth who have:

- been bullied or cyberbullied
- depression

Table 4.4 Risk and protective factors for cyberbullying others.

	Protective factors	Risk factors
Child	• Communicates and interacts well with others • Can regulate big emotions and feelings, especially anger and frustration • Uses technology responsibly • Has digital citizenship skills, especially using the internet for good causes	• Are aggressive or bully others "in person" such as at school or other places • Engages in rule-breaking behavior (e.g., at school, home) • Are impulsive • Lacks empathy for others and struggles to see others' perspectives • Justifies harmful or aggressive behavior • Mental health problems, including depression and anxiety • Excessively uses technology or uses technology in inappropriate ways (e.g., has multiple Instagram accounts under pseudonyms)
Family	• Parental support and warmth • Parental guidance and restrictions on device use appropriate with child's developmental level	• Overcontrolling/authoritarian or overly permissive parenting styles • No parental restrictions or monitoring of device use
Peers	• Feels accepted and supportive by peers • Peer group encourages positive and prosocial behaviors	• Feels rejected by peers • Peers engage in rule-breaking behavior. • Peer group normalizes or encourages bullying (e.g., thinks it is justified).
School	• Views school as a safe and positive place • Feels satisfied with their school experience • Sees teachers speak up when bullying or unkind comments are said at school	• Bullying and other aggressive behavior happen frequently at school. • The school day is unstructured and/or unsupervised and there are unclear rules and expectations regarding behavior. • Teachers and other adults do not stop bullying when it occurs at school.
Community	• Views neighborhood as a safe and positive place • Involved in extracurricular activities through their school and community	• Violent behavior happens frequently in their neighborhood or extracurricular activities without negative consequences.

- significant negative thoughts about themselves (e.g., low self-worth, low self-esteem)
- thoughts of suicide or previous suicide attempts
- engaged in physical self-harm (i.e., harming your own body on purpose such as cutting or burning yourself)

LGBTQ+ youth are also more at risk for engaging in digital self-harm (Patchin et al., 2023). Why would a person, particularly a teenager who may be concerned about their social status or online identity, post harmful or humiliating content about themselves so publicly? This certainly is an emerging area of research, and some reasons can be found in Table 4.5.

Table 4.5 Motivations for digital self-harm.

Possible reason for digital self-harm	Example
To be funny, to get a reaction, or to get attention from peers	Jax was not invited to a school leadership retreat over the weekend, although many of his friends were invited. Feeling bored and a little sorry for himself, he posts a self-deprecating meme of himself eating McDonalds alone in his sweatpants.
To "test" their relationships with their peers and friends	Dylan creates a fake Snapchat account and makes it look like the account belongs to a girl who attends a school nearby. She adds multiple people from her school as friends and talks bad about herself to them from the fake account to see who would defend her.
To gain sympathy from their peers or adults in their lives (i.e., sadfishing)	Nancy has a fake Instagram account under a pseudonym. She sends herself hurtful messages saying awful things about herself in the NGL app, where the sender's name remains anonymous. She then uploads those as her Instagram stories asking why she is unlovable and hated by everyone.
Show toughness or resilience to stressful events	Leanne posts an unflattering photo of herself from her friend Emma's Instagram account. Leanne confronts Emma, asks her why she would post such a terrible picture, and starts a school campaign to raise awareness about cyberbullying. Leanne's teachers praise her for the way she has handled the situation and Emma is ostracized at school and on social media groups.

Source: Information adapted from Soengkoeng and Moustafa (2022) and Patchin and Hinduja (2017).

In addition to the motivations stated in Table 4.5, youth who are experiencing stressful situations that may feel overwhelming, such as feeling rejected by their peers, having conflicts with peers or their significant other, failing a class, experiencing bullying or harassment, or discrimination may also be implicated in youth motivations to engage in digital self-harm. Overall, digital self-harm is a complex behavior, and youth engaging in these behaviors have ongoing mental health challenges (e.g., anxiety, depression, suicidal behavior) in need of support. Digital self-harm likely results from overwhelming negative feelings, and we should view this behavior as a cry for help in need of support from adults and peers.

In this chapter, we discussed the definitions and criticisms surrounding the definition of cyberbullying, and examples of cyberbullying were provided. We provided information on how often cyberbullying is experienced and the impact of cyberbullying on youth. Finally, we took a deep dive into why youth may cyberbully others and why some youth may be more (or less) likely to be cyberbullied or to cyberbully others. In the next chapter, we describe how families can help to prevent cyberbullying and related behavior, including digital self-harm. Later chapters in this book will describe in detail how families and schools can respond in helpful ways to cyberbullying and related behavior.

References

Ansary, N. S. (2020). Cyberbullying: Concepts, theories, and correlates informing evidence-based best practices for prevention. *Aggression and Violent Behavior, 50*, 101343. https://doi.org/10.1016/j.avb.2019.101343.

Barlett, C. P., Kowalski, R. M., & Wilson, A. M. (2024). Meta-analyses of the predictors and outcomes of cyberbullying perpetration and victimization while controlling for traditional bullying perpetration and victimization. *Aggression and Violent Behavior, 74*, 101886. https://doi.org/10.1016/j.avb.2023.101886.

Bayraktar, F., Machackova, H., Dedkova, L., Cerna, A., & Ševčíková, A. (2014). Cyberbullying: The discriminant factors among cyberbullies, cybervictims, and cyberbully-victims in a Czech adolescent sample. *Journal of Interpersonal Violence, 30*(18), 3192–3216. https://doi.org/10.1177/0886260514555006.

References

Bronfenbrenner, U. (1979). *The ecology of human development: Experiments by nature and design*. Harvard University Press.

Centers for Disease Control and Prevention. (2024). *Youth risk behavior survey data summary & trends report: 2013–2023*. U.S. Department of Health and Human Services. https://www.cdc.gov/yrbs/dstr/index.html.

Charaschanya, A., & Blauw, J. (2017). A study of the direct and indirect relationships between online disinhibition and depression and stress being mediated by the frequency of cyberbullying from victim and perpetrator perspectives. *Scholar: Human Sciences*, *9*(2), 275–301. http://www.assumptionjournal.au.edu/index.php/Scholar/article/view/3003/1926.

Chen, L., Ho, S. S., & Lwin, M. O. (2016). A meta-analysis of factors predicting cyberbullying perpetration and victimization: From the social cognitive and media effects approach. *New Media & Society*, *19*(8), 1194–1213. https://doi.org/10.1177/1461444816634037.

Cheung, C. M. K., Wong, R. Y. M., & Chan, T. K. H. (2020). Online disinhibition: Conceptualization, measurement, and implications for online deviant behavior. *Industrial Management & Data Systems*, *121*(1), 48–64. https://doi.org/10.1108/imds-08-2020-0509.

Cook, C. R., Williams, K. R., Guerra, N. G., Kim, T. E., & Sadek, S. (2010). Predictors of bullying and victimization in childhood and adolescence: A meta-analytic investigation. *School Psychology Quarterly*, *25*(2), 65–83. https://doi.org/10.1037/a0020149.

Farrington, D. P., Zych, I., Ttofi, M. M., & Gaffney, H. (2023). Cyberbullying research in Canada: A systemic review of the first 100 empirical studies. *Aggression and Violent Behavior*, *69*, 101811. https://doi.org/10.1016/j.avb.2022.101811.

Fisher, B. W., Gardella, J. H., & Teurbe-Tolon, A. R. (2016). Peer cybervictimization among adolescents and the internalizing and externalizing problems: A meta-analysis. *Journal of Youth and Adolescence*, *45*, 1727–1743. https://doi.org/10.1007/s10964-016-0541-z.

Falla, D., Ortega-Ruiz, R., da Costa Ferreira, P., Veiga Simão, A. M., & Romera, E. M. (2023). The effect of cyberbullying perpetration on empathy and moral disengagement: Testing a mediation model in a three-wave longitudinal study. *Psychology of Violence*, *13*(5), 436–446. https://doi.org/10.1037/vio0000472.

Falla, D., Romera, E. M., & Ortega-Ruiz, R. (2021). Aggression, moral disengagement, and empathy: A longitudinal study within the interpersonal dynamics of bullying. *Frontiers in Psychology, 12*, 703468. https://doi.org/10.3389/fpsyg.2021.703468.

Fredrick, S. S., & Demaray, M. K. (2018). Peer victimization and suicidal ideation: The role of gender and depression in a school-based sample. *Journal of School Psychology, 67*, 1–15. https://doi.org/10.1016/j.jsp.2018.02.001.

Fredrick, S. S., Coyle, S., & King, J. (2023). Middle and high school teachers' perceptions of cyberbullying and digital citizenship. *Psychology in the Schools, 60*(6), 1958–1978. https://doi.org/10.1002/pits.22844.

Fredrick, S. S., Ettakel, I., Domoff, S. E., & Nickerson, A. B. (2024). Patterns of child and adolescent digital media use: Associations with school support, engagement, and cyber victimization. *Psychology of Popular Media*. Advance online publication. https://doi.org/10.1037/ppm0000570.

Fredrick, S. S., Jenkins, L. N., & Dexter, C. M. (2021). Resiliency in young adulthood and associations among retrospective peer victimization and internalizing problems. *Journal of Child & Adolescent Trauma, 14*, 367–379. https://doi.org/10.1007/s40653-021-00342-4.

Gardella, J. H., Fisher, B. W., & Teurbe-Tolon, A. R. (2017). A systematic review and meta-analysis of cyber-victimization and educational outcomes for adolescents. *Review of Educational Research, 87*(2), 283–308. https://doi-org.gate.lib.buffalo.edu/10.3102/0034654316689136.

Gladden, R. M., Vivolo-Kantor, A. M., Hamburger, M. E., & Lumpkin, C. D. (2014). *Bullying surveillance among youth: Uniform definitions for public health and recommended data elements, version 1.0*. Atlanta, GA: National Center for Injury Prevention and Control, Centers for Disease Control and Prevention and U.S. Department of Education.

Hinduja, S., & Patchin, J. W. (2023). *Bullying beyond the schoolyard: Preventing and responding to cyberbullying* (3rd ed.). Corwin.

Joinson, A. N. (1998). Causes and effects of disinhibition on the Internet. In J. Gackenbach (Ed.) *The psychology of the Internet* (pp. 43–60). New York: Academic Press.

Jones, L. M., & Mitchell, K. J. (2015). Defining and measuring youth digital citizenship. *New Media & Society, 18*(9), 2063–2079. https://doi.org/10.1177/1461444815577797.

Katzer, C., Fletchenhauer, D., & Belschak, F. (2009). Cyberbullying: Who are the victims? A comparison of victimization in internet chatrooms and victimization in school. *Journal of Media Psychology, 21*(1), 1073–1137. https://doi.org/10.1027/1864-1105.21.1.25.

Kowalski, R. M., Limber, S. P., & McCord, A. (2019). A developmental approach to cyberbullying: Prevalence and protective factors. *Aggression and Violent Behavior, 45*(1), 20–32. https://doi.org/10.1016/j.avb.2018.02.009.

Liu, C., Liu, Z., & Yuan, G. (2021). Cyberbullying victimization and problematic internet use among Chinese adolescents: Longitudinal mediation through mindfulness and depression. *Journal of Health Psychology, 26*(14), 2822–2831. https://doi.org/10.1177/1359105320934158.

Mitchell, K. J., Jones, L. M., Turner, H. A., Shattuck, A., & Wolak, J. (2016). The role of technology in peer harassment: Does it amplify harm for youth? *Psychology of Violence, 6*(2), 193–204. https://doi.org/10.1037/a0039317.

Mulvey, K. L., Hoffman, A. J., Gönültaş, S., Hope, E. C., & Cooper, S. M. (2018). Understanding experiences with bullying and bias-based bullying: What matters and for whom? *Psychology of Violence, 8*(6), 702–711. https://doi.org/10.1037/vio0000206.

Nickerson, A., Fredrick, S., Sun, L., & Harrison, D. (2024). Cyberbullying, digital technology, and social media use: Research and practical implications for U.S. schools. In J. S. Hong, H. C. O. Chan, A. L. C. Fung, & J. Lee (Eds.), *Handbook of school violence, bullying and safety*. Edward Elgar Press.

Nicolai, S., Geffner, R., Stolberg, R., & Yaruss, J. S. (2018). Retrospective experiences of cyberbullying and emotional outcomes on young adults who stutter. *Journal of Child & Adolescent Trauma, 11*(1), 27–37. https://doi.org/10.1007/s40653-018-0208-x.

Neumayer, F., Jantzer, V., Lerch, S., Resch, F., & Kaess, M. (2023). Traditional bullying and cyberbullying victimization independently predict changes in problematic internet gaming in a longitudinal sample. *Journal of Adolescent Health, 73*(2), 288–295. https://doi.org/10.1016/j.jadohealth.2023.03.013.

Olweus, D. (1993). *Bullying at school: What we know and what we can do.* Blackwell Publishing.

Olweus, D., & Limber, S. P. (2018). Some problems with cyberbullying research. *Current Opinion in Psychology, 19*, 139–143. https://doi.org/10.1016/j.copsyc.2017.04.012.

Pabian, S., & Vandebosch, H. (2019). Perceived long-term outcomes of early traditional and cyberbullying victimization among emerging adults.

Journal of Youth Studies, 24(1), 91–109. https://doi.org/10.1080/13676261.2019.1695764.

Patchin, J. W., & Hinduja, S. (2006). Bullies move beyond the schoolyard: A preliminary look at cyberbullying. *Youth Violence and Juvenile Justice, 4*(2), 148–169. https://doi.org/10.1177/1541204006286288.

Patchin, J. W., & Hinduja, S. (2017). Digital self-harm among adolescents. *Journal of Adolescent Health, 61*(6), 761–766. https://doi.org/10.1016/j.jadohealth.2017.06.012.

Patchin, J. W., & Hinduja, S. (2022). Cyberbullying among Asian American youth before and during the COVID-19 pandemic. *Journal of School Health, 93*(1), 82–87. https://doi.org/10.1111/josh.13249.

Patchin, J. W., & Hinduja, S. (2024). *2023 cyberbullying data*. Cyberbullying Research Center. https://cyberbullying.org/2023-cyberbullying-data.

Patchin, J. W., Hinduja, S., & Meldrum, R. C. (2023). Digital self-harm and suicidality among adolescents. *Child and Adolescent Mental Health, 28*(1), 52–59. https://doi.org/10.1111/camh.12574.

Peter, I.-K., & Petermann, F. (2018). Cyberbullying: A concept analysis of defining attributes and additional influencing factors. *Computers in Human Behavior, 86*, 350–366. https://doi.org/10.1016/j.chb.2018.05.013.

Pharo, H., Clark, S., Graham, M., Gross, J., & Hayne, H. (2011) Risky business: Executive function, personality, and reckless behavior during adolescence and emerging adulthood. *Behavioral Neuroscience, 125*(6), 970–978. https://doi.org/10.1037/a0025768.

Rose, C. A., & Tynes, B. M. (2015). Longitudinal association between cybervictimization and mental health along U.S. adolescents. *Journal of Adolescent Health, 57*(3), 305–312. https://doi.org/10.1016/j.jadohealth.2015.05.002.

Schacter, H. L., & Juvonen, J. (2018). Dynamic changes in peer victimization and adjustment across middle school: Does friends' victimization alleviate distress? *Child Development, 90*(5), 1738–1753. https://doi.org/10.1111/cdev.13038.

Soengkoeng, R., & Moustafa, A. A. (2022). Digital self-harm: An examination of the current literature with recommendations for future research. *Discover Psychology, 2*, 19. https://doi.org/10.1007/s44202-022-00032-8.

Steinberg, L. (2005). Cognitive and affective development in adolescence. *Trends in Cognitive Sciences, 9*(2), 69–74. https://doi.org/10.1016/j.tics.2004.12.005.

Substance Abuse and Mental Health Services Administration. (n.d). *Risk and protective factors.* https://www.samhsa.gov/sites/default/files/20190718-samhsa-risk-protective-factors.pdf.

Suler, J. (2004). The online disinhibition effect. *CyberPsychology & Behavior, 7*(3), 321–326. https://doi.org/10.1089/1094931041291295.

Udris, R. (2014). Cyberbullying among high school students in Japan: Development and validation of the Online Disinhibition Scale. *Computers in Human Behavior, 41,* 253–261. https://doi.org/10.1016/j.chb.2014.09.036.

Vaillancourt, T., Faris, R., & Mishna, F. (2017). Cyberbullying in children and youth: Implications for health and clinical practice. *The Canadian Journal of Psychiatry, 62*(6), 368–373. https://doi.org/10.1177/0706743716684791.

Vogels, E. A. (2022, December). *Teens and cyberbullying 2022.* Pew Research Center. https://www.pewresearch.org/internet/2022/12/15/teens-and-cyberbullying-2022/.

Wachs, S., & Wright, M. (2018). Associations between bystanders and perpetrators of online hate: The moderating role of toxic online disinhibition. *International Journal of Environmental Research and Public Health, 15*(9), 2030. https://doi.org/10.3390/ijerph15092030.

Wachs, S., Wright, M. F., & Vazsonyi, A. T. (2019). Understanding the overlap between cyberbullying and cyberhate perpetration: Moderating effects of toxic online disinhibition. *Criminal Behaviour and Mental Health, 29*(3), 179–188. https://doi.org/10.1002/cbm.2116.

Zych, I., Farrington, D. P., & Ttofi, M. M. (2019). Protective factors against bullying and cyberbullying: A systematic review of meta-analyses. *Aggression and Violent Behavior, 45,* 4–19. https://doi.org/10.1016/j.avb.2018.06.008.

Zych, I., Ortega-Ruiz, R., & Del Ray, R. (2015). Systematic review of theoretical studies on bullying cyberbullying: Facts, knowledge, prevention, and intervention. *Aggression and Violent Behavior, 23,* 1–21. https://doi.org/10.1016/j.avb.2015.10.001.

5

Helping Children Navigate Social and Digital Life

There are many ways that parents and educators can help children and adolescents socialize safely online, such as helping them to develop their social-emotional competence (e.g., skills in communication, respect, perspective-taking, emotion-regulation). Parents and educators can also help guide children and teens through responsible digital media use (e.g., not sharing passwords, understanding their "digital footprint," digital media etiquette in person and online). We begin this chapter by providing guidance on how to help children and teenagers build positive peer relationships and support their social-emotional competencies. We also review effective parenting styles and strategies associated with reduced cyberbullying and problematic social media use. Specific strategies for promoting safe media use are provided, such as how to talk about social media and guide youth in making good choices (including how to support their friends and peers), if and when to give children smartphones, setting limits, and using options for monitoring. Finally, we highlight resources parents and educators can use to guide these efforts.

Supporting Social-Emotional Competencies and Building Positive Peer Relationships

Helping children navigate their increasingly complicated social and digital worlds may seem overwhelming. We talk to many parents who say things like, "I am glad I did not have to grow up in the world my kids do" and grandparents who exclaim that they are relieved that when they

Cyberbullying: Helping Children Navigate Digital Technology and Social Media,
First Edition. Stephanie Fredrick, et al.
© 2025 John Wiley & Sons, Inc. Published 2025 by John Wiley & Sons, Inc.

raised their children, social media did not exist. Some points raised in Chapter 4 were that children are better protected from the effects of cyberbullying when they have support from their friends, and when they can regulate emotions like anger and sadness during stressful situations (Zych et al., 2019). Given this, teaching and guiding children in developing these social-emotional competencies becomes a way that parents and educators can help prevent some of these problems. There are also several parenting practices that have been related to children's prosocial behavior (that is, behavior that benefits others, such as helping and supporting others who are hurting; Eisenberg, 2006) and reduced bullying behavior.

What can parents do to help children develop social-emotional competence and prosocial behavior? Recent meta-analyses (studies that compile findings across several other research studies) have identified parenting styles that relate to children being more prosocial (van der Storm et al., 2022; Wong et al., 2021) and having better self-regulation (Goagoses et al., 2023). Two components of effective parenting styles are (1) warmth/responsiveness to children's needs and (2) positive behavioral control (having clear rules and expectations; Baumrind, 1971; Wong et al., 2021). The concept of parenting styles on these dimensions goes back several decades to the work of psychologist Diana Baumrind (Baumrind, 1971). She found that authoritative parents who were high in both components (warmth/responsiveness and behavioral control) had children with the most prosocial behavior. Research has found that parents who are high on one of these dimensions but low on the other are more likely to have children who engage in less prosocial behavior. Authoritarian parents are very controlling, but they do not balance this with being warm and responsive to their child's needs. Their focus is on obedience to strict rules, and children tend to not share their feelings or problem-solve with their parents. On the other hand, permissive parents encourage their children to share their feelings and are warm and responsive; however, they do not discourage problem behavior by making clear rules and enforcing consequences. Let us look at scenarios of these three different parenting styles:

- *Authoritative (↑ warmth/responsiveness, ↑ behavioral control).* Amaya is raised in a home knowing that her basic (food, water, clothing, and shelter) and other needs (affection, communication, and quality time) will be met. She is expected to follow her parents' rules and decisions, and she is told why the rules and decisions are made. When she behaves in kind and responsible ways (for example, doing chores, helping her sibling, saying thank you), she is rewarded with praise or other positive things (for example, stickers on a behavior chart for which she earns a reward if she gets a certain number of stickers at the end of the week). When she breaks rules or does not meet behavioral expectations, her parents use consequences that are logical. For example, if Amaya hits her brother, she is put in a brief time-out to calm down and her parents work with her on better strategies to express her frustration and anger. Amaya shows kindness to others in person and in digital environments, and when she sees others being cyberbullied, she tries to comfort them or tell the person doing it to stop.

- *Authoritarian (↓ warmth/responsiveness, ↑ behavioral control).* Evan's parents are very strict and expect him to conform to the high expectations they have of him in all aspects of life. When he makes mistakes or disagrees with what they want for him, his parents apply strict consequences. For example, when he questioned why he had to wait until he was in high school before getting a smartphone, they replied by saying that they were the parents and could make the decisions, and his attitude made them think he should not get smartphone privileges until he turned 16. When Evan becomes upset or wants attention or affection, he is called weak and told to toughen up. Evan uses the school computers to spread mean messages about some of the younger, smaller boys in the school.
- *Permissive (↑ warmth/responsiveness, ↓ behavioral control).* Renee has always been showered with love and affection by her family. She is confident that whatever she needs will be provided for her, and anything that she wants to do, her family will make happen. When she behaves in problematic ways, such as insulting her mother for the way she dresses, there are no consequences. Renee and a few of her other friends started getting social media accounts when they were 10 years old and flaunted this in front of other students who were not allowed to have these. When the teacher informs Renee's parents that her phone use is disruptive to others, the parents say that Renee is mature for her age and should be able to do what she wants.

These examples are not meant to say that parents who are too strict or too permissive will have children that cyberbully others, but rather, we share these to show how a balanced parenting style helps youth develop skills and behaviors that will help them to make good choices. In fact, a 10-year follow-up study of adolescents whose parents had participated in a program to teach positive parenting strategies (such as talking with children, showing affection and praise, setting rules, and using logical consequences) were less likely to bully their peers, although the effects were not found for cyberbullying (Kim et al., 2021).

Research has shown a relationship between positive parenting practices and reduced bullying and cyberbullying (Hinduja & Patchin, 2022; Nocentini et al., 2019). Similar to the authoritative parenting style described, these parenting practices include warmth, support, autonomy, and structure (Elsaesser et al., 2017; Hinduja & Patchin, 2022), as well as communication, supervision and monitoring, and parental involvement (Elsaesser et al., 2017; Nocentini et al., 2019). In contrast, negative parenting, including conflict and aggression, abuse and neglect, and rejection, is associated with children's bullying and cyberbullying behavior (Hinduja & Patchin, 2022; Nocentini et al., 2019). It is likely that this contributes to a cycle of violence, as children learn and then perpetuate the aggression they have experienced.

Some research has found that positive parenting practices may also protect children from problematic use of social media. In a study of Dutch adolescents, positive parenting (such as being warm and supportive, having behavioral control through supervision, rules, and discipline, and allowing children to express their thoughts and ideas) was the most important factor associated with less problematic and risky use of social media (Geurts et al., 2022). A meta-analysis found a small, negative association between authoritative parenting style (i.e., warmth, control) and problematic internet use in adolescence (Lukavská et al., 2022).

As discussed in Chapter 4, positive peer interactions and support from peers is also associated with a lower likelihood of cyberbullying (Zych et al., 2019). Parents can support these positive relationships the same way that they promote their children's social-emotional competence. For example, children whose parents are warm and responsive, allow them to express emotions, validate feelings, and help them manage various emotions are more likely to behave in prosocial and empathic ways that contribute to better peer relationships (Spinrad & Gal, 2018). Parents can also help structure play dates, encourage their children to take the perspective of others, discuss qualities of good friends, and help them to value their own identities to cultivate positive peer influences and minimize peer pressure (DeAngelis, 2023).

Promoting Safe Media Use

There is an enormous expectation for parents to protect their children in the online world, which can be anxiety producing, especially since even experts do not agree on advice on how to do this (Harris & Jacobs, 2023)! The parenting styles and strategies discussed above help children and adolescents develop social-emotional competencies that promote positive behavior, but they do not specifically address how to promote safe media use. Recently, the U.S. Surgeon General (2023) and the American Psychological Association (APA, 2023) have released guidance about social media use that has implications for parents and educators. This guidance surrounds what adults can do to model responsible behavior on social media, promote and teach about healthy online use, set limits, monitor use, and look out for signs of problematic use.

Model Responsible Behavior on Social Media

Children often model their behavior after what they see the adults around them do. It is not surprising that if they see their parents use social media responsibly, children and adolescents are likely to do the same. Parents should be mindful of how much they are using their devices and what they are doing with them. Both parental screen time and parental phubbing (using smartphones during mealtimes or when talking to or spending time with their child) have been associated with adolescents' more problematic social media use (Geurts et al., 2022; Nagata et al., 2024). Therefore, adults should strive to keep the content they post positive, avoid over-sharing, and set limits on use. For example, talking to and spending quality time with children when not in front of a digital device, charging smartphones overnight in a room other than the bedroom, and sharing positive examples of posts and connections with others through social media are ways to model responsible behavior.

Promote Healthy Online Use

There are many practices adults engage in to guide their children in online spaces, sometimes referred to as joint media engagement (as discussed in Chapter 2) or active mediation of use (for example, talking about online activities, sharing or co-using media) and active mediation of internet safety, which are activities used to promote safe and responsible behavior online (Livingstone et al., 2015). Some of the recommended practices and resources are highlighted in the following text.

Talk About Online Lives

Conversations about healthy online behavior should happen early and continue as children develop (Harris & Jacobs, 2023). The more open and validating parents are about their children's online lives, the more likely youth will be to share concerns and ask for advice. It is the quality, rather than the frequency, of the conversations about internet use that seems to make the most impact. More specifically, when children feel comfortable and taken seriously by their parents when they talk about internet use, they are less likely to develop problems with internet use (van den Eijnden et al., 2010). Youths report wanting their parents to teach them about cyberbullying and using digital media in a relatable rather than overly serious way through conversations, personal stories, and concrete examples (Cassidy et al., 2018).

Since digital media is such a constant in our lives, it makes sense to talk about our experiences, both positive and negative, with it. Asking children to show you their favorite YouTube channel and who they like to follow on Instagram allows them to share their interests. You can also share aspects that you enjoy, such as connecting with family and friends who live far away, playing interactive games like Words with Friends, and sharing funny reels. Parents can also give examples of mistakes they have made, such as having someone post an unflattering photo or post they do not agree with on their page because they did not select the option to review posts that they are tagged in. In contrast, if we only talk about digital media as problematic or if adults are overly concerned about it, children may not want to share their thoughts and concerns.

Choosing the right time and place to have these conversations can also be important. If the child has just come home from school or is in a bad mood, it is likely not the time to bring up these issues as they may want to unwind. We have found that bringing up these things when doing something together like driving, eating, taking a walk, or even around bedtime can lead to more natural conversations. Using a conversational tone, even when asking questions, will also help put children at ease. *Constant Companion: A Week in the Life of Young Person's Smartphone Use* (Radesky et al., 2023) provides helpful talking points for parents to ask their children about media use, for example:

- What apps do you spend the most time on?
- How have you seen algorithms work in your social media?
- Are there notification settings you can turn off to be less annoying?

Co-use Media

As discussed in Chapter 2, co-use is when children share technology with someone else (such as a parent or teacher) that allows for discussion, sharing of perspectives and experiences, and teaching how to use certain devices (Kolb, 2016). Co-use is more common when children are younger, and parents with higher education and more positive attitudes toward digital media are more likely to do this (Wahyuningrum et al., 2020). There are pros and cons of co-use. For example, if adults simply view/experience the media together in a passive way (with no discussion or active selection of the media), they may be sending a message that they condone problematic aspects of it, as in the case of watching violent videos. In contrast, when adults use connective co-use, where they are actively intending to share the digital media experience to connect with their child, the experience may be more positive. A study found that when parents discuss digital media and engage in connective co-use, their children have a lower risk of cyberbullying (Padilla-Walker et al., 2018). There is also educational software created specifically for co-use, which allows adults to work with children synchronously to write, draw, and create screencasts (see Kolb, 2016). Some of our own examples and those of parents in a Facebook group have some examples of co-use, such as:

- going to museums and splitting up, and taking photos of favorite artwork and sending them to each other
- following science teachers on TikTok and doing experiments together

- using Happyfeed (www.happyfeed.co), a gratitude app, to reflect on positive moments each day and share with each other via the pod feature
- families sharing funny memes about mutual interests (e.g., travel, pets) via Instagram messenger
- having a family BeReal to see what each other are doing
- sharing Spotify and Netflix accounts to see what other family members are listening to and watching
- gaming together (either through shared server or through correspondence chess apps or other means)

Engage in Active Mediation

Active mediation is when parents engage with their children to discuss, explain, and guide children in appropriate use of digital media and internet safety (Chen et al., 2023; Livingstone et al., 2015). There are many free and helpful resources, highlighted later in this chapter, which adults can use to provide this guidance. We have listed a few examples in Table 5.1 of what parents might do to guide their children's digital media use.

Adults should also do their best to educate themselves about the apps their children are using and the safety and family features they offer. The internetmatters.org (2024) *Guide to Apps* is a great resource, and it also offers step-by-step guidelines for setting up parental controls. Commonsensemedia.org also provides reviews of apps (www.commonsensemedia.org/app-reviews), including ages they are appropriate for, what they are designed to do, ease of use/play, representation of diversity, positive messages, and content issues (e.g., violence, sex, language, alcohol, and drug use).

Most digital media platforms also have family centers and resources. For example, Snapchat's Family Center (parents.snapchat.com) includes a YouTube series that helps parents understand how it works and the safety protections in place. The center also explains how messaging works, community guidelines, safeguards (e.g., protecting from unwanted contact, no tolerance for severe harm, age-appropriate content, reporting tools, age requirements), and parental controls and resources. Instagram has a webpage (https://about.instagram.com/community/parents) for parents that details the tools, resources, and

Table 5.1 Examples of active mediation strategies.

Strategy	Examples
Protect privacy	• Change privacy settings to control who sees posts • Set permissions for apps • Only accept friend/follower requests from people you know • Avoid sharing personal information (phone number, address, and credit card information) online • Google yourself to see what others can see
Keep information secure	• Use strong passwords • Log out when using public/shared devices • Do not share passwords (except with parents)
Be mindful of your digital footprint	• Remember that what you post is permanent and could be seen by family members, employers, and others. • Delete questionable or unflattering content. • Show examples of positive posts and content (e.g., thanking teachers on parent websites for schools instead of insulting school)
Think critically	• Remember that posts may not be accurate reflections of people's real lives (filters, selective content) • Algorithms are used by social media sites to steer us toward content/products (body/weight, politics, self-harm) • Question the evidence/source (social media platforms are not scientific sources) • Be sure to check identities/safe procedures whenever exchanging money, and avoid scams (ads claiming "free," "you've won," "I need help – send money.")
Prevent and resolve online issues	• Be aware that sharing nude pictures of minors is considered child pornography • Report cyberbullying and online abuse to trusted adult and/or social media platform (https://cyberbullying.org/report). • Report exploitation to CyberTipline (https://report.cybertip.org/; 1-800-THE-LOST), Take it Down (https://takeitdown.ncmec.org/)
Explore interests and connections	• Choose apps and platforms that nurture creativity and connection • Find communities of support

Sources: Strategies and examples adapted from Children and Screens (2024b); Harris and Jacob (2023); U.S. Surgeon General (2023).

features built-in for youth to have safe and positive experiences. These include options for, but not limited to blocking, filtering, anonymous reporting, connecting to crisis support resources, choosing who can comment on posts, applying caption warnings, using prompts (i.e., safety notices) to encourage youth to be cautious in conversations, using parental supervision tools (e.g., to set time limits, view accounts followed by teen, approve app purchase/download, and receive purchase notifications), managing ads, and hiding more age-inappropriate content. Roblox also has information for parents, safety, and moderation (en.help.roblox.com/hc/en-us/categories/200213830-Parents-Safety-and-Moderation) including information about safety features (e.g., filters, blocking users, monitoring activity, account restrictions) and resources on their digital safety initiative.

Beyond the controls that are built into the apps, adults can also help children to think critically about the information they are seeing on digital media, such as asking if a person sharing information on mental health has credentials to make these claims or is instead relying on personal experience or being paid as an influencer (Klein, 2024). Internetmatters.org also has a quiz called "Find the Fake," (https://www.internetmatters.org/issues/fake-news-and-misinformation-advice-hub/find-the-fake/) that parents can compete with their children to test their knowledge on detecting and preventing the spread of fake news and misinformation.

Support Youth to Engage in Bystander Intervention in Online Spaces

As mentioned in Chapter 3, youth are very likely to see harmful or hateful content on digital media, so in addition to preparing them for it, adults can also help support them to engage in bystander intervention. Most bystander intervention approaches provide youth with several different options, such as intervening directly to address the issue, providing a distraction, reporting the abuse, and/or supporting the person harmed (Doumas et al., 2021; Nickerson et al., 2024). Strategies that can be used to respond to microaggressions and cyberbullying in digital environments also include identifying and calling out the problem (i.e., making the invisible visible), directly confronting the perpetrator, providing education, or getting other support (Awad & Connors, 2023).

Table 5.2 Examples of bystander intervention strategies for cyberbullying.

Cyberbullying situation	How can bystanders intervene?
Someone posted on a Kayla's social media account that everyone hates her and she should kill herself	• Post a comment calling out the problem and supporting the person harmed ("This is so wrong. Stay strong, Kayla – luv u!")
Rex, an 11-year old, plays on an online gaming platform with some of his friends, but older players send constant rude and offensive messages in the chat	• Report the abuse to the online gaming platform • Tell Rex he should not have to deal with it and advise that he disable the chat feature
Tonya sends a partially nude photo of herself to her boyfriend, John. After they break up, John shares it on his social media accounts	• Tell John that is uncool and that he can be charged with child pornography • Reach out to Tonya to empathize ("I am sorry that happened"); tell her to contact takeitdown.ncmec.org to have the image removed

Source: Adapted from Awad and Connors (2023) and Nickerson et al. (2024).

Table 5.2 provides some cyberbullying situations and examples of how bystanders can intervene.

Set Limits

The choice about if and when to allow a child to have a smart device can be a difficult one. On the one hand, it seems like *everyone* in schools and the neighborhood has one and that is how they connect and relate, and parents may not want their kids to be left out. On the other hand, there are so many concerns and cautions about what smart devices can do (limit physical and face-to-face social activity and expose children to content that may lead to depression, anxiety, self-harm, cyberbullying, and exploitation) that impressionable young people may not and should not have to encounter, and parents may feel a desire to limit and protect them. It may be helpful for adults to know the age at which other children have these phones. According to Common Sense Media, about one-third of 8- and 9-year-old children have smartphones, just over half (i.e., 53%) of 11-year-olds have one, and by age 14, 91% of teens have one, with the highest percentage (97%) occurring at age 17 (Rideout et al., 2022).

Deciding If and When to Give a Child a Smartphone

Children and Screens (2024a) offers some helpful considerations for families in their *Smartphones: Assessing Readiness* tip sheet. First, it is important to be intentional about the device to start with, and it is best to avoid simply giving children their parents' old phones because there tend not to be controls on them. Instead, many families choose to start their child out with a flip phone (e.g., TCL Flip 2, Nokia 2780 Flip) or a kid-centric smartphone (e.g., Bark Phone, Pinwheel, iPhone SE) that allow children options to call, text, or take pictures yet limits or blocks access to web, social media, and other apps. Depending on the phone, they either do not allow access to social media or the web, or they have controls that allow parents to limit screen time, block content, review text message, and call history, filter messages from unknown people, and/or screen messages and social media for harmful content (e.g., bullying, depression, alcohol, guns, pornography).

Every child is different in terms of development and behaviors that signal readiness. Parents can look for signs that their child is showing responsibility, as it can help to pair these with the privilege of having a smartphone (Children and Screens, 2024a). For example, are they contributing by making lunches, babysitting for others, and/or being able to have conversations and engage in coming up with rules about devices? Parents can also consider the extent to which the child is able to talk about the considerations in Table 5.1, such as maintaining privacy and handling the challenges with things said in text or on social media. There may also be unique needs for neurodivergent children (for example, those with autism or attention deficit hyperactivity disorder). For safety reasons, parents may be especially concerned with wanting to locate them. Smartphones may also be too distracting due to sensory issues, or they may be helpful for allowing more independence, using features to organize things, and pursuing interests (Children and Screens, 2024a).

Because smartphone usage is so tied in with the peer group, it can be helpful to work with others in a community to have common standards. A specific example of this is "Wait Until 8th" (www.waituntil8th.org/), a pledge parents make where they promise to not give their child a smartphone until at least the end of 8th grade. It works by having at least 10 families from a given school and grade make the pledge, thus empowering families to rally together and resist the notion that everyone else has one.

Families with children from the same grade and school are given each other's emails and names so that they can be connected.

Many adults may not be aware of the federal rules about children's online privacy. The Children's Online Privacy Protection Act of 1998 (known as COPPA) imposes restrictions on websites and online services to give parents control over what information is collected from children under the age of 13. The rule applies to websites and other online services, including apps and smart toys, which collect and use information from children. COPPA requires that they post clear online privacy policies, require parental consent to collect information, provide parents access to their child's personal information, and maintain confidentiality and security, among other rules. A helpful resource is *Complying with COPPA: Frequently Asked Questions* (Federal Trade Commission, 2020).

In February 2019, the social networking app TikTok agreed to pay $5.7 million in civil penalties to settle the Federal Trade Commission's complaint that they failed to notify parents and obtain consent for the collection of private information from children under the age of 13 and did not delete personal information about children per parental request (Federal Trade Commission, 2019). The lawsuit raised many issues, one of which was the lack of education and awareness that parents have about COPPA, especially considering that almost half of children under the age of 13 have social media profiles (Ortiz, 2020). COPPA is in the process of being strengthened further to limit push notifications and strengthen data security, among other changes, designed to shift the burden from parents to website providers for ensuring safe and secure digital environments for children (Federal Trade Commission, 2023).

Setting Rules About Digital Technology Use

Regardless of when a child gets a smartphone, in this digital age, they almost always have access to digital technology at home, through school, and/or with friends or other adults. Therefore, it is important to have rules and expectations about how, when, and in what ways digital technology will be used. As discussed in Chapter 4, youth with lower levels of technology use are less likely to be involved in cyberbullying (Zych et al., 2019). Spending too much time on social media or using it in unhealthy ways, such as comparing oneself to unrealistic beauty and appearance standards, can interfere with functioning (APA, 2023). Therefore, parents should set limits on their children's digital media use so that it does not interfere with getting enough sleep (approximately eight hours per night), physical activity, and socialization (APA, 2023). Specific rule setting about Internet use (for example, limiting use, not allowing during mealtimes or in the bedroom) is associated with a lower chance of being an at-risk/problematic social media user (Geurts et al., 2022). Because youth interact so often with their friends in the digital world, it can also be helpful to talk with other parents to create shared expectations around social media use (U.S. Surgeon General, 2023). Table 5.3 provides some suggestions for limits that families can set.

Negotiation about roles and boundaries for smartphone use can be stressful and the source of conflict between parents and children (Radesky et al., 2023). Parents tend to be pessimistic about their child's digital media use – many are concerned that they will lose control of their children's online behavior and that the devices will have a negative impact on the parent–child relationship (Benedetto & Ingrasia, 2021; Danet, 2020). Parents may need to remember that children today are

Table 5.3 Setting limits on digital devices: guidance for families.

Strategy
Set up parental controls and privacy settings (see https://www.internetmatters.org/parental-controls/#choose-parental-controls-guide) for parental control apps as well as step-by-step guides for smartphones, social media, video games, and other • Manage screen time (set limits) • Disable the ability for children to install apps without password/parental permission • Restrict content
Maintain healthy sleep habits • Turn off digital devices within one hour of bedtime • Charge in a room outside the bedroom • Silent notifications during bedtime hours
Keep devices off during mealtime
Collaborate with your child to come up with a more specific plan (see American Academy of Pediatrics or Wait Until 8th for templates)

Source: Strategies and examples adapted from American Academy of Pediatrics (n.d.), Shannon (2023), and U.S. Surgeon General (2023).

digital natives, growing up with and being well-versed with technology, whereas many parents are digital immigrants, still learning and adopting (Prensky, 2001). Parents' attitudes toward digital media make a difference in their behavior. Studies have shown that when parents have more positive perceptions, they are more likely to engage in active mediation strategies (e.g., co-using, communicating, and guiding use), whereas negative perceptions are associated with being more restrictive (Wahyuningrum et al., 2020).

Engaging in active mediation, such as open family communication, and using positive parenting and setting rules about internet use is related to safer online behavior and a lower chance of problematic use of social media (Benedetto & Ingrassia, 2021; Geurts et al., 2022). Limit setting is also related to lower screen time and less problematic use of social media and digital technology, whereas screen use in bedrooms and during mealtimes is associated with more problematic use (Nagata et al., 2024). Setting these limits is important, and although it can be challenging, doing it in a positive, mutually respectful way is likely to lead to the best outcomes.

Monitor Use

As discussed in Chapter 4, the adolescent brain is not fully developed to control impulses – yet it is highly sensitive to things like attention and feedback from peers – all of which can make social media highly appealing (APA, 2023). In our increasingly digitized world, youth may have trouble disconnecting and keeping to the limits set on their social media use. Therefore, parental monitoring becomes really important. There are a wide range of ways that parents can monitor their children's use, from having conversations with them about what they are doing to becoming friends or followers on their children's social media accounts, to using apps and controls. We believe the decisions about how to monitor should be made based on the child's age and maturity level, the platforms they are using and how they are used, and the parents' preferences and skills. For example, parents may start out with much more close monitoring and mediating, then as their children enter adolescence, typically after the age of 13, this monitoring tends to decrease (Wahyuningrum et al., 2020).

Having active communication, where adults have two-way communication with their children about what they do on digital technology and social media, asking questions, listening, and coaching (APA, 2023) are an important way to monitor use without being overly restrictive. Adults can ask open-ended questions (e.g., What are you doing on social media these days? How has social media affected your friends?) and listen and validate their children's responses (Choukas-Bradley, 2022). Although we may have the urge when a child talks about a negative experience on social media to minimize it by saying something like "that drama shouldn't bother you" or to lecture (for example, "I told you that if you spent all your time on that phone it would lead to this"), it is better to listen and validate. Parents can say things like "It sounds like that you felt left out" or "I can see how that would make you mad." This allows the child to feel heard, keep talking, and be more open to advice about how to cope with different situations.

It is important to note that installing parental controls and monitoring applications can require a lot of time and upkeep (Radesky et al., 2023) – and research is mixed at best about their effectiveness, particularly if used reactively. For example, restrictive mediation of internet use for adolescents has been associated with less problematic use but more gaming disorders (Lukavská et al., 2022). Parental use of reactive restrictions (e.g., remove access to digital technology as punishment) is associated with more problematic use by their children (Geurts et al., 2022; Nagata et al., 2024). Of course, it is difficult to draw conclusions about this, as we do not know for sure if the restrictions lead to the problematic use, or if children's risky behaviors lead to parents being more restrictive, or if both occur.

Also related to monitoring children's digital media use is adults being able to recognize signs of problematic use. Examples of problematic use were discussed in Chapter 3, and Chapter 6 of this book reviews warning signs. In addition to the guidance, provided in this book, there are a number of free online resources that parents and educators can use, which are described further in the text.

Resources for Parents and Educators

American Academy of Pediatrics Family Media Plan (www.healthychildren.org/English/fmp/Pages/MediaPlan.aspx): Families create a profile for each family member and can use the template to set priorities, find media balance, communicate about media, encourage kindness and empathy, promote digital privacy and safety, and designate screen-free zones.

Bark (www.bark.us/): This company has a phone and an app (both of which cost a fee) that include a variety of monitoring and parental controls for children's devices. These features include monitoring texts and apps, receiving alerts when there is content that is concerning, blocking websites and apps, setting limits on screen time, tracking device location, and pausing or disabling internet access.

Childrenandscreens.org: The international non-profit organization, Children and Screens: Institute of Digital Media and Child Development, seeks to understand and address questions about media's impact on children through objective research and interdisciplinary dialogue. They are also committed to educating the public by offering tip sheets on a range of topics (e.g., cyberbullying, digital addiction, artificial intelligence, and mental health), hosting events (e.g., #AskTheExperts webinars on topics such as media use and attention, copycat behavior, and social contagion, as well as digital media use for neurodivergent youth, algorithms, radicalization, and mental health).

Commonsensemedia.org: This organization provides ratings and reviews for parents (and by parents and kids, in addition to their content reviewers) about all digital media, including movies, television, games, apps, and others. It is a one-stop place to find out age-appropriate apps, their positive features, as well as concerns and cautions about anything from content to ease of use to hidden costs. There is also helpful guidance about children's age, topic (e.g., screen time and social media), and platform.

Cyberbullying Research Center (cyberbullying.org): Focused primarily on issues of cyberbullying, this website provides resources for parents, educators, and students about this topic, as well as guidance about social media apps, bullying and cyberbullying laws by state, and informative blogs about trends and topics (e.g., takeaways from U.S. Surgeon General's Advisory on Social Media, AI Risks and Potential for Harm, Digital Self-Harm). Also very helpful is updated contact information for social media apps, gaming, and online platforms about where to report abuse: https://cyberbullying.org/report

Internetmatters.org: Find information on how to set up devices safely with parental controls, learn about apps, get tips about communicating about online safety, and many other resources. There are also options for getting personalized online safety toolkits.

Netsmartz (https://www.missingkids.org/netsmartz/home): The National Center for Missing Children, who operate the CyberTipline to report child sexual exploitation online and offline, has an online safety program called Netsmartz. It provides videos and activities to help guide children to become aware of risks online and make safe choices. They also provide PowerPoint presentations for multiple audiences, tip sheets, and trainings.

waituntil8th.org: For parents looking to connect with other families to pledge not to give their child a smartphone until at least the end of 8th grade, log onto this site. If at least 10 families from the same school and grade make the pledge, they are provided with each other's contact information. The website has lists of schools with active pledges, stories of communities that have done this, smartphone family plans, and other resources.

References

American Academy of Pediatrics. (n.d.). *Family media plan.* https://www.healthychildren.org/English/fmp/Pages/MediaPlan.aspx.

American Psychological Association (APA). (2023, May). *Health advisory on social media use in adolescence.* https://www.apa.org/topics/social-media-internet/health-advisory-adolescent-social-media-use.

Awad, M. N., & Connors, E. H. (2023). Active bystandership by youth in the digital era: Microintervention strategies for responding to social media-based microaggressions and cyberbullying. *Psychological Services, 20*(3), 423–434. https://doi.org/10.1037/ser0000549.

Baumrind, D. (1971). Current patterns of parental authority. *Developmental Psychology, 4* (1, Pt.2), 1–103. https://doi.org/10.1037/h0030372.

Benedetto, L., & Ingrassia, M. (2021). Digital parenting: Raising and protecting children in media world. In L. Benedetto & M. Ingrassia (Eds.), *Parenting: Studies by an ecocultural and transactional perspective* (pp. 127–148). InTechOpen. https://doi.org/10.5772/intechopen.92579.

Cassidy, W., Faucher, C., & Jackson, M. (2018). What parents can do to prevent cyberbullying: Students' and educators' perspectives. *Social Sciences, 7*(12), 251. https://doi.org/10.3390/socsci7120251.

Chen, L., Liu, X., & Tang, H. (2023). The interactive effects of parental mediation strategies in preventing cyberbullying on social media. *Psychology Research and Behavior Management, 16*, 1009–1022. https://doi.org/10.2147/PRBM.S386968.

Children and Screens. (2024a). *Smartphones: Assessing readiness.* https://www.childrenandscreens.org/learn-explore/research/introducing-a-smartphone-assessing-readiness/.

Children and Screens. (2024b). *Smartphones: Preparing for healthy use.* https://www.childrenandscreens.org/learn-explore/research/smartphone-introduction-preparing-for-healthy-use/.

Children's Online Privacy Protection Act of 1998, 15 U.S.C. 6501–6505.

Choukas-Bradley, S. (2022, April 17). *How to talk with your kids about social media: 4 tips for better conversations.* Psychology Today. https://www.psychologytoday.com/us/blog/psychology-adolescence/202204/how-talk-your-kids-about-social-media.

Danet, M. (2020). Parental concerns about their school-aged children's use of digital devices. *Journal of Child and Family Studies, 29*(10), 2890–2904. https://doi.org/10.1007/s10826-020-01760-y.

DeAngelis, T. (2023, January 13). *How to help kids navigate friendships and peer relationships.* American Psychological Association. https://www.apa.org/topics/parenting/navigating-friendships.

Doumas, D. M., Midgett, A., & Hausheer, R. (2021). A pilot study testing the efficacy of a brief, bystander bullying intervention: Reducing bullying victimization among high school students. *Professional School Counseling, 25*(1), 1–11. https://doi.org/10.1177/2156759X211018651.

Eisenberg, N. (2006). Prosocial behavior. In G. G. Bear & K. M. Minke (Eds.), *Children's needs III: Development, prevention, and intervention* (pp. 313–324). National Association of School Psychologists.

Elsaesser, C., Russell, B., Ohannessian, C. M., & Patton, D. (2017). Parenting in a digital age: A review of parents' role in preventing adolescent cyberbullying. *Aggression and Violent Behavior, 35,* 62–72. https://doi.org/10.1016/j.avb.2017.06.004.

Federal Trade Commission. (2019, February 27). *Video social networking app Muiscal.ly agrees to settle FTC allegations that it violated children's privacy law.* https://www.ftc.gov/news-events/news/press-releases/2019/02/video-social-networking-app-musically-agrees-settle-ftc-allegations-it-violated-childrens-privacy.

Federal Trade Commission. (2020, January). *Complying with COPPA: Frequently asked questions.* https://www.ftc.gov/business-guidance/resources/complying-coppa-frequently-asked-questions#A.%20General%20Questions.

Federal Trade Commission. (2023, December 20). *FTC proposes strengthening children's privacy rule to further limit companies' ability to monetize children's data.* https://www.ftc.gov/news-events/news/press-releases/2023/12/ftc-proposes-strengthening-childrens-privacy-rule-further-limit-companies-ability-monetize-childrens.

Geurts, S. M., Koning, I. M., Vossen, H. G., & van den Eijnden, R. J. (2022). Rules, role models or overall climate at home? Relative associations of different family aspects with adolescents' problematic social media use. *Comprehensive Psychiatry, 116,* 152318. https://doi.org/10.1016/j.comppsych.2022.152318.

Goagoses, N., Bolz, T., Eilts, J., Schipper, N., Schuetz, J., Rademacher, A., Vesterling, C., & Koglin, U. (2023). Parenting dimensions/styles and emotion dysregulation in childhood and adolescence: A systematic review and meta-analysis. *Current Psychology, 42*(22), 18798–18822. https://doi.org/10.1007/s12144-022-03037-7.

Harris, L. E., & Jacobs, J. A. (2023). Emerging ideas. Digital parenting advice: Online guidance regarding children's use of the Internet and social media. *Family Relations, 72*(5), 2551–2568. https://doi.org/10.1111/fare.12813.

internetmatters.org. (2024). *Guide to apps.* https://www.internetmatters.org/resources/apps-guide/.

Kim, J. H., Hahlweg, K., & Schulz, W. (2021). Early childhood parenting and adolescent bullying behavior: Evidence from a randomized intervention at ten-year follow-up. *Social Science & Medicine, 282,* 114114. https://doi.org/10.1016/j.socscimed.2021.114114.

Klein, A. (2024, April 24). *A deep dive into TikTok's sketchy mental health advice.* Education Week. https://www.edweek.org/technology/a-deep-dive-into-tiktoks-sketchy-mental-health-advice/2024/04.

Kolb, L. (2016). *Co-use and technology: A magic mix*. Edutopia. https://www.edutopia.org/blog/co-use-technology-magic-mix-liz-kolb.

Livingstone, S., Mascheroni, G., Dreier, M., Chaudron, S., & Lagae, K. (2015). *How parents of young children manage digital devices at home: The role of income, education and parental style*. London: EU Kids Online, LSE.

Lukavská, K., Hrabec, O., Lukavský, J., Demetrovics, Z., & Király, O. (2022). The associations of adolescent problematic internet use with parenting: A meta-analysis. *Addictive Behaviors, 135*, 107423. https://doi.org/10.1016/j.addbeh.2022.107423.

Nagata, J. M., Paul, A., Yen, F., Smth-Russack, Z., Shao, I. Y., Al-shoaibi, A. A. A., Ganson, K. T., Testa, A., Kiss, O., He, J., & Baker, F. C. (2024). Associations between media parenting practices and early adolescent screen use. *Pediatric Research*. Advance online publication. https://doi.org/10.1038/s41390-024-03243-y.

Nickerson, A. B., Manges, M. E., Casella, J., Huang, Y., Bellavia, G. M., Livingston, J., Jenkins, L. N., & Feeley, T. H. (2024). Bystander intervention in bullying and sexual harassment training: Mixed-method evaluation. *Journal of Prevention and Health Promotion, 5*(1), 6–34. https://doi.org/10.1177/26320770231200230.

Nocentini, A., Fiorentini, G., Di Paola, L., & Menesini, E. (2019). Parents, family characteristics and bullying behavior: A systematic review. *Aggression and Violent Behavior, 45*, 41–50. https://doi.org/10.1016/j.avb.2018.07.010.

Ortiz, K. (2020). Underage social media use and COPPA. *Journal of Gender, Social Policy, and the Law*. https://jgspl.org/underage-social-media-usage-and-coppa/.

Padilla-Walker, L. M., Coyne, S. M., Kroff, S. L., & Memmott-Elison, M. K. (2018). The protective role of parental media monitoring style from early to late adolescence. *Journal of Youth and Adolescence, 47*, 445–459. https://doi.org/10.1007/s10964-017-0722-4.

Prensky, M. (2001). Digital natives, digital immigrants part 1. *On the Horizon, 9*(5), 1–6. https://doi.org/10.1108/10748120110424816.

Radesky, J., Weeks, H. M., Schaller, A., Robb, M., Mann, S., & Lenhart, A. (2023). *Constant companion: A week in the life of a young person's smartphone use*. San Francisco, CA: Common Sense. https://www.commonsensemedia.org/sites/default/files/research/report/2023-cs-smartphone-research-report_final-for-web.pdf.

Rideout, V., Peebles, A., Mann, S., & Robb, M. B. (2022). *Common Sense census: Media use by tweens and teens, 2021*. San Francisco, CA: Common Sense.

Shannon, B. (2023, September 7). *My kid just got an iPhone: Help!* https://www.waituntil8th.org/blog/my-kid-just-got-a-phone-help.

Spinrad, T. L., & Gal, D. E. (2018). Fostering prosocial behavior and empathy in young children. *Current Opinion in Psychology, 20*, 40–44. https://doi.org/10.1016/j.copsyc.2017.08.004.

U.S. Surgeon General's Advisory. (2023). *Social media and youth mental health*. U.S. Public Health Service. https://www.hhs.gov/sites/default/files/sg-youth-mental-health-social-media-advisory.pdf.

van den Eijnden, R. J., Spijkerman, R., Vermulst, A. A., van Rooij, T. J., & Engels, R. C. (2010). Compulsive internet use among adolescents: Bidirectional parent–child relationships. *Journal of Abnormal Child Psychology, 38*(1), 77–89. https://doi.org/10.1007/s10802-009-9347-8.

van der Storm, L., van Lissa, C. J., Lucassen, N., Helmerhorst, K. O., & Keizer, R. (2022). Maternal and paternal parenting and child prosocial behavior: A meta-analysis using a structural equation modeling design. *Marriage & Family Review, 58*(1), 1–37. https://doi.org/10.1080/01494929.2021.1927931.

Wahyuningrum, E., Suryanto, S., & Suminar, D. R. (2020). Parenting in digital era: A systematic literature review. *Journal of Educational, Health and Community Psychology, 9*(3), 226–258. https://doi.org/10.12928/jehcp.v9i3.16984.

Wait Until 8th. www.waituntil8th.org.

Wong, T. K., Konishi, C., & Kong, X. (2021). Parenting and prosocial behaviors: A meta-analysis. *Social Development, 30*(2), 343–373. https://doi.org/10.1111/sode.12481.

Zych, I., Farrington, D. P., & Tofi, M. M. (2019). Protective factors against bullying and cyberbullying: A systematic review of meta-analyses. *Aggression and Violent Behavior, 45*, 4–19. https://doi.org/10.1016/j.avb.2018.06.008.

6

Families Role in Recognizing and Responding to Problematic Online Behaviors

As was discussed in Chapters 2 and 3, children and adolescents are spending more time online and with their devices and with that may come a variety of potential problematic behaviors. Concerns have risen broadly about "problematic internet use" among youth (PIU; Saletti et al., 2021). PIU is a term often utilized by researchers and definitions of PIU have varied widely. Other terms or related behaviors in research include internet addiction, addictive phone use, social media addiction, and problematic technology use (Fredrick et al., 2023; Kuss & Lopez-Fernandez, 2016). However, labeling problematic or excessive internet/technology use as "addictive" has been met with criticism (despite the term being used quite frequently in news and other media outlets trying to grab your attention). The American Academy of Pediatrics (AAP) recommends avoiding the term "technology addiction" as a catch-all term because it obscures specific nuanced issues that a child might be dealing with regarding technology. Not all PIU activities are alike and may include behaviors such as excessive online gaming, problematic social media use, pornography, and/or cyberbullying (Kircaburun et al., 2019; Saletti et al., 2021). The AAP suggests that a child or teenager may be engaging in problematic technology use if they are utilizing devices in ways that have detrimental physical and social impacts on their life (e.g., significant loss of sleep, weight loss/gain, failing classes or skipping school, withdrawing from friends/family). Although some adults may think that all youth today are engaging in problematic technology or internet use, reported ranges range from

Cyberbullying: Helping Children Navigate Digital Technology and Social Media, First Edition. Stephanie Fredrick, et al.
© 2025 John Wiley & Sons, Inc. Published 2025 by John Wiley & Sons, Inc.

about 1% to 26% of adolescents across multiple countries, including the United States (Saletti et al., 2021).

The goal of this chapter is to help parents recognize when their child may be engaging in problematic online behaviors. The chapter also reviews strategies for parents on how to respond to problematic online behaviors. Since problematic online behavior can include a wide variety of behaviors, this chapter focuses on cyberbullying involvement, problematic social media use, addictive gaming, and digital self-harm.

Warning Signs

In order to respond and intervene with problematic internet use, parents have to be aware that a problem exists. Thus, the first step is for parents to know the warning signs for youth engaged in a variety of problematic internet behaviors. A warning sign is a behavior that *may* indicate there is a problem or that a problem may occur in the immediate future. They can be thought of as traffic warning signs (those traffic signs that are yellow with black letters). If you see a traffic warning sign, you will likely slow down, be more aware of your surroundings, and be prepared to stop. This can also be applied to warning signs for PIU: if parents see one or more of these behaviors, they should increase their awareness and involvement in their child's device use. For all PIU, parents can watch for warning signs; however, parents should also engage in ongoing conversations with their children and adolescents about their online activities, as was discussed in detail in Chapter 5. Engaging in continual ongoing conversations about any online behavior will help parents know what their child is doing online and encourage future discussions when parents notice any warning signs. For example, a parent might start a conversation by asking their child questions like, "What's your favorite video game or YouTube channel?" or "Who do you follow on Instagram or Twitch, and why do you like them?" As was discussed in Chapter 5, finding appropriate times to ask these types of questions is important, such as when you are driving, before bedtime, taking a walk, or doing another activity together that your child enjoys (and not when they are irritable or in a bad mood). Warning signs for cyberbullying involvement are listed in Table 6.1.

Table 6.1 Warning signs for cyberbullying involvement.

Warning signs for cyberbullying others

- Switches out of apps/games or hides their screen when others are around
- Does not want to talk about or share what they are doing online
- Has multiple online accounts
- Lacks empathy toward others
- Uses devices throughout the night and gets upset when they do not have access to their device
- Is overly concerned with their social status
- Engages in aggressive behavior toward others in person

Warning signs for being cyberbullied

- Appears upset when on their device
- Hides their device from parents
- Unexpectedly stops using their devices or suddenly uses devices excessively
- Does not want to go to school
- Shows changes in both eating and sleeping habits
- Shows symptoms of depression such as losing interest in things they used to enjoy or being withdrawn from friends/family
- Avoids talking about online activities

Source: Information adapted from Hinduja and Patchin (2024).

How these warning signs may actually appear in youth is described next with examples of fictitious individuals named Sam (perpetrator) and Jesse (victim). Sam, who is cyberbullying others, always closes his phone or shuts his laptop screen when his parents walk by him. He always wants to be on his phone and gets angry when he is not able to be on it. He talks about his friends with a large emphasis on people who are popular according to him and he does not seem to demonstrate empathy or sympathy for peers going through tough things (and even sometimes laughs about it). When his parents try to talk to him about his device use he gets angry, storms away, or changes the subject. We need to consider that it is challenging for parents to be aware of specific online activities of their child (e.g., that their child is cyberbullying others). For instance, it would be nearly impossible for a parent to know that Sam makes racially and sexually derogatory comments on friends' Instagram posts, or that Sam is using his phone to copy and paste harmful messages from a private conversation with a friend into a group chat. This is why it is important to monitor these more general warning signs and consider whether your child is showing signs of readiness (e.g., social-emotional competence, responsibility) for autonomous device (e.g., smartphone) use, as was discussed in Chapter 5.

For Jesse, who is being cyberbullied, her parents notice that she seems more down than usual, is not eating as much, and has recently been having trouble sleeping at night. When she is on her phone, she seems upset and is in a bad mood more often than not even when not on her phone. She tells her parents she does not like school and gets stomachaches before school every day and asks if she can stay home. She also does not want to hang out with her friends anymore, even when encouraged by her parents. Again, it is important to pay close attention to these signs since Jesse could be experiencing cyberbullying and is certainly showing symptoms of depression.

It is important to note that none of these warning signs definitively means a child is cyberbullying others or being cyberbullied; however, the more warning signs a child demonstrates, the more likely they may be involved in cyberbullying. It is recommended to check in with your child displaying any of these behaviors because they are concerning and could be indicative of other problems as well, such as mental health problems. As noted in the warning signs, both those who cyberbully others and who are being cyberbullied may avoid or hide what they are doing or experiencing online (Hinduja & Patchin, 2024); thus, beyond watching for warning signs, parents are encouraged to talk to their children about their online behaviors and experiences. Although youth are often encouraged to tell an adult if they are being bullied, the majority of them do not tell adults about their victimization (Bjerald et al., 2021), as was discussed in Chapter 4. As such, it is important to keep an open dialogue about children's online experiences. There are excellent resources for engaging in discussions with your child on the Cyberbullying Research Center website (see Cyberbullying Scenarios Talking to Teens about Online Harassment on www.cyberbullying.org; Hinduja & Patchin, 2023a). As discussed in Chapter 5, preventative discussions with your child about social media use, device use, and what they do online will make it easier to approach more difficult conversations as children get older or are actually involved in problematic online behavior.

According to the American Psychological Association (APA), warning signs for problematic social media use in youth include:

- not being able to stop using social media;
- allowing social media to interfere with other life activities (e.g., relationships, school, and sleep);
- putting a lot of effort into making sure they have access to social media;
- always wanting to be on social media or spending more time on social media than planned; and
- using deceptive behavior to have access to social media use (APA, 2023).

Here is an example of what these risk factors might look like for Jesse. Jesse is a middle school girl who is always on her phone. She scrolls for hours and hours and forgets to do things she had planned. At times when she is not supposed to be on her phone she will tell her parents she just has to check something really quick and will go onto social media. Although her parents make her charge her phone overnight in the kitchen, she will sneak out of her bedroom in the middle of the night to check her social media accounts. She has stopped engaging in activities she used to enjoy doing with her family and friends and her grades in school have started to suffer.

Youth addicted to gaming may demonstrate behaviors similar to problematic social media use, but instead of using social media, they spend time in gaming. It is important to note that Internet Gaming Disorder (IGD) is recognized in the American Psychiatric Association's *Diagnostic and Statistical Manual of Mental Disorders* (DSM-5-TR; APA, 2022), which is the manual used by psychologists and other mental health practitioners to diagnose mental health disorders. The key focus for addictive gaming would be that youth allow gaming to negatively impact areas of their life such as schoolwork, physical health, personality, mental health, and relationships. They may end up socially isolating from other friends or neglecting activities besides gaming (Institute of Digital Media and Child Development, 2024). It is also important to note that there are some commonly co-occurring symptoms and disorders with gaming addiction. Youth addicted to gaming are more likely to have symptoms of depression, social anxiety, Attention-Deficit/Hyperactivity Disorder (ADHD), sleep disorders, and Autism Spectrum Disorder (ASD; Pluhar et al., 2019). It is thought that because youth are spending increasing amounts of time online they have less time for engaging in enjoyable activities with family and friends, which leads to more loneliness and symptoms of depression (Kuss & Lopez-Fernandez, 2016). An adolescent boy addicted to gaming may appear like the following description of Karim. Karim spends significant amounts of time gaming every day. He stays up very late gaming into the early morning hours after his parents go to bed even though he is supposed to be off the computer at that time. He started to lose some of the friends he used to hang out with in person and only hangs out with online gaming friends. He has gained some weight and is not playing basketball in the driveway like he used to enjoy. His grades have started to drop and he seems more sad lately when he is not gaming.

A less commonly known behavior is digital self-harm or presenting oneself as if they were being cyberbullied by others (more information on digital self-harm can be found in Chapter 4). Warning signs for digital self-harm, sometimes referred to as Fictitious Online Victimization (FOV), are less well understood (Soengkoeng & Moustafa, 2022). Warning signs for digital self-harm overlap considerably with warning signs for being cyberbullied and may include the following:

- Talks about themselves in very negative ways and has low self-worth
- Engages in physical self-harm (i.e., harming their body on purpose such as cutting or burning themselves) or has thoughts of suicide or had previous suicide attempts
- Has signs of problematic social media use (as described above), suddenly uses devices excessively, hides device use from parents, and/or avoids talking about online activities
- Shows symptoms of depression, such as losing interest in things they used to enjoy, being withdrawn from family and friends, and shows changes in eating and sleeping habits

As mentioned in Chapter 4, stressful situations such as being rejected by peers, having a conflict with a significant other, or failing a class may all heighten the risk of engaging in digital self-harm, and these types of situations should also be monitored as parents watch for warning signs. Digital self-harm behaviors are challenging for parents because if your child tells you they are being cyberbullied you want to carefully approach the conversation of who may be cyberbullying them and not assume they did it themselves, especially given the small number of youth who engage in this behavior. However, it is important for parents to be aware of this possibility.

Responding to Cyberbullying Involvement

Should you find out your child has been involved with cyberbullying, whether they are being cyberbullied or they are cyberbullying others, there are a variety of things you can do to assist your child. First, if you find out your child has been bullied online, there are five things you can do:

1. Stay Calm: It is important to stay calm as you help your child/adolescent navigate the situation. They will follow your lead and it is important to model being calm in order to problem-solve the situation. You may feel upset and have strong emotions to manage when someone has hurt your child. If you do not think you can remain calm, take a break or wait until you are able to process the event with your child more calmly.
2. Provide Support: It is important to listen to your child's experience in a nonjudgmental manner (Cassidy et al., 2018). This may be a very significant experience for your child, so acknowledging their sadness or struggle is important. If your child was the one who told you about their experience, you should express appreciation to them for sharing this with you. If you found out from someone besides your child that they were bullied online, this is a good opportunity to let them know they can share things with you and that you are here to support them. Additionally, it may be beneficial to assist your child in obtaining counseling or therapy to support their mental health.
3. Collect Evidence: You should collect evidence of the online victimization that has occurred toward your child (Hinduja & Patchin, 2023b). This could involve taking screenshots of the incident(s) or printing out the exchange(s). The only time this would not be appropriate is if the evidence involves an inappropriate or sexual photo of a minor online. In that situation, it is recommended that you do not obtain copies of the images (see Chapter 9 for more information on this).

4. **Report:** Talk to your child about reporting the incident. To whom you report the incident will vary depending on the situation or the platform where the bullying occurred. If the perpetrator is from your child's school, it is best to report the incident to the school for the school staff to handle. If it is anonymous, unfortunately, you do not have a specific individual to report; however, you can still report the incident to the school for the school staff to be aware of the situation. Additionally, any cyberbullying can be reported to the platform that it happened on (e.g., TikTok, Instagram). Each of the social media platforms has a way to report bullying incidents. Depending on the severity of the incident you may also need to contact the police. This would be necessary if any threats were made or sexually explicit photos were shared (see Chapter 9 for more information).
5. **Monitor:** Once you report the incident, you want to make sure that you monitor the school staff's response or the response of the platform where you reported the incident. The goal is to make sure that cyberbullying stops. You may want to continue talking with your child to stay informed about whether the behavior stopped. You may also want to continue educating your child about how to handle cyberbullying in the future.

Youth often say that adults are not helpful when they report to them that they are being cyberbullied (see Chapter 4). Keeping this in mind, we recommend that parents, as much as possible, allow their child to take the lead on problem-solving solutions. We often hear from youth that adults can sometimes get overinvolved (such as getting really angry and immediately calling the bully's parents, which can make the situation worse, or calling the school before the parent is calm and the child is comfortable with this plan). Listening to your child and coming up with possible strategies or solutions that make them feel safe, supported, and validated is the most important thing and will likely reassure them that they can continue to talk to you about stressful situations in the future.

However, some parents will have the opposite problem, finding out that their child is bullying others online. This information may be hard for parents to acknowledge. It is not easy to hear that your child is engaging in behaviors that are hurtful to others. However, you want to be sure to address the situation. Again, there are five steps you can take to approach this situation:

1. **Stay Calm:** Staying calm is the same first step whether your child is being cyberbullied or cyberbullying others. As a parent, you want to be able to approach your child calmly and talk about the situation. In order to move through the following steps, you will need to be able to communicate calmly with your child and problem-solve together.
2. **Investigate and Stop the Bullying:** The most important immediate goal is to stop the bullying. In order to stop the cyberbullying, you are going to need to know what has been happening and learn from your child the extent of the situation (Hinduja & Patchin, 2023b). The overall goal of this step is to ensure that the bullying stops and that there is no more bullying going forward. You may need to provide consequences for your child's harmful online behaviors (Hinduja & Patchin, 2014), such as restricting device use.
3. **Provide Support:** It will be important to determine the reasoning behind why your child is engaging in cyberbullying and that may require outside additional support beyond what you as a parent can provide. It may be helpful to get your child counseling to help them work through any issues they may be experiencing. It could also be helpful to model empathy for the person or people who were harmed in the situation.
4. **Remediate:** Either via a counselor or working with your own child, it will be helpful to develop a way to remediate the harm done by cyberbullying (Hendry et al., 2023). That could include removing what they had posted and/or writing an apology letter to the person they harmed. It may also include letting the school or police know about the situation. Although it may be hard to report your own child's behavior to the school or the police, this may be an important step to follow up and make sure to remediate and stop the behaviors. For example, it may mean that your child could face consequences for their actions imposed by the school. This remediation step will be very unique to the situation and the child involved.
5. **Monitor:** It will be important to make sure that the cyberbullying did stop and that bullying is not continuing online or in person. It may also be necessary to provide more supervision of your child's online behaviors through parental monitoring or using parental controls on devices.

In the following text, we offer a few broad comments for parents on responding to cyberbullying. If your child was cyberbullied, you want to make sure not to encourage your child to retaliate against the perpetrator.

This can backfire and make things worse for your child and is not a recommended solution. In addition, it is not typically recommended that parents reach out to the parents of the perpetrator. Again, this strategy can make things worse for your child and the parents may not be ready to hear this information from you and be ready to problem-solve. Of course, this may vary depending on your relationship with the other parents and the situation. However, typically it is best to leave these discussions to school personnel or other professionals (Hinduja & Patchin, 2024).

Responding to Problematic Social Media Use and Gaming

Social media and gaming are not inherently good or inherently bad and both of these tools can be used in negative (e.g., bullying, exclusion) or positive (e.g., making new friends, engaging in social activities) ways. In addition, these may be very important activities to your child and you do not want to discount the value they may add to your child's life when used appropriately (Institute of Digital Media and Child Development, 2024). Appropriate social media use is influenced by the maturity of the adolescent and that can vary across ages as youth mature at different rates. However, early adolescence (ages 10 to 14) is thought to be a more at-risk time for problematic internet use. During early adolescence, it is important to provide adult monitoring with autonomy increasing as youth get older and show more responsibility (APA, 2023). An example of what parental monitoring with autonomy might look like is allowing Jesse, who is in high school, to play video games as long as she goes to bed by 10 pm on weeknights. However, one night Jesse is playing a cooperative game online with friends that will end 5 to 10 minutes after 10 pm. In this case, she is able to ask her parents to stay up a few more minutes to finish up the game and not let her teammates down. If Jesse started a new game at 10:10 p.m., her parents would hold her accountable to the house rules by providing a logical consequence, such as not allowing her to play video games the following night. As discussed in Chapter 5, research on social media use shows that both setting social media limits and boundaries along with discussing and coaching your children about social media use produces the best outcomes for youth (APA, 2023).

For both problematic social media and gaming use, the interventions recommended for parents are similar. First, it is important to be aware of the warning signs for potential problematic social media and gaming noted earlier in this chapter. If parents have concerns, they can do the following things:

1. Engage in Communication: The first course of action would be to have an open and honest conversation with your child about your concerns (Feinberg & Robey, 2009). Then, engage in a discussion about how you plan to move forward to support them with their behaviors. It will be important to continue to have open conversations about their social media or gaming use. Be sure to encourage your children to come to you should they see anything or have any negative experiences online.
2. Set Clear Limits and Guidelines: After discussing your concerns, the next step would be to set limits and boundaries for your child's device use (Feinberg & Robey, 2009; Espelage & Hong, 2017). Setting limits for your child can include not only how much time they engage in the activities, but also what social media sites or games they are allowed to utilize or whom they are allowed to interact with on these sites. This may require you to set parental controls and monitoring tools in place on the various social media sites, apps, or games. It is important to consider the child's age when monitoring youth and still encourage open communication. Parental controls and monitors on adolescents may incentivize secret profiles and lack of communication with parents about their social challenges. Be sure to reward your children for following the limits and provide logical consequences when they do not follow the limits.
3. Encourage Healthy Social Media and Gaming Use: As noted earlier and throughout Chapters 2 and 3, there are positive aspects of social media (e.g., social support) and gaming (e.g., having fun with friends). You can talk to your child about the good aspects of these activities while still making them aware of any negative repercussions that can also be part of the experience. Help your child recognize the difference between unhealthy and healthy social media and gaming use (Hinduja & Patchin, 2023b).
4. Be a Good Role Model for Your Technology Use: Your child may see you being on your devices and learn those behaviors. For example,

are there times you are with your child and distracted by your own social media use? Be sure to monitor your own use of technology and be a good role model for your child (Ben-Joseph, 2018). You may also ask your children to engage with you on social media or online games so you learn more about it. More information on this is discussed in Chapter 5.

5. Promote Other Activities: Encourage your child to engage in activities that encourage your child to be off social media and games. This could be encouraging more family time with no phones, encouraging sports or clubs, or time with friends in person.
6. Get Support: It may be necessary to reach out to others for support. As noted earlier, problematic social media or gaming is closely associated with mental health problems. School personnel, psychologists, or family therapy can support your child and family in changing the problematic online behavior, recognizing triggers for engaging in it, and supporting positive mental health (Pluhar et al., 2019; Stevens et al., 2019; Yang et al., 2023). More clinical interventions, such as those provided by a psychologist or physician, are described in more detail in the next section.

Outside Interventions for Problematic Online Behavior

One of the most commonly utilized and empirically validated psychological therapies to support your child with problematic gaming use is cognitive behavior therapy (CBT; Pluhar et al., 2019; Stevens et al., 2019; Yang et al., 2023). CBT is based on the belief that psychological difficulties are based on unhelpful ways of thinking and patterns of unhelpful behaviors. CBT treatment helps youth change their unhelpful thoughts and behavioral patterns (APA, 2017). A meta-analysis published in 2019 summarized the results of 12 studies on the use of CBT for Internet Gaming Disorder (IGD) and found that CBT was highly effective at decreasing symptoms of both IGD and co-occurring symptoms of depression and moderately effective at decreasing co-occurring symptoms of anxiety. The researchers concluded that CBT is a potentially promising treatment of IGD, but more research is needed

(Stevens et al., 2019). CBT can be provided through both individual and group therapy. Additionally, there have been some types of CBT that have been revised to specifically focus on internet addiction (CBT-IA) that focuses on controlling habits, changing thoughts that lead to addictive internet behaviors, and treating underlying mental health concerns (Pluhar et al., 2019).

Another form of therapy that is utilized for problematic internet use or gaming addiction is dialectical behavior therapy (DBT). DBT is a form of CBT that helps youth with emotional regulation. It is suggested that DBT may be especially helpful for youth who game to avoid or deal with emotions (Pluhar et al., 2019). Some of the skills taught in DBT include distress tolerance and learning ways to cope with emotions that do not rely on the use of devices or gaming. Families can look for therapists who provide either CBT or DBT as a way to treat their child's problematic aspects of media use or gaming. It is important to note that more successful interventions for problematic internet use include psychoeducation (e.g., teaching about symptoms) and family involvement (Shoemaker Brino et al., 2022). Some research on CBT for additive gaming has shown that involving parents in treatment will result in more positive outcomes for youth (e.g., lower dropout rates for therapy; González-Bueso et al., 2018; Pluhar et al., 2019).

Sports interventions, including a wide range of sports, is another promising approach to reduce problematic online behavior, including PIU. This strategy supports the idea of parents suggesting alternative activities for their child to engage in to assist with less time online and less problematic internet behavior (Yang et al., 2023). When youth are spending significant amounts of time online, they are less active. Participating in regular exercise, such as sports, provides increased sleep and physical and mental functioning, and can assist in reducing internet addiction. However, more research is needed on the specifics of physical/sports interventions (Yang et al., 2023).

Finally, there has been some research on the use of psychopharmacology, or medication, to treat PIU. However, research has found mixed results regarding the use of psychopharmacology to reduce symptoms of internet addiction (Kuss & Lopez-Fernandez, 2016; Yang et al., 2023). Additionally, the use of psychopharmacology is commonly utilized with psychological therapy, such as CBT and DBT as described above.

Responding to Digital Self-Harm

Digital self-harm is a more recently discovered phenomenon and thus, does not have a significant amount of empirical literature available to better understand and treat it. As discussed in Chapter 4, research has shown that youth who engage in digital self-harm are more likely to have symptoms of depression or engage in self-harm offline. Youth who engage in digital self-harm may have been cyberbullied and may be seeking a response or attention from others (Patchin & Hinduja, 2017). Regardless of the reason behind your child engaging in digital self-harm, it is very likely a loud cry for help. Similar to the steps above regarding responding to cyberbullying, if you find out your child has been engaging in digital self-harm, discuss it with them in a calm, nonjudgmental manner. Due to the overlap between digital self-harm, mental health problems, and other risky behavior (such as harming themselves in person or suicidal thoughts), it is likely necessary that your child receive support from a professional to treat any underlying issues (e.g., depression and low self-esteem). Both CBT and DBT therapy have been found to be effective for self-harm and suicidal ideation (Hawton et al. 2016; Kothgassner et al., 2021). Thus, although there is no significant research on interventions for digital self-harm, these would be appropriate interventions to support youth who self-harm digitally as well.

Summary

The internet is not inherently a good or a bad thing for youth; it depends on how youth are utilizing it. As a parent, it is important to be aware of the warning signs for when internet use does become problematic. This chapter reviewed the warning signs and ways to respond to problematic online behaviors, including cyberbullying, problematic social media use, addictive gaming, and digital self-harm. Open communication between parents and their children is crucial to recognize when they need to intervene. There are a variety of strategies that parents can utilize when they feel their child is exhibiting warning signs for problematic use, including reaching out to the school and other professionals for support. The next chapter will discuss the school's role in responding to cyberbullying and other problematic online behavior.

References

American Psychiatric Association. (2022). *Diagnostic and statistical manual of mental disorders* (5th ed., text rev.). https://doi.org/10.1176/appi.books.9780890425787.

American Psychological Association. (2017). *What is cognitive behavioral therapy?* https://www.apa.org/ptsd-guideline/patients-and-families/cognitive-behavioral.

American Psychological Association. (2023). *Health advisory on social media use in adolescence.* https://www.apa.org/topics/social-media-internet/health-advisory-adolescent-social-media-use.

Ben-Joseph, E. P. (2018). *How to prevent cyberbullying (for parents).* Kids Health. https://kidshealth.org/en/parents/cyberbullying.html.

Cassidy, W., Faucher, C., & Jackson, M. (2018). What parents can do to prevent cyberbullying: Students' and educators' perspectives. *Social Sciences, 7*(12), 251. https://doi.org/10.3390/socsci7120251.

Espelage, D. L., & Hong, J. S. (2017). Cyberbullying prevention and intervention efforts: Current knowledge and future directions. *Canadian Journal of Psychiatry, 62*(6), 374–380. https://doi.org/10.1177/0706743716684793.

Feinberg, T., & Robey, N. (2009). Cyberbullying: Intervention and prevention strategies. *National Association of School Psychologists, 38*(4), 22–24. http://www.sonetbull-platform.eu/wp-content/uploads/repository/Users/lianmcguire/cyberbullying%20%5BLian%20McGuire%5D.pdf.

Fredrick, S. S., Domoff, S. E., & Avery, K. L. (2023). Peer cyber-victimization and addictive phone use: Indirect effects of depression and anxiety among college students. *Cyberpsychology: Journal of Psychosocial Research on Cyberspace, 17*(3), Article 6. https://doi.org/10.5817/CP2023-3-6.

González-Bueso, V., Santamaría, J. J., Fernández, D., Merino, L., Montero, E., Jiménez-Murcia, S., Del Pino-Gutiérrez, A., & Ribas, J. (2018). Internet gaming disorder in adolescents: Personality, psychopathology and evaluation of a psychological intervention combined with parent psychoeducation. *Frontiers in Psychology, 9,* 787. https://doi.org/10.3389/fpsyg.2018.00787.

Hawton, K., Witt, K. G., Salisbury, T. L., Arensman, E., Gunnell, D., Hazell, P., Townsend, E., & van Heeringen, K. (2016). Psychosocial interventions following self-harm in adults: a systematic review and meta-analysis.

Lancet Psychiatry, 3(8), 740–750. http://dx.doi.org/10.1016/S2215-0366(16)30070-0.

Hendry, B. P., Hellsten, L. A. M., McIntyre, L. J., & Smith, B. R. (2023). Recommendations for cyberbullying prevention and intervention: A western Canadian perspective from key stakeholders. *Frontiers in Psychology, 14*, 1067484. https://doi.org/10.3389/fpsyg.2023.1067484.

Hinduja, S., & Patchin, J. W. (2014). *Cyberbullying: Identification, prevention, and response*. Cyberbullying Research Center. https://cyberbullying.org/Cyberbullying-Identification-Prevention-Response.pdf.

Hinduja, S., & Patchin, J. W. (2023a). *Social media and tech misuse scenarios*. Cyberbullying Research Center. https://cyberbullying.org/Social-Media-and-Tech-Misuse-Scenarios.pdf.

Hinduja, S., & Patchin, J. W. (2023b). *What to do when your child is cyberbullied: Top ten tips for parents*. Cyberbullying Research Center. https://cyberbullying.org/tips-for-parents-when-your-child-is-cyberbullied.pdf.

Hinduja, S., & Patchin, J. W. (2024). *Bullying beyond the schoolyard: Preventing and responding to cyberbullying* (3rd ed.). Corwin.

Institute of Digital Media and Child Development. (2024). *Video gaming 101: Healthy vs problematic gaming*. Children and Screens. https://www.childrenandscreens.org/learn-explore/research/video-gaming-101-healthy-vs-problematic-gaming/.

Kircaburun, K., Kokkinos, C. M., Demetrovics, Z., Király, O., Griffiths, M. D., & Çolak, T. S. (2019). Problematic online behaviors among adolescents and emerging adults: Associations between cyberbullying perpetration, problematic social media use, and psychosocial factors. *International Journal of Mental Health and Addiction, 17*, 891–908. https://doi.org/10.1007/s11469-018-9894-8.

Kothgassner, O. D., Goreis, A., Robinson, K., Huscsava, M. M., Schmahl, C., & Plener, P. L. (2021). Efficacy of dialectical behavior therapy for adolescent self-harm and suicidal ideation: A systematic review and meta-analysis. *Psychological Medicine, 51*(7), 1057–1067. https://doi.org/10.1017/S0033291721001355.

Kuss, D. J., & Lopez-Fernandez, O. (2016). Internet addiction and problematic Internet use: A systematic review of clinical research. *World Journal of Psychiatry, 6*(1), 143–176. https://doi.org/10.5498/wjp.v6.i1.143.

Patchin, J. W., & Hinduja, S. (2017). Digital self-harm among adolescents. *The Journal of Adolescent Health: Official Publication of the Society for*

Adolescent Medicine, 61(6), 761–766. https://doi.org/10.1016/j.jadohealth.2017.06.012.

Pluhar, E., Kavanaugh, J. R., Levinson, J. A., & Rich, M. (2019). Problematic interactive media use in teens: Comorbidities, assessment, and treatment. *Psychology Research and Behavior Management, 12*, 447–455. https://doi.org/10.2147/PRBM.S208968.

Saletti, S. M. R., Van den Broucke, S., & Chau, C. (2021). The effectiveness of prevention programs for problematic Internet use in adolescents and youths: A systematic review and meta-analysis. *Cyberpsychology: Journal of Psychosocial Research on Cyberspace, 15*(2), Article 10. https://doi.org/10.5817/CP2021-2-10.

Shoemaker Brino, K. A., Derouin, A. L., & Silva, S. G. (2022). Problematic Internet use in adolescents and implementation of a social media hygiene protocol. *Journal of Pediatric Nursing, 63*, 84–89. https://doi.org/10.1016/j.pedn.2021.10.011.

Soengkoeng, R., & Moustafa, A. A. (2022). Digital self-harm: An examination of the current literature with recommendations for future research. *Discover Psychology, 2*(1), 19. https://doi.org/10.1007/s44202-022-00032-8.

Stevens, M. W. R., King, D. L., Dorstyn, D., & Delfabbro, P. H. (2019). Cognitive-behavioral therapy for Internet gaming disorder: A systematic review and meta-analysis. *Clinical Psychology & Psychotherapy, 26*(2), 191–203. https://doi.org/10.1002/cpp.2341.

Yang, H., Guo, H., Zhu, Z., Yuan, G., Zhang, X., Zhang, K., Lu, X., Zhang, J., Du, J., Shi, H., Jin, G., & Zhang, Z. (2023). Intervention of Internet addiction and smartphone addiction: An umbrella review of systematic reviews and meta-analyses. *Current Addiction Reports, 11*, 125–148. https://doi.org/10.1007/s40429-023-00536-w.

7

Schools' Role in Preventing Cyberbullying and Other Forms of Cyber Aggression

Schools are vital in preventing cyberbullying and other online aggressive or problematic behaviors because they serve as foundational environments where students learn and practice social skills. Research shows that students' experiences of cyberbullying, whether as victims or perpetrators, are closely linked to how they perceive their school's climate and safety (Kowalski et al., 2019) and as discussed in Chapter 4, the school environment is an important risk or protective factor for cyberbullying and other online aggressive behaviors. A lack of teacher support and unclear school rules about cyberbullying can lead to higher rates of this harmful behavior among students (Kowalski et al., 2019). On the positive side, a supportive school climate and students feeling satisfied with their school experience can help protect against cyberbullying (Kowalski et al., 2019; Zych et al., 2019). In this chapter, we discuss the roles and effectiveness of school-wide programs and practices, including social-emotional learning, digital citizenship programs, positive behavior and intervention support, restorative justice approach, and trauma-informed practices in preventing bullying and cyberbullying incidents and alleviating its negative impacts on youth mental health and school engagement. Practical guidance is provided about how to utilize the support and resources from the above-mentioned school-wide practices to support your child's school in their prevention efforts.

Cyberbullying: Helping Children Navigate Digital Technology and Social Media, First Edition. Stephanie Fredrick, et al.
© 2025 John Wiley & Sons, Inc. Published 2025 by John Wiley & Sons, Inc.

The Importance of Schools and Family Involvement in Cyberbullying Prevention

Within the structured and supportive setting of a school, educators can introduce comprehensive digital citizenship education, teaching students about the ethical use of technology, the consequences of online actions, and strategies for safe internet use. Schools can also implement and enforce robust anti-cyberbullying policies that clearly define unacceptable behaviors and outline appropriate consequences, creating a culture of accountability. Moreover, the school setting allows for regular monitoring and early identification of behavioral changes or signs of distress (as indicated in Chapter 6) that might indicate a student is involved in or affected by online aggression. By promoting a positive school climate that emphasizes respect, empathy, and inclusion, schools can mitigate the factors that contribute to cyberbullying. Additionally, schools can provide supporting resources, such as counseling and peer support groups, to address the emotional and psychological needs of students impacted by online aggression (Hinduja & Patchin, 2014). Through positive school climate, teaching and instructional support, policy enforcement, early intervention, and supportive resources, schools play a critical role in preventing cyberbullying and other online risk behaviors, fostering a safer and more respectful community both online and offline (Llorent et al., 2021).

As indicated throughout the book, parents and caregivers also play a critical role in preventing cyberbullying. When children see their parents engaged and concerned about their online experiences, they are more likely to develop a sense of accountability and empathy toward their peers (Ji et al., 2024; Tomasello & Vaish, 2019). Let us consider the following example: Julie shows her mom a text from her track teammate Leah, who has repeatedly been unkind to her. The message says, "What do you think of Kim?" – another teammate and close friend of Leah. Julie's mom reminds her daughter that Kim could eventually see anything she writes and encourages Julie to consider why Leah is asking this question. As a family, they work together to come up with strategies, such as ways to change the subject or respond kindly and firmly to end the conversation. In this situation, Julie's mom helped Julie stay responsible for what she texts and avoid participating in what could turn into cyberbullying. By staying informed about the signs of cyberbullying and understanding the potential online risks your children may face, you can better support and potentially even guide them.

Family involvement is crucial for school-wide efforts to address cyberbullying and other online risks within school communities (Elasesser et al., 2017). As parents, your active participation in school initiatives can significantly enhance the effectiveness of these efforts. By talking with school staff to learn about technology etiquette, parents can better model appropriate behavior and reinforce school values at home. For example, as many parents know, children love using their smartphone cameras. It is important for parents to remind their children that taking pictures of classmates – who are minors – without consent violates their privacy and goes against school policies. This partnership between home and school ensures that children receive consistent messages about online safety and fostering a safer digital environment. Thus, your involvement contributes to a supportive and proactive school community.

What Is a Multi-tiered Support System?

To understand the school's systematic effort in providing targeted support to students, including support that helps address bullying, cyberbullying, and other problematic online behaviors, it is important to learn about the concept of a Multi-Tiered System of Support (MTSS). MTSS is a school framework designed to provide targeted support to meet students' individual needs, as well as support the entire school community (Fredrick, n.d.). It is widely used in U.S. schools. In 2019, 55% of districts or schools in the United States reported using MTSS frameworks, and by 2023, this number had increased to 74% (Pendharkar, 2023). The MTSS framework typically includes three tiers of support (American Institutes for Research, 2024; PBIS Rewards, n.d.). Here is how it works:

- **Tier 1 with universal prevention services**: This level includes prevention programs that teach social-emotional skills to all students, aiming to be effective for approximately 75% to 90% of the student population. These programs are often integrated into regular classroom activities. Schools use data from general screenings to identify if any groups of students might need additional support.

- **Tier 2 with selective prevention services**: At this stage, schools provide targeted support for about 10% to 25% of students who may need extra help. These students might work with educators or specialists, like school counselors, to improve their academic and social skills.
- **Tier 3 with indicated intervention services**: This level offers intensive, individualized support for less than 10% of students who need more substantial help with social or behavioral issues. Tier 3 often includes special education services and involves close collaboration with mental health counselors. In some cases, students may be referred to community-based services for further assistance.

The MTSS framework has been widely applied to support students' learning and growth across academic, social, emotional, and behavioral domains. In the context of cyberbullying, MTSS involves three tiers of intervention. The first tier focuses on creating a positive and inclusive school climate through education and awareness programs that teach all students about respectful online behavior. The second tier provides additional support for students who may be at risk of being involved in cyberbullying, offering group interventions and counseling. The third tier offers intensive, individualized support for students who are significantly impacted by cyberbullying, whether as victims or perpetrators. By being aware of how MTSS works, parents can collaborate with the school to ensure that their child receives the appropriate level of support, helping to create a safer and more supportive online environment for everyone. In this chapter, we focus on discussing effective school-wide (Tier 1) programs that are widely used by schools for *preventing* cyberbullying and other forms of online risk behaviors. Chapter 8 details how to partner with your child's school if your child is involved in bullying and cyberbullying.

Social and Emotional Learning and School-wide Digital Citizenship Programs

Social and emotional learning (SEL) focuses on helping students develop important social and emotional skills while also creating a caring, safe, and positive school environment. When implemented at the school-wide level, SEL is aligned and has a complementary relationship with MTSS (Jackson et al., 2021), as SEL can provide strategies, programs, and support through a tiered system (Yang & Dong, 2023). This chapter focuses on SEL at Tier 1.

Some core skills focused by SEL include managing strong emotions, navigating relationships, working effectively with others, solving difficult problems, and making responsible decisions (CASEL, n.d.). For example, teachers may shake up a glitter ball to visually represent how emotions can feel overwhelming (Momentous Institute, n.d.). They then explain that emotions, like glitter, will eventually settle if students take time to pause and breathe. This simple SEL tool helps students understand emotional control and encourages reflection on managing feelings. Another SEL tool is role-playing, where students act out scenarios to practice social and emotional skills. This hands-on activity allows students to experience different perspectives, express their emotions, and practice empathy (Everyday Speech, n.d.). These strategies can be taught by your child's classroom teacher or another staff member, such as the school counselor.

Developing these skills is crucial for your child's positive life experiences. When taught at school and supported, children are more likely to succeed academically, have a positive attitude toward themselves and school, and are less likely to experience internal and external problems (Cipriano et al., 2023; Corcoran et al., 2018; Durlak et al., 2011). Another key element of the SEL approach is fostering a positive school climate. In this approach, everyone in the school – teachers, staff, and families – works together to support students' social and emotional growth (Yang et al., 2018). SEL can be integrated into daily school activities and interactions, helping students connect with others, learn and practice positive behaviors, and build important social skills. For example, during group projects, students are encouraged to set goals, collaborate, and provide constructive feedback to their peers. These interactions build important communication, teamwork, and conflict resolution. In this way, SEL is naturally integrated into academic tasks, supporting both personal and social development for all students.

Existing research underscores the importance of SEL in preventing cyberbullying. For instance, Espelage et al. (2015) found among 3,651 6th-grade students that a social-emotional learning program (i.e., Second Step Middle School Program) reduced student delinquency, bullying, and cyberbullying. Moreover, Yang et al. (2021) found that higher levels of SEL skills including decision-making and self-management were linked to lower rates of being cyberbullied among 15,227 U.S. students. Similarly, Schoeps et al. (2018) found that an emotional skills program reduced cyberbullying among 148 students. As parents, your involvement in supporting SEL skills, such as perspective taking and empathy, at home likely reinforces what your child learns at school, promoting a safer and more respectful environment both online and offline.

Digital Citizenship Programs (DCPs) are designed to educate students on how to use technology and the internet safely, responsibly, and respectfully (Vega & Robb, 2019). Digital citizenship programs cover essential topics such as online privacy, cyberbullying, digital footprints, and appropriate online behavior. By integrating these lessons into the curriculum, schools can equip students with the skills they need to navigate the digital world confidently and ethically. It helps students understand the impact of their online actions, promotes positive online interactions, and prepares them for a connected world, ensuring they grow into responsible digital citizens. Research highlights the effectiveness of these programs. For instance, Jones and Mitchell (2016) found that U.S. youth with stronger digital citizenship skills are less likely to engage in online harassment, such as cyberbullying, and more likely to exhibit supportive behavior as online bystanders. Similarly, Zhong et al. (2021) discovered that Chinese students with higher levels of digital literacy and adherence to online etiquette experienced fewer incidents of cyberbullying. Understanding and following digital laws and regulations also was associated with a decrease in both cyberbullying victimization and perpetration. As parents, your involvement in supporting digital citizenship at home, as was detailed in Chapter 5, reinforces what your child learns at school.

SEL and DCP are deeply interconnected in addressing cyberbullying and online aggressive behaviors and promoting a positive and safe school environment (Fredrick et al., 2023). SEL focuses on building students' emotional intelligence, empathy, and self-regulation, which are essential for understanding and managing interactions with others, both in person and online. These skills help students respond to conflicts and handle online disputes more constructively. Simultaneously, DCP educates students about responsible online behavior, including how to protect their privacy, recognize cyberbullying, and respond appropriately to online aggression. Thus, schools often integrate these two approaches to create a comprehensive framework. This more comprehensive approach ensures that students are well prepared to navigate both in-person and digital worlds respectfully and ethically.

To equip parents with resources to be effectively engaged in school-wide integrated efforts connecting SEL and DCP, Common Sense Education (resources for educators provided by Common Sense Media) provides some practical recommendations across the five domains of SEL competencies and different development stages (Common Sense Education, n.d.). In the following text, we provide a summary of the recommendations shared by Common Sense Education (see Tables 7.1–7.5)[1] to highlight some practical strategies for parents, which will foster and supplement school efforts in promoting both SEL and digital citizenship practices.

Self-awareness involves recognizing and understanding one's emotions, thoughts, and values, as well as how they influence behavior in various situations. It includes the ability to identify personal strengths and weaknesses, fostering a grounded sense of confidence and purpose (CASEL, n.d.).

Self-management refers to the capability to regulate one's emotions, thoughts, and actions in different circumstances, which aims to achieve personal goals and aspirations. Skills such as delayed gratification, managing stress, and staying motivated to accomplish both individual and collective objectives are examples of self-management (CASEL, n.d.).

Responsible decision-making is about making thoughtful and constructive choices concerning personal behavior and social interactions. It involves considering ethical standards and safety concerns and assessing the potential outcomes of various actions for the well-being of oneself and others (CASEL, n.d.).

---

[1] The tables (7.1–7.5) illustrate a summary of a structured guide designed to help educators, parents, and students understand how SEL principles apply to digital life and online interactions. Each table adapts SEL domains to the digital world, outlining what students should learn at different grade levels about interacting with technology and the internet. The tables provide specific recommendations for parents on guiding their children to understand responsibilities from Common Sense Education. (2021). *SEL in digital life: Skills and dispositions progression chart.* [Infographic]. Common Sense Education. https://docs.google.com/document/d/1Eb07J2xsgqYRqbdGZOVC3VvnnVN5b_ioEUbRjgrYz1Y/edit.

Table 7.1 Fostering self-awareness in the digital world: parental guidance by grade level.

Grade levels	Self-awareness
K–2	**My feelings when using technology** • Encourage open discussions about their feelings when using technology. • Help your child recognize emotions like excitement or frustration during screen time. • Guide them to reflect on which online activities bring joy and which may cause distress. • Support them in making positive choices by identifying online activities that promote well-being.
Grades 3–5	**Our responsibilities online** • Teach your child the connection between their online behaviors and emotions. • Discuss how their actions can affect others, emphasizing kindness and respect. • Encourage conversations about being responsible and thoughtful when using technology. • Model responsible online behavior by demonstrating respectful interactions.
Grades 6–8	**Oversharing and your digital footprint** • Explain the concept of a digital footprint and its long-term impact. • Encourage your child to think before sharing personal information online. • Discuss the importance of maintaining privacy and setting boundaries on social media.
Grades 9–12	**Who are you on social media?** • Support your teen in reflecting on how they present themselves online. • Discuss the benefits and drawbacks of sharing different aspects of their identity on social media. • Help them define what healthy and positive use of technology looks like for them. • Encourage mindful representation of themselves in the digital world and promote critical thinking about their online image.

Table 7.2 Fostering self-management in the digital world: parental guidance by grade level.

Grade levels	Self-management
K–2	**Saying goodbye to technology** • Help your child develop strategies to manage their emotions when it is time to put devices away. • Encourage routines that allow for smooth transitions between online and offline activities. • Model how to "say goodbye" to technology by setting family-wide limits on screen time.
Grades 3–5	**My media balance** • Guide your child in reflecting on how their media choices impact their emotions and overall well-being. • Support them in developing their own sense of a healthy balance between media use and other activities, like outdoor play or reading. • Establish a family media plan emphasizing fun and balance in digital consumption.
Grades 6–8	**Checking our digital habits** • Encourage your child to identify which online activities support their emotional health and which may be draining. • Work with your child to create a plan that balances screen time with offline hobbies, socializing, and physical activities. • Regularly review their digital habits together, making adjustments when necessary to promote well-being.
Grades 9–12	**Screen time: how much is too much?** • Help your teen develop personalized strategies for balancing media use with other priorities, like schoolwork and sleep. • Discuss how some apps and platforms are designed to be addictive and encourage critical thinking about how they use technology. • Support your teen in setting boundaries to avoid excessive screen time and staying mindful of their digital consumption habits.

Table 7.3 Fostering responsible decision-making in the digital world: parental guidance by grade level.

Grade levels	Responsible decision-making
K–2	**Traveling safety online** • Teach your child basic online safety rules, such as asking for permission before using a device or going online. • Emphasize the importance of not talking to strangers online and only interacting with people they know in real life. • Help them understand what to do when they experience negative feelings while using technology, like stepping away or asking for help.
3–5	**How can you be an online superhero?** • Explain the responsibilities that come with owning or using a device, such as keeping personal information safe. • Help your child understand the difference between private and personal information and why it is important to keep certain details private. • Encourage them to take ownership of their online safety by being proactive and thoughtful in their interactions.
6–8	**Who are you talking to online?** • Help your child identify potential risks and opportunities that come with talking to people online, especially those they have not met in person. • Teach them how to stay safe in these interactions, such as not sharing personal details or meeting strangers in real life without adult supervision. • Encourage critical thinking about whom they interact with and how to verify if someone is trustworthy.
9–12	**Perspectives on posting** • Discuss the responsibilities your child has when posting information about others online, including how their posts may affect others' privacy and reputations. • Help them reflect on how their digital footprint can impact their own reputation and future opportunities. • Encourage thoughtful posting habits, reminding that once something is online, it can be difficult to take back.

Table 7.4 Fostering relationship skills in the digital world: parental guidance by grade level.

Grade levels	Relationship skills
K–2	**Use your heart when you are online** • Teach your child the importance of kindness when interacting with others online. • Encourage them to reflect on actions they can take to be respectful and considerate, such as putting their device away when someone is talking to them or if a friend invites them to play. • Model these behaviors at home by showing kindness and attentiveness in online and offline interactions.
Grades 3–5	**Gaming with positivity** • Encourage your child to show empathy toward others when gaming online. • Help them understand the importance of considering other people's perspectives during communication or gameplay. • Teach strategies for de-escalating conflicts that arise in online games and knowing when it is time to step away from a negative situation.
Grades 6–8	**Friendships and social media** • Guide your child in developing positive relationships both online and offline, discussing the importance of meaningful connections. • Help them reflect on how constant connectivity through social media might affect their emotions and relationships, encouraging balance. • Discuss potential social stressors, like the number of followers or likes, and help them manage these pressures in a healthy way.
Grades 9–12	**Friendships and boundaries online** • Encourage your child to reflect on how devices and the internet influence their friendships. • Help them identify the qualities of healthy and supportive relationships and what makes those relationships rewarding. • Guide your child in establishing healthy boundaries when using social media to connect with friends, fostering a balance between online and offline relationships.

Table 7.5 Fostering social awareness in the digital world: parental guidance by grade level.

Grade levels	Social awareness
K–2	**Standing up to online meanness** • Help your child understand how online meanness can make others feel hurt or sad. • Encourage your child to identify kind ways to respond to mean comments they see online. • Model empathy and kindness in your own online interactions, showing how to stand up for others without being confrontational.
Grades 3–5	**The words we choose** • Encourage your child to reflect on the impact their words can have on others when communicating online. • Teach them about cyberbullying, helping them understand what it is and how to recognize it. • Encourage them to be an upstander – someone who stands up to bullying by offering support to victims and reporting harmful behavior.
Grades 6–8	**Dealing with digital drama** • Help your child understand how communication online can escalate into digital drama or conflict. • Teach them strategies to de-escalate conflicts, such as stepping away from the conversation or using calm and respectful language. • Encourage them to think before they post, reminding them that their words can influence situations positively or negatively.
Grades 9–12	**The impacts of online hate speech** • Help your child understand how online environments can contribute to the spread of hate speech. • Encourage your child to develop cultural awareness and empathy, teaching them how to support their peers when confronted without online hate. • Discuss the importance of reporting hate speech and standing against harmful rhetoric in ways that promote inclusivity and respect.

Relationship skills encompass the ability to create and maintain healthy and encouraging relationships while effectively navigating interactions with diverse individuals and groups. Key components include clear communication, active listening, cooperation, collaborative problem-solving, constructive conflict resolution, and offering or seeking help when necessary (CASEL, n.d.).

Social awareness involves the ability to understand and empathize with people from different backgrounds, cultures, and situations. It includes showing compassion, understanding social norms in various contexts, and recognizing the resources and support available within families, schools, and communities (CASEL, n.d.).

Positive Behavior Intervention Support

Positive behavior intervention support (PBIS) is a structured framework that schools use to promote positive and reduce aggressive or rule-breaking behavior. The overall goal of PBIS is to teach students about clear expectations regarding behavior and then reinforce expected behaviors over time (Center on PBIS, n.d.). PBIS is a long-term and evidence-based approach that aims to foster safe, supportive, and inclusive learning environments (Houchens et al., 2017). Schools using PBIS adopt a range of practices tailored to students' varying needs, from school-wide strategies (Tier 1) to small group and individualized interventions (Tiers 2 and 3; Center on PBIS, n.d.). Within the MTSS framework, PBIS helps educators implement strategies to support positive behavior at multiple levels: (1) Tier 1 universal strategies to guide all students toward positive behavior; (2) Tier 2 targeted interventions for students who require additional help; and (3) Tier 3 intensive, personalized support for students facing more significant challenges.

Behavior expectations are typically stated as three positively stated school-wide rules (e.g., be safe, be respectful, be responsible). Teachers teach and model behavior expectations during a brief session at the beginning of the school year and conduct short, regular follow-ups to reinforce expectations in areas where disrespectful behavior might still occur, such as the cafeteria, playground, or parking lot. Students are recognized and reinforced for engaging in positive behaviors through verbal praise from teachers and/or with incentives such as a PBIS ticket (which are often tied to other incentives, such as lunch with the principal, a pajama day, or a homework pass). PBIS aligns closely with SEL: while PBIS primarily focuses on teaching and managing behavior, SEL emphasizes teaching social and emotional skills often necessary for students to be able to follow school behavior expectations. Schools that utilize PBIS have shown decreases in student discipline referrals and suspension rates and improved student academic performance (Lee & Gage, 2020).

School-based bullying prevention is often integrated into PBIS and may involve teaching students and adults to recognize bullying, respond appropriately, educate others, and create a positive, preventive environment. One such example is a simple, school-wide strategy to remove triggers for bullying (or related aggressive behavior) and teach students to use the "stop signal" when they experience or witness disrespectful behavior. If the behavior continues, students are taught to "walk" away and, if necessary, "talk" to an adult (Ross & Horner, 2013). This approach may be most appropriate in elementary schools with younger kids. All adults in the school are trained to (1) encourage and praise students for using the stop routine; (2) practice these skills with students daily to ensure they become second nature; and (3) follow a universal routine for addressing reports of problem behavior, providing clear and predictable responses. These additional strategies are essential for the success of the intervention. They help students apply the stop/walk/talk skills in various environments and ensure they know how adults will respond when incidents are reported. This approach empowers students to handle minor issues independently while providing a clear rule for seeking adult help appropriately.

As parents, understanding this strategy can help you support your child in using these skills both in and out of school, promoting a safer and more respectful environment. You can also play an active role in supporting your children to apply the stop–walk–talk strategies to cope with cyberbullying issues in and beyond the school context (Ross et al., n.d.). Following are some activities you can engage your child at home after they become familiar with PBIS in school. By engaging in these activities, you can reinforce the lessons your child learns at school and help them navigate online interactions safely and respectfully. It is important to keep in mind that not all PBIS schools will utilize the specific stop/walk/talk signals and to discuss with your child's school how they utilize PBIS and how you can support their efforts at school.

1. **Review the School Rules**: Discuss the following three positively stated school-wide rules with your child.
   - **Be Safe**: Emphasize the importance of keeping hands and feet to themselves.
   - **Be Respectful**: Encourage them to use phrases such as "Someone I know ..." instead of naming others when sharing examples.
   - **Be Responsible**: Remind them to practice what they have learned outside the classroom.
2. **Relate School Rules to Digital Behavior**: Talk about how school-wide rules apply to text messaging, emails, and other digital technologies.
   - **Being Kind and Respectful**: Highlight that this means saying only nice things about other students, both in person and online.
   - **Examples of Not Being Respectful or Kind**:
     - Repeatedly sending offensive, rude, or insulting emails and text messages.
     - Posting cruel gossip or rumors to damage someone's reputation or friendships.
     - Sharing someone's secrets online.
3. **Review Stop/Walk/Talk Signals**: Go over the verbal and physical actions your child should use when they encounter or witness disrespectful behavior online. For example, if a child encounters a chat thread where people are mocking someone for posting incorrect information about an animal, they might brainstorm helpful responses with their parents. A parent might suggest that the child respond assertively by typing, "We all make mistakes. That's not very respectful." They could also advise the child to privately check in with the person being targeted, such as by sending a message like, "Hey, are you okay? Those people are being a bit harsh." Alternatively, the parent may suggest that the child make a lighthearted joke or distraction within the thread to diffuse the situation ("What even is a horse?").
4. **Practice Responses**: Discuss your child's various cyberbullying scenarios (e.g., how they might respond if someone sends them a message that is rude or offensive).
5. **Reward Positive Behavior**: Acknowledge and reward your child for their participation and appropriate behavior.

School-wide and Classroom-wide Mindfulness Programs

Many schools recognize the benefits of implementing school-based mindfulness programs, which teach children to become aware of their thoughts, emotions, and behaviors. These programs may be part of the school's SEL strategies, are typically guided by teachers, and aim to equip students with skills for managing their emotional and mental well-being. Although there is limited research evidence supporting the linkage between mindfulness practices and cyberbullying, mindfulness can be particularly beneficial for students who may be inclined to act out or who have experienced bullying, as it helps them identify and manage escalating feelings before acting on them (Georgiou et al., 2020). By fostering greater self-awareness and emotional regulation, mindfulness programs can play a crucial role in cyberbullying prevention. They can enable students to respond to online conflicts thoughtfully and calmly, reducing the likelihood of reactive, harmful behavior.

Public health agencies often provide resources on mindfulness for children and families, supporting the integration of these practices both in school and at home. This holistic approach not only helps prevent cyberbullying, but also promotes a healthier, more supportive school environment. Here are some simple mindfulness exercises you can do with your child to help them develop focus and calm (National Education Association, 2015):

- **Breathing Exercise**: Encourage your child to sit with a straight back. Have them breathe in while silently saying "I am" and breathe out saying "Peace." Repeat this 3–5 times. Ask them to feel their breath rising from their abdomen through their chest and lungs. You can refer to these as "elevator breaths" for visual aid. Have them count to two as they breathe in, hold for another two counts, and release for another two counts. Repeat this cycle.
- **Body Scan Meditation**: Watch Jon Kabat-Zinn's Body Scan video on YouTube with your child. This guided meditation helps quiet the body and mind by focusing attention on different parts of the body.
- **Mindful Walking**: Have your child walk slowly in a circle or line, either inside or outside. Encourage them to concentrate on their feet, muscles, and sensations, doing this in silence to increase awareness.

- **Passing Objects**: In a circle or row, have your child and their friends pass an object that needs careful attention (like a bell that should not ring or a cup of water that should not spill). They should do this without speaking, only noticing their movements and sensations.
- **Mindful Work/Reading**: Have your child focus on a task or reading material. Ring a bell to start and end the exercise. They should work quietly and put their full attention on what they are doing.

Remind your child that if bothersome thoughts arise during these activities, they should return to their breath. Encourage them to listen to and feel their breathing to anchor themselves back to the present moment and continue with the task at hand.

Restorative Justice Approaches

A restorative justice approach focuses on building a positive school community by addressing conflicts and harmful behaviors through dialogue and mutual understanding rather than punitive measures. Although describing restorative justice practices goes beyond the scope of this book, it often involves a trained facilitator bringing together the victim(s), the perpetrator(s), and any affected community members to discuss the impact of the behavior and collaboratively find solutions to repair the harm. As we discuss in Chapter 8, it is often recommended that educators meet with the perpetrator and the victim of bullying and cyberbullying separately. This is due to the power imbalance between the two (or more) students and a meeting together may create more conflict (e.g., forcing the perpetrator to apologize; the perpetrator may retaliate or use the meeting as an excuse to further harass the victim). However, restorative justice approaches encourage student accountability, empathy, and healing among all parties involved and may be helpful in addressing situations that involve peer conflict and preventing future bullying and cyberbullying. Studies have demonstrated that schools implementing restorative practices see significant reductions in school violence and improvements in school climate and student relationships (Duncan, 2016). A specific study in Pittsburgh Public Schools revealed that these practices improved school climate and reduced suspension days, particularly benefiting high school students (Critical Social Epidemiology Research Collaborative, n.d.). Additionally, middle school students who experienced restorative practices reported better social skills and less cyberbullying victimization (Critical Social Epidemiology Research Collaborative, n.d.). These findings highlight the potential of restorative practices to create a more supportive and inclusive school environment.

Many of the practical strategies discussed in Chapter 6, such as fostering a home environment where children feel safe discussing their online experiences, encouraging positive online behavior through modeling and clear expectations, and engaging with your child in collaborative problem-solving when issues arise, align with restorative justice approaches.

Trauma-Informed Programs

As discussed in Chapter 4, cyberbullying and other types of online aggression and violence can cause significant emotional and psychological harm, leading to long-term effects such as anxiety, depression, posttraumatic stress disorder (PTSD), and even suicidal thoughts (Hinduja & Patchin, 2010; Kowalski et al., 2014). Research has shown that children who experience adverse childhood experiences (ACEs) are at increased risk of depression and being bullied during early adolescence (Blum et al., 2019). Furthermore, being a victim of bullying is itself considered an ACE (NASEM, 2016), highlighting the necessity of a traumainformed approach in prevention efforts. In relation to cyberbullying, Nagata et al. (2023) conducted a longitudinal study with 10,317 participants, revealing that those with ACEs, which are traumatic and distressing events occurring during childhood, are at greater risk of experiencing cyberbullying. This underscores the critical role of trauma-informed frameworks in preventing cyberbullying.

Trauma-informed programs focus on creating a safe and supportive environment for students by recognizing and addressing the impact of trauma. For example, programs like the Cognitive Behavioral Intervention for Trauma in Schools (CBITS; Jaycox et al., 2012) and Bounce Back (Langley et al., 2015) are designed to help students process and cope with trauma. CBITS is aimed at reducing symptoms of PTSD in older students (Jaycox et al., 2012), while Bounce Back is an adaptation for younger children, focusing on building resilience (Langley et al., 2015). In the context of MTSS, trauma-informed programs address student needs across different tiers of intervention. Some interventions are designed specifically for students who have experience with trauma, while others are implemented school-wide. These strategies aim to improve culture and climate throughout the school and often align with other efforts at the school, such as SEL and restorative practices (American Institutes for Research, n.d.). These practices help build a positive school climate, foster strong relationships, and support students' emotional and mental well-being. Key aspects include being aware of potential triggers for trauma, showing compassion rather than judgment, and giving students a safe space to express their feelings. Schools also use restorative practices to minimize punitive discipline and encourage a growth mindset. By involving families, building trust, and prioritizing both student and educator wellness, trauma-informed practices aim to support all students effectively and create a nurturing educational experience. As parents, understanding the importance of these approaches allows you to advocate for and support their implementation, ensuring your child and their peers are protected and supported in their school environment.

Summary

This chapter highlighted how various school-wide programs and practices can help prevent and address bullying and cyberbullying. These include social-emotional learning, digital citizenship education, positive behavior support, restorative justice approaches, and trauma-informed practices. Keep in mind that not all schools will implement all these strategies and ask your child's school about what they are doing to prevent bullying and cyberbullying (if you are not already aware). It can also be helpful to be more formally involved in school prevention efforts and parents can be involved through the school's parent–teacher association (PTA) or on other school or district committees that need parent representatives. Understanding your child's school prevention initiatives is crucial, as they can offer valuable resources to support your child at school, home, and online. By actively engaging with these programs and working closely with your child's school, you can better address and prevent issues related to cyberbullying and its impact on your child's mental health and school experience. The next chapter will explore ways to communicate with the school if your child is involved in bullying and cyberbullying.

References

American Institutes for Research. (2024). *Essential components of MTSS for success*. https://mtss4success.org/essential-components.

American Institutes for Research. (n.d.). *Trauma-sensitive schools*. Center on Multi-Tiered System of Supports. https://www.air.org/resource/trauma-sensitive-schools.

Blum, R. W., Li, M., & Naranjo-Rivera, G. (2019). Measuring adverse child experiences among young adolescents globally: Relationships with depressive symptoms and violence perpetration. *Journal of Adolescent Health, 65*(1), 86–93. https://doi.org/10.1016/j.jadohealth.2019.01.020.

CASEL. (n.d.). *What is the CASEL framework?* CASEL. Retrieved July 26, 2024, from https://casel.org/fundamentals-of-sel/what-is-the-casel-framework/.

Center on PBIS. (n.d.). *What is PBIS?* PBIS.org. https://www.pbis.org/pbis/what-is-pbis.

Cipriano, C., Strambler, M. J., Naples, L. H., Ha, C., Kirk, M., Wood, M., Sehgal, K., Zieher, A. K., Eveleigh, A., McCarthy, M., Funaro, M., Ponnock, A., Chow, J. C., & Durlak, J. (2023). The state of evidence for social and emotional learning: A contemporary meta-analysis of universal school-based SEL interventions. *Child Development, 94*(5), 1181–1204. https://doi.org/10.1111/cdev.13968.

Common Sense Education. (n.d.). *Digital citizenship resources for family engagement*. Retrieved July 26, 2024, from https://www.commonsense.org/education/family-resources.

Corcoran, R. P., Cheung, A. C., Kim, E., & Xie, C. (2018). Effective universal school-based social and emotional learning programs for improving academic achievement: A systematic review and meta-analysis of 50 years of research. *Educational Research Review, 25*, 56–72. https://doi.org/10.1016/j.edurev.2017.12.001.

Critical Social Epidemiology Research Collaborative. (n.d.). *Restorative practices in schools: Research summary*. Retrieved July 26, 2024, from https://criticalsocialepi.org/resources/fact-sheets/restorative-practices-in-schools/.

Duncan, S. H. (2016). Cyberbullying and restorative justice. In R. Navarro, S. Yubero, & E. Larrañaga (Eds.) *Cyberbullying across the globe* (pp. 239–257). Springer International Publishing. https://doi.org/10.1007/978-3-319-25552-1_12.

Durlak, J. A., Weissberg, R. P., Dymnicki, A. B., Taylor, R. D., & Schellinger, K. B. (2011). The impact of enhancing students' social and emotional learning: A meta-analysis of school-based universal interventions. *Child Development, 82*(1), 405–432. https://doi.org/10.1111/j.1467-8624.2010.01564.x.

Elsaesser, C., Russell, B., Ohannessian, C. M., & Patton, D. (2017). Parenting in a digital age: A review of parents' role in preventing adolescent cyberbullying. *Aggression and Violent Behavior, 35,* 62–72. https://doi.org/10.1016/j.avb.2017.06.004.

Espelage, D. L., Low, S., Van Ryzin, M. J., & Polanin, J. R. (2015). Clinical trial of second step middle school program: Impact on bullying, cyberbullying, homophobic teasing, and sexual harassment perpetration. *School Psychology Review, 44*(4), 464–479. https://doi.org/10.17105/spr-15-0052.1.

Everyday Speech. (n.d.). *Understanding the power of SEL role-playing scenarios: Practical tools for personal growth.* Everyday Speech. https://www.everydayspeech.com/blog/sel-role-playing-scenarios.

Fredrick, L. (n.d.). *A comprehensive guide to MTSS.* Panorama Education. Retrieved July 26, 2024, from https://www.panoramaed.com/blog/mtss-comprehensive-guide.

Fredrick, S. S., Coyle, S., & King, J. A. (2023). Middle and high school teachers' perceptions of cyberbullying prevention and digital citizenship. *Psychology in the Schools, 60*(6), 1958–1978. https://doi.org/10.1002/pits.22844.

Georgiou, S. N., Charalambous, K., & Stavrinides, P. (2020). Mindfulness, impulsivity, and moral disengagement as parameters of bullying and victimization at school. *Aggressive Behavior, 46*(1), 107–115. https://doi.org/10.1002/ab.21876.

Hinduja, S., & Patchin, J. W. (2010). Bullying, cyberbullying, and suicide. *Archives of Suicide Research, 14*(3), 206–221. https://doi.org/10.1080/13811118.2010.494133.

Hinduja, S., & Patchin, J. W. (2014). *Bullying beyond the schoolyard: Preventing and responding to cyberbullying.* Corwin Press.

Houchens, G. W., Zhang, J., Davis, K., Niu, C., Chon, K. H., & Miller, S. (2017). The impact of positive behavior interventions and supports on teachers' perceptions of teaching conditions and student achievement. *Journal of Positive Behavior Interventions, 19*(3), 168–179. https://doi.org/10.1177/1098300717696938.

Jaycox, L. H., Kataoka, S. H., Stein, B. D., Langley, A. K., & Wong, M. (2012). Cognitive behavioral intervention for trauma in schools. *Journal of Applied School Psychology, 28*(3), 239–255. https://doi.org/10.1080/15377903.2012.695766.

Ji, X., Feng, N., & Cui, L. (2024). The serial mediation role of parent–child attachment and empathy in the relationship between parental technoference and social anxiety. *Current Psychology, 43*, 24418–24428. https://doi.org/10.1007/s12144-024-06109-y.

Jones, L. M., & Mitchell, K. J. (2016). Defining and measuring youth digital citizenship. *New Media & Society, 18*(9), 2063–2079. https://doi.org/10.1177/1461444815577797.

Kowalski, R. M., Giumetti, G. W., Schroeder, A. N., & Lattanner, M. R. (2014). Bullying in the digital age: A critical review and meta-analysis of cyberbullying research among youth. *Psychological Bulletin, 140*(4), 1073–1137. https://doi.org/10.1037/a0035618.

Kowalski, R. M., Limber, S. P., & McCord, A. (2019). A developmental approach to cyberbullying: Prevalence and protective factors. *Aggression and Violent Behavior, 45*, 20–32. https://doi.org/10.1016/j.avb.2018.02.009.

Langley, A. K., Gonzalez, A., Sugar, C. A., Solis, D., & Jaycox, L. (2015). Bounce back: Effectiveness of an elementary school-based intervention for multicultural children exposed to traumatic events. *Journal of Consulting and Clinical Psychology, 83*(5), 853–865. https://doi.org/10.1037/ccp0000051.

Lee, A., & Gage, N. A. (2020). Updating and expanding systematic reviews and meta-analyses on the effects of school-wide positive behavior interventions and supports. *Psychology in the Schools, 57*(5), 783–804. https://doi.org/10.1002/pits.22336.

Llorent, V. J., Farrington, D. P., & Zych, I. (2021). School climate policy and its relations with social and emotional competencies, bullying and cyberbullying in secondary education. *Revista de Psicodidáctica (English ed.), 26*(1), 35–44. https://doi.org/10.1016/j.psicoe.2020.11.002.

Momentous Institute. (n.d.). *Settle your glitter*. https://momentousinstitute.org/resources/settle-your-glitter.

Nagata, J. M., Trompeter, N., Singh, G., Raney, J., Ganson, K. T., Testa, A., Jackson, D. B., Murray, S. B., & Baker, F. C. (2023). Adverse childhood experiences and early adolescent cyberbullying in the United States. *Journal of Adolescence, 95*(3), 609–616. https://doi.org/10.1002/jad.12124.

National Academies of Sciences, Engineering, and Medicine NASEM. (2016). *Preventing bullying through science, policy, and practice.* Washington, DC: National Academic Press.

National Education Association. (2015, October 2). *Are mindful students less likely to bully? NEA Today.* Retrieved July 26, 2024, from https://www.nea.org/nea-today/all-news-articles/are-mindful-students-less-likely-bully.

PBIS Rewards. (n.d.). *What is MTSS?* https://www.pbisrewards.com/blog/what-is-mtss/.

Pendharkar, E. (2023, November 9). *What we know about multi-tiered systems of supports (MTSS), in charts.* Education Week. Retrieved July 26, 2024, from https://www.edweek.org/teaching-learning/what-we-know-about-multi-tiered-system-of-supports-mtss-in-charts/2023/11.

Ross, S., Horner, R., & Stiller, B. (n.d.). *Bully prevention in positive behavior support.* Education and Community Supports. Retrieved July 26, 2024, from https://assets-global.website-files.com/5d3725188825e071f1670246/5d6ff1ec72843e4ad1d44b55_bullyprevention_es.pdf.

Schoeps, K., Villanueva, L., Prado-Gascó, V. J., & Montoya-Castilla, I. (2018). Development of emotional skills in adolescents to prevent cyberbullying and improve subjective well-being. *Frontiers in Psychology, 9,* 2050. https://doi.org/10.3389/fpsyg.2018.02050.

Tomasello, M., & Vaish, A. (2019). Linking parent–child and peer relationship quality to empathy in adolescence: A multilevel meta-analysis. *Journal of Youth and Adolescence, 48*(10), 2033–2043.

Vega, V., & Robb, M. B. (2019). *The Common Sense census: Inside the 21st-century classroom* (pp. 5–55). San Francisco, CA: Common Sense Media.

Yang, C., Bear, G. G., & May, H. (2018). Multilevel associations between school-wide social–emotional learning approach and student engagement across elementary, middle, and high schools. *School Psychology Review, 47*(1), 45–61. https://doi.org/10.17105/SPR-2017-0003.V47-1.

Yang, C., Chen, C., Lin, X., & Chan, M.-K. (2021). School-wide social emotional learning and cyberbullying victimization among middle and high school students: Moderating role of school climate. *School Psychology, 36*(2), 75–85. https://doi.org/10.1037/spq0000423.

Yang, C., & Dong, Q. (2023). Best practices in school-wide social and emotional learning. In P. L. Harrison, S. L. Proctor, & A. Thomas (Eds.), *Best practices in school psychology*: Vol. 2. *Students, systems, and family services* (7th ed., pp. 317-326). National Association of School Psychologists.

Zhong, J., Zheng, Y., Huang, X., Mo, D., Gong, J., Li, M., & Huang, J. (2021). Study of the influencing factors of cyberbullying among Chinese college students incorporated with digital citizenship: From the perspective of individual students. *Frontiers in Psychology, 12*, 621418. https://doi.org/10.3389/fpsyg.2021.621418.

Zych, I., Baldry, A. C., Farrington, D. P., & Llorent, V. J. (2019). Are children involved in cyberbullying low on empathy? A systematic review and meta-analysis of research on empathy versus different cyberbullying roles. *Aggression and Violent Behavior, 45*, 83-97. https://doi.org/10.1016/j.avb.2018.03.004.

8

School-Family Partnership

Despite best efforts in prevention, bullying and cyberbullying still occur, and it is important for families and schools to partner to best support the child. The focus of the chapter is to provide recommendations for parents whose children have been bullied or cyberbullied on how and to whom to communicate concerns, whom to share information (e.g., documentation), and how to best advocate for the child. We also provide guidance for parents whose children are involved as perpetrators and bystanders or witnesses of bullying and cyberbullying. Finally, we provide suggestions for how educators can best partner with families.

Communicating with the School

As shared in Chapter 6, if you find out your child has been bullied online, after staying calm, listening, providing support, and getting the information about what happened, reporting it to school is an important next step. Although this strategy is often recommended, it can be confusing to know how and to whom to report, what to share, and what to expect in response. Next, we list some frequently asked questions and answers for parents.

Cyberbullying: Helping Children Navigate Digital Technology and Social Media, First Edition. Stephanie Fredrick, et al.
© 2025 John Wiley & Sons, Inc. Published 2025 by John Wiley & Sons, Inc.

Whom Should I Contact at the School If My Child Is Being Cyberbullied?

Even though cyberbullying can happen 24 hours a day, 7 days a week, often outside of school hours, it can impact your child in school. Most state anti-bullying laws include cyberbullying (Hinduja & Patchin, 2023) and require schools to respond if this occurs (more information on this can be found in Chapter 9). To find out who to contact at your school, you can search the school or district website with the keyword "bullying" or "reporting bullying" to find out how to report. We tested this by randomly selecting schools in 10 different states and found the online report form and/or number to call within seconds.

Some states use a standardized reporting tool that can be used for bullying, cyberbullying, and other safety concerns (e.g., Safe2tell https://safe2tell.org in Colorado, Safe2Say Something https://www.safe2saypa.org in Pennsylvania). Some of these reporting systems also have training videos or public service announcements about the importance of reporting and how to make a report (e.g., STOPit https://www.youtube.com/watch?v=BTzDhSIqe4M&t=126s). Other states require schools to have an anti-bullying specialist/coordinator (e.g., New York, New Jersey) who handles reports. The coordinator may be a school administrator (e.g., principal, assistant/vice principal), mental health professional (e.g., school counselor, school psychologist), or other educator with appropriate training to handle bullying and cyberbullying. If you are not able to find information about whom to report to, you can always call the school and ask to speak with the principal.

You and your child may have concerns about reporting the cyberbullying to the school – and these are important to consider. In fact, a study of parents whose middle or high school student had been bullied revealed that less than one-quarter of them (23%) contacted the school (Lindstrom Johnson et al., 2019). About half of the time, parents and teachers do not know about bullying because children do not tell, often due to fear of retaliation (from the person doing the bullying and/or from other peers) or they think it will not help or even make things worse (Mishna et al., 2006). As was mentioned in Chapter 4, other reasons youth do not report cyberbullying to parents include being afraid that their device will be taken away, or they may not view it as cyberbullying, they may not know how to talk about it, or they may think they should be able to handle it on their own (PACER's National Bullying Prevention Center, 2020). When parents do find out about bullying, they are most likely to try to talk with their child first (Lindstrom Johnson et al., 2019), and advise on how to handle it (e.g., separate from the other person, get help from an adult, or offering other suggestions; Brown et al., 2013; Cooper & Nickerson, 2013). Parents are more likely to report to the school if the bullying continues for some time and their child has an adverse response to it (Brown et al., 2013).

Some youth may be reluctant to have the bullying reported because they worry about being seen as a "rat" or a tattle, fear of retaliation, concern that reporting might make the situation worse, or because they consider the people doing it to be their friends (PACER National Bullying Prevention Center, n.d.). While it is important that parents help their children to be empowered in cases of bullying, concerns related to emotional and physical safety also need to be addressed. Parents can help their children to feel comfortable with a report being made to the school by talking to them about self-advocacy, explaining the difference between tattling and telling, explaining how involving the school can help to keep them safe, and explaining that true friends do not intentionally and repeatedly hurt each other (PACER Teens Against Bullying, 2018).

There is also a possibility that your child may be experiencing bullying at the hands of a teacher or staff member in their school, or that a teacher is actively or passively supporting the bullying and allowing it to continue. Although the vast majority of teachers and school staff do not mistreat their students, a review of the bullying literature showed that the percentage of students in the United States who reported experiencing at least one instance of teacher bullying ranging from 1.2% to 88% across studies (Gusfre et al., 2023). Experiencing bullying by a teacher can impact children's mental health, well-being, and academic performance (Gusfre et al., 2023), so it is important to take action if this occurs. As the teacher is the subject of the report, it can be helpful to go directly to a staff member you trust such as the principal, school social worker, school counselor, or school psychologist.

What Information Should I Share?

Regardless of who you contact at the school, you should be prepared to share the information and documentation you have about the bullying or cyberbullying incident(s), including who, what, where, when, and why. You do not have to have all of this information to make a report, as the school may be able to find out some of it. Below we list some of the common information that is included in an incident report. If you have this, it will be helpful to have ready to share when you contact the school:

- Name, role (student, parent, staff, administrator, and other), and contact information of reporter – note: many schools allow this to be anonymous
- Date of report
- School
- Date and time of bullying incident
- *Who* was involved
  - *Person who was bullied* (alleged target/victim) – name, age, grade, school
  - *Person/people doing the bullying* (alleged perpetrator) – name, age, grade, school (some reporting systems may ask for more information such as description of person)
  - *Witnesses* – names, age, grade, school
- *Where* the incident occurred (on school grounds, bus, at school-sponsored activity, online, on the way to school or way to home from school, or other)
  - If cyberbullying, the platform used (e.g., Instagram, Snapchat, and text) and link
- *What* happened (description of the incident; be as specific as possible)
  - If you have documentation (screenshots, etc.), this can often be uploaded/shared
- *Why* – although not always asked about, it can be important to know the context. For example: Has this happened before? Did the bullying involve race/color/ethnicity, national origin, religion, sex, gender expression or identity, perceived sexual orientation, socioeconomic status, disability, weight, or appearance? What is the relationship of the people involved? Was this purposeful (was there an intent to harm)? What was the impact (was there physical injury, psychological harm, school absence, etc.)? How are the people involved reacting (e.g., showing remorse or continuing despite harm)? Has anyone else been notified?
- Certification of accuracy of information and report made in good faith

Although your emotions may (understandably!) be running high, it is important to try to be as calm, factual, and thorough as possible when reporting. Unfortunately, schools report that sometimes it seems like some parents are just looking for someone to blame and are distrustful (Su et al., 2021). In our work with schools and educators, we often hear educators say that parents are quick to assume the worst of them (e.g., that they are ignoring all instances of bullying and doing nothing about bullying prevention/intervention). They wish parents knew that they also want what is best for the child and that they are on the same team. Keeping documentation, learning about the school's policy for handling bullying, and working to collaborate on an action plan are helpful strategies for parents to advocate for their children (PACER's National Bullying Prevention Center, 2019).

What Should I Expect from the School?

Although state laws and policies have some variation, most state anti-bullying laws and policies require that schools receiving public funding promptly investigate and respond to any reports of bullying and cyberbullying (Stopbullying.gov, 2023). Further, a range of federal civil rights laws prohibit discrimination on the basis of disability, sex, race, and national origin (U.S. Department of Education, n.d.). More information, including common components to state laws and policies, is provided in Chapter 9. To find out about the key components in your state laws and policies applicable to publicly funded schools, go to https://www.stopbullying.gov/resources/laws/key-components.

The best practice is for the school administrator (or another trained person that the administrator has designated) to conduct interviews, separately and privately, with each individual involved (Florida Department of Education [FDOE], Office of Safe Schools, 2022). The involved people include the alleged perpetrator(s), victim/target, and witness(es); the victim and perpetrator should never be interviewed together (Florida Department of Education [FDOE], Office of Safe Schools, 2022). Therefore, you should expect that the school will ask your child about what happened if you make a report. In the interview, your child will likely be asked about (FDOE, Office of Safe Schools, 2022; New York Center for School Safety [NYCSS], 2024):

- What happened (a description of the incident)
- Who was involved (number of people, identities; includes target, perpetrator(s), and witnesses) and the relationships between people involved
- How often it has happened (have there been past or continuing incidents?)
- Where it happened
- How the incident affected the people involved (negative impact on the educational environment [missing school or classes or other effects], imbalance of power, emotional distress, physical injury, and damaged belongings)
- If there is any evidence to share (e.g., screenshots, photos, notes, and physical damage)
- If there are others involved who might help the school understand what happened

The school should also gather other relevant information about the incident, such as social media posts (NYCSS, 2024). With the information gathered from interviews and other sources, the school makes a determination about whether the incident meets the criteria for bullying/cyberbullying (or related behaviors in the policy, such as harassment or discrimination), and how to respond. In many states, schools are required to notify parents of all students involved in a bullying incident (Stopbullying.gov, 2023). Even if the investigation reveals that the incident did not meet the criteria to be considered bullying or cyberbullying (which may happen due to things like not having a substantive impact on education, having students report that it was a two-way conflict, etc.), it does not mean that an incident did not occur, and your child's safety should still be taken seriously (NYCSS, 2024).

Schools should take steps to end bullying and cyberbullying, create a more positive school climate without hostility, and safeguard the students involved (NYCSS, 2024). A school official should meet with the perpetrator to review the anti-bullying policy and reinforce the values of school community. Other consequences may include loss of privilege, reassignment of classes or seats (in class and on the bus), written apology or reparation (NYSCSS, 2024), suspension, and if the behavior was determined to be a criminal act, the school will report it to law enforcement (FDOE, 2022; Stopbullying.gov, 2023). The person who did the bullying may also need to be taught alternative behaviors such as empathy, conflict resolution, or self-regulation, and/or be referred for additional support (NYSCSS, 2024). Safeguards and support for the student being bullied can be documented in a safety plan that may include separation, supervision, check-in person or place, connection with friends or other peers with whom the child feels safe, and/or a referral to counseling or other mental health services (FDOE, 2022; NYSCSS, 2024; Stopbullying. gov, 2023). The approach used to address the situation may be different based on the age of the child and other circumstances. For example, research has shown that working with perpetrators and other peers to instill concern and support for the target of bullying is more effective in elementary schools and for long-term or ongoing victimization, whereas direct sanctions (e.g., strong message that bullying must stop) is more effective in short-term victimization in middle and high school (Garandeau et al., 2014). There should be follow-up with the child to see how effective the plan is (and to determine whether the bullying has stopped), and the plan should be revised if needed (NYSCSS, 2024).

What if your child is in a private school? Although private schools do not have the same mandates as described above for schools that receive public funding, most fall under accrediting bodies that have standards for student behavior (including bullying and cyberbullying), and expectations for it to be addressed in terms of policy, discipline, counseling, and other procedures (see, for example, New England Association of Schools and Colleges, 2024). Private schools tend to have even more discretion when it comes to bullying; they often have smaller classes, autonomy about who can be enrolled and excluded/removed, and more parental involvement, so there may be more adults involved (Rosenkrantz, 2021). You should definitely reach out to a teacher, counselor, dean of students, or other trusted adult at the school if you are concerned about bullying or cyberbullying.

The Bullying Is Still Happening: How Can I Best Advocate for My Child?

It can be incredibly difficult and disheartening to see a child continue to experience bullying after reporting it, but this can sometimes happen. In an interview study, most families of middle school children who had been bullied (all from different schools) perceived that the school was unwilling or unable to enforce their school's anti-bullying policy (Brown et al., 2013). In surveys of parents of children with disabilities who had been bullied, many parents also believed that the schools' response was unhelpful or could have been handled better (Pimm, 2012; Rapp, 2023). Although it is completely understandable that parents may feel frustrated, angry, and helpless in these situations, it is best to try to channel that into trying to collaborate and problem-solve. We highly recommend requesting a meeting with the school if this happens. PACER's National Bullying Prevention Center (2019) offers some helpful guidance for these meetings, including:

- Find out who will attend the meeting
- Prepare to state the problem clearly (with supporting evidence if available)
- Go in with a problem-solving perspective
- Offer some potential solutions
- Make a list of questions
- Listen to input from others, paraphrasing or asking clarifying questions to understand
- Emphasize concern for your child instead of blaming or accusing
- Summarize the next steps

If you have followed the school's procedures and worked with them but feel your child is not safe or is not being supported, it may be time to take it to the next level. Depending on who you have contacted previously, this may include the school's anti-bullying coordinator, the principal, the school district's superintendent, the Board of Education, or even your state board of education or office of civil rights (NYSCSS, 2024). Many states also have school safety centers that provide guidance for parents who are in these situations. Throughout the process, keep clear documentation of the communication, and strive to provide the facts of the situation and refer to the school's anti-bullying policy and/or other relevant laws. You should also be aware that certain instances of cyberbullying may rise to the level of harassment or discrimination. If the behavior limits a student's educational opportunities based on race, color, or national origin (including English language proficiency and ethnic characteristics), sex (including sexual orientation, gender identity or expression, pregnancy, or parental status), disability, or age, you can file a complaint with the Office for Civil Rights (U.S. Department of Education, 2010).

These processes, especially at the state and federal level, can be quite lengthy and stressful, so it is important to carefully consider this and the ultimate goal when pursuing your options. Focusing on your child's well-being is the first priority. One way to do this is to seek the help of a licensed mental health professional. This can be done by contacting your insurance provider, the school, or your pediatrician, or by finding professionals through organizations such as Mental Health America (2024) or the American Psychological Association (2024).

Sometimes families decide that removing the child from the school environment is the only option to end the bullying or cyberbullying. Most states allow for some level of school choice or the option to select a school, which differs from your geographically based assigned school. Most states have open enrollment policies that allow families to use state funding to enroll their children in alternate publicly funded schools. These local and state laws may vary geographically by the inclusion of out-of-district schools, charter schools, and magnet schools. State laws also dictate whether open enrollment policies are mandated, or if schools and districts can choose to opt in. Although most families who enroll their children in private schools pay out-of-pocket for the tuition, some states provide private school choice options with financial support. This financial support can come in the form of vouchers or scholarships, state-funded education savings accounts, or tax credits and deductions. The availability of and eligibility to participate in these programs vary greatly at the state and local levels. Lastly, all US states allow parents to choose to homeschool their children, although homeschooling requirements also vary by state (Congressional Research Service, 2024).

How Can I Work with the School If My Child Is Cyberbullying Others?

As difficult as it is to find out your child is being cyberbullied, it may be just as hard if not harder to find out that your child is bullying others. Parents may feel guilt, shame, anger, and/or disbelief that their child could do such a thing (Su et al., 2021). As described in greater detail in Chapter 6, remaining calm and discussing the situation with your child to find out more about what happened is important. Parents are less inclined to contact the school when their child is doing the cyberbullying as opposed to being cyberbullied by others (Stuart et al., 2022). Schools, and particularly school-based mental health professionals (such as school counselors, social workers, and school psychologists), have expertise in children's behavior and can help work with you and your child to learn other alternatives to behaving aggressively. In collaboration with the school, remediation plans, meaningful consequences (e.g., increased supervision at school or home and revoking device privileges), and skill-building approaches (e.g., social skills training and/or counseling/therapy) can be implemented. Reaching out to express concern and request help for your child is likely to be more successful than having the only interactions with the school to be reactive or around discipline for the behavior.

How Can I Work with the School If My Child Is a Bystander of Cyberbullying?

Even if your child has not been involved in cyberbullying as a target or perpetrator, it is very likely that they have witnessed it happening. Research shows that 88% of adolescents say they have seen cyberbullying on social media, although most ignore it as opposed to helping (Lenhart et al., 2015). Experimental studies, where youth are shown real cyberbullying situations, also show that the majority do not intervene (Allison & Bussey, 2016; Dillon & Bushman, 2015). Some things that make youth more likely to intervene in cyberbullying include being younger, female, having social skills, holding anti-bullying attitudes, having previous experience of being bullied, and believing they can make a difference (Lambe et al., 2019).

Research shows that the parent–child relationship and the specific messages you send about what to do in bullying situations make a difference (Grassetti et al., 2018; Lambe et al., 2019; Nickerson et al., 2008; Pozzoli & Gni, 2013). A secure parent–child attachment relationship and the expectations parents have for their child about defending victims make it more likely that they will intervene with traditional bullying (Nickerson et al., 2008; Pozzoli & Gni, 2013) and cyberbullying (Lambe et al., 2019). An interesting study that included home observations of the specific advice parents gave their 4th- and 5th-grade children about what to do in bullying situations showed that their peers at school reported that they took these actions (Grassetti et al., 2018). More specifically, when parents advised their child to help or comfort the person being bullied, peers reported that their child intervened to help, whereas caregivers who told their child not to get involved were more likely to have peers say that their child stayed passive or joined in when the bullying was happening (Grassetti et al., 2018).

As discussed in Chapter 5, you can also talk about how they can respond when they see cyberbullying. Specific examples are included in that chapter for intervening directly to call out the problem, reporting the cyberbullying, and supporting the person being harmed (Awad & Connors, 2023; Nickerson et al., 2024). Perhaps it is not surprising that parents are more likely to teach their children to stand up for victims when they have knowledge of the schools' anti-bullying interventions (Banks et al., 2020). As detailed in Chapter 7, it is important for parents to pay attention to what schools are teaching their children in this regard and also for schools to share this information with parents so that there are consistent messages about how children can engage in bystander intervention when they see bullying and cyberbullying.

How Educators Can Best Partner with Families?

Thus far, we have focused on communicating and working with the school in instances of cyberbullying, which can be a stressful and emotional experience for all involved, and one that is greatly facilitated by strong partnerships between schools and families. Effective school–family collaboration leads to better relationships and improved mental health for children (Sheridan et al., 2019). In this section, we provide recommendations for educators and schools about how they can form authentic and successful partnerships with families. We focus on two-way communication and shared decision-making, both generally and specifically in relation to cyberbullying and bullying.

Engage in Effective Two-Way Communication

One of the most important aspects of effective partnerships is having understandable, respectful communication using families' preferred methods (Garbacz et al., 2022; Witte et al., 2021). Proactively, schools should reach out to parents and families about values, practices, and policies (Garbacz et al., 2022). It is also important to have multiple methods, including but not limited to email, phone, postal, apps, and face-to-face communication, and for schools to share both good and bad news with families (Witte et al., 2021). Educators should focus on the strengths of students and families (Garbacz et al., 2022), approaching them with transparency, empathy, and without judgment (Witte et al., 2021).

With regard to bullying and cyberbullying, schools can provide education about bullying prevention, digital citizenship, and safe social media usage (Doss & Crawford, 2023; Kolbert et al., 2014; Su et al., 2021). A meta-analysis found that these parent programs (both those delivered through home visits or the school) significantly reduced rates of bullying and victimization (Chen et al., 2021). In our own experience and as found in research (Su et al., 2021), parents often do not attend these types of events at school. Finding out from parents what they want to learn about, offering education in the community instead of at the school (Witte et al., 2021), and sharing information when families may be at school for other events (conferences, concerts, and celebrations) may help to overcome some of these barriers.

When parents report concerns about bullying or cyberbullying, the way schools communicate with them may be one of the most important factors in how they will respond (Englehart, 2014). One of the most common complaints from parents whose children have been bullied is about the poor communication between the family and the school, with parents perceiving that they were not being kept informed about what the school was doing (Brown et al., 2013; Pimm, 2012; Rapp, 2023). The way the school communicates also makes a difference. As a former teacher and principal – and now a superintendent – Joshua Englehart (2014) explains that school leaders often focus too much on the procedural details of investigating and finding out if the behavior meets the criteria of bullying. This can come off as dismissive of the real concern, which is about a child feeling unsafe or unhappy at school. Therefore, in the initial communication, educators should focus on the child (not on other children, staff, and policies) and what can be done to make them feel safe (Englehart, 2014). Parents of children with disabilities who had been bullied have shared that processing the bullying incidents with school personnel helped them in reducing their anger (Rapp, 2023). Concrete examples of what schools can do is to say things like:

- "Tell me about what happened."
- "I am so sorry to hear this. I can see how this is upsetting for you and your child."
- "Let's talk about some ways that we can work together to support your child."

Continuing to check in and communicate with both the child and parent also shows respect and support (Englehart, 2014).

Of course, school leaders will still need to follow their policy and proceed with an investigation, and parents should be kept informed about this. Paying attention to language is important. As Mishna and colleagues (2006) noted, sometimes adults use accusatory and emotionally laden terms when describing children's behavior (e.g., nasty, awful, conniving, vicious, manipulative, and playing the victim), which can be counter-productive. Schools should focus on the process they took, emphasizing how they will ensure that the victim is checked in with and cared about (Englehart, 2014). Parents are often frustrated when they feel like the school did not address the bullying with the perpetrator or their parents (Brown et al., 2013). Parents often report that the school "did nothing," which may be more of a reflection of the school not making the steps known and visible to parents (Englehart, 2014). This is sometimes tricky, as the Family Educational Rights and Privacy Act of 1974 prohibits schools from sharing personally identifiable information (PII) about another student from their education records. Therefore, a school cannot tell the family of a victimized child what the discipline was for the perpetrator unless the conduct the student was disciplined for poses a significant risk to the safety and well-being of others (although cyberbullying may not rise to that level – see Cyberbullying Research Center, 2009). Therefore, schools should focus on the process they took, emphasize that they took action with all involved, and focus on what they are doing with regard to the parent's own child, while partnering with the parents in shared decision-making.

Focus on Shared Decision-Making

Another vital component of effective school–family collaboration is establishing a structure for shared decision-making (Garbacz et al., 2022; Witte et al., 2021). This can happen proactively by including parents on committees and teams that make decisions about policies, practices, and programs at the school and district, surveying families for their input, and holding forums to get feedback (Garbacz et al., 2022; Witte et al., 2021). This value and focus on shared decision-making should also apply to cyberbullying situations. Oftentimes, parents believe that schools blamed their child who was the target or victim (e.g., saying it was their behavior or interpretation, offering solutions for what the victimized child should do) or downplayed the situation (Brown et al., 2013; Pimm, 2012), indicating that they did not feel heard, valued, or part of the process for what would happen. There are many things that may contribute to this disconnect between the goals of parents and the response of schools. These include complexities and different perspectives in determining what is not bullying and cyberbullying (Campbell et al., 2019; Liu et al., 2023; Mishna et al., 2006; Tang et al., 2024), and not partnering effectively in how to respond (Brown et al., 2013; Mishna et al., 2006; Pimm et al., 2012; Rapp, 2023).

As discussed in more detail in Chapters 1 and 4, and elsewhere in this book, bullying and cyberbullying have some specific defining characteristics that can be hard to distinguish from other behaviors. Sometimes there is disagreement or complexity in terms of what is normal behavior compared to bullying, especially surrounding intent and if the people involved are or had been friends (Mishna et al., 2006). When a friend teases someone and says they are joking, if a person leaves someone out of a group chat when talking about plans, and if a teen says or does things to get attention or express that they are attracted to someone, the lines can become blurred between acceptable behavior and bullying or cyberbullying depending on the specific situation/behaviors, intent, and resulting harm (Mishna et al., 2006). In a study comparing parent and school faculty perspectives, educators were more accurate than parents in identifying bullying (although there were no differences in cyberbullying detection), and a large proportion of both groups incorrectly interpreted situations as bullying and cyberbullying when they were not (Campbell et al., 2019). Studies that have compared child and parent reports of the child's bullying and cyberbullying experiences have found that they only agree a low-to-moderate degree about the occurrence of this victimization (Dudley et al., 2023; Liu et al., 2023; Tang et al., 2024). When adults do not witness the behaviors and are overwhelmed with other demands, it can be challenging to make these determinations, especially with more covert behavior and/or if adults think the students are exaggerating (Mishna et al., 2006). Therefore, it is possible that some situations that cause distress to children may not be interpreted by the school as bullying or cyberbullying.

Parents, educators, and students also may differ in how they think the cyberbullying should be dealt with. At the end of the day, all are invested in making sure that cyberbullying stops, but they may disagree on the path to get to that aim. For example, school counselors perceive a need for parents to have an active role in setting rules and expectations and monitoring their children's online behaviors (Su et al., 2021), and parents report trusting their children's online behaviors more than educators do (Nguyên & Mark, 2014). Parents also perceive their monitoring and overseeing of their children's online behavior to be higher than their children perceive it to be (Wahyuningrum et al., 2020). As discussed in Chapter 5, there are some proactive strategies that parents can use, but none of these guarantee that a child would not be involved in cyberbullying or other problematic online behaviors.

Families often focus on and expect that schools should make the bullying and cyberbullying stop by disciplining the perpetrator(s). Although an important component of effective interventions for bullying includes firm disciplinary sanctions for perpetrators (e.g., serious talk and loss of privilege; Ttofi & Farrington, 2011), schools should also be focusing on opportunities for growth and more positive behavior (Chin et al., 2012). Studies with parents of children who had been bullied revealed that they felt supported when they were listened to and the schools took direct action to address the bullying with the person doing the behavior (e.g., speaking with them right after, moving them away from the target, making an apology, instilling empathy, and reviewing bullying policies), as well as provided support for the targeted child (e.g., creating circles of friends for the bullied student and telling who to report to if it happened again; Brown et al., 2013; Pimm, 2012).

We hope that it is clear from this chapter that it takes a village to respond to cyberbullying through a strong school–family partnership. This includes clear communication, a problem-solving approach, and a genuine respect for others. There are also some specific strategies and actions that can be taken whether the child's involvement is as a target, a perpetrator, or a bystander. Next, we will explore the legal implications of cyberbullying and related online risky behavior, including when families and schools should get law enforcement involved.

References

Allison, K. R., & Bussey, K. (2016). Cyber-bystanding in context: A review of the literature on witnesses' responses to cyberbullying. *Children and Youth Services Review, 65*, 183–194. https://doi.org/10.1016/j.childyouth.2016.03.026.

American Psychological Association. (2024). *Psychology locator.* https://locator.apa.org/.

Awad, M. N., & Connors, E. H. (2023). Active bystandership by youth in the digital era: Microintervention strategies for responding to social media-based microaggressions and cyberbullying. *Psychological Services, 20*(3), 423–434. https://doi.org/10.1037/ser0000749.

Banks, C. S., Blake, J. J., & Lewis, K. (2020). Collaborating with parents to increase proactive bystander messages. *Professional School Counseling, 23*(1), https://doi.org/10.1177/2156759X20912741.

Brown, J. R., Aalsma, M. C., & Ott, M. A. (2013). The experiences of parents who report youth bullying victimization to school officials. *Journal of Interpersonal Violence, 28*(3), 494–518. https://doi.org/10.1177/0886260512455513.

Campbell, M., Whiteford, C., & Hooijer, J. (2019). Teachers' and parents' understanding of traditional and cyberbullying. *Journal of School Violence, 18*(3), 388–402. https://doi.org/10.1080/15388220.2018.1507826.

Chen, Q., Zhu, Y., & Chui, W. H. (2021). A meta-analysis on effects of parenting programs on bullying prevention. *Trauma, Violence, & Abuse, 22*(5), 1209–1220. https://doi.org/10.1177/152483802091.

Chin, J. K., Dowdy, E., Jimerson, S. R., & Rime, W. J. (2012). Alternatives to suspensions: Rationale and recommendations. *Journal of School Violence, 11*(2), 156–173. http://dx.doi.org/10.1080/15388220.2012.652912.

Congressional Research Service. (2024). *Overview of public and private school choice options.* https://crsreports.congress.gov/product/pdf/IF/IF10713.

Cooper, L., & Nickerson, A. B. (2013). Parent retrospective recollections of bullying and current views, concerns, and strategies to cope with children's bullying. *Journal of Child and Family Studies, 22*, 526–540. https://doi.org/10.1007/s10826-012-9606-0.

Cyberbullying Research Center. (2009, August 22). *FERPA and the identity of students who cyberbully others.* https://cyberbullying.org/ferpa-and-the-identity-of-students-who-cyberbully-others.

Dillon, K. P., & Bushman, B. J. (2015). Unresponsive or un-noticed: Cyberbystander intervention in an experimental cyberbullying context. *Computers in Human Behavior*, *45*, 144–150. https://doi.org/10.1016/j.chb.2014.12.009.

Doss, K. M., & Crawford, S. H. (2023). Parent education: A key aspect in prevention and intervention of bullying in school communities. *National Youth Advocacy and Resilience Journal*, *6*(2), 1–32. https://doi.org/10.20429/nyarj.2023.060201.

Dudley, M. J., Nickerson, A. B., Seo, Y. S., & Livingston, J. A. (2023). Mother-Adolescent agreement concerning peer victimization: Predictors and relation to coping. *Journal of Child and Family Studies*, *32*(10), 3134–3147. https://doi.org/10.1007/s10826-023-02567-3.

Englehart, J. M. (2014). Attending to the affective dimensions of bullying: Necessary approaches for the school leader. *Planning and Changing*, *45*(1), 19–30. https://eric.ed.gov/?id=EJ1145630.

Family Educational Rights and Privacy Act of 1974, 20 U.S.C. § 1232g (1974).

Florida Department of Education, Office of Safe Schools. (2022). *Model policy against bullying and harassment for K-12 schools*. https://www.fldoe.org/core/fileparse.php/20086/urlt/10-5.pdf.

Garandeau, C. F., Poskiparta, E., & Salmivalli, C. (2014). Tackling acute cases of school bullying in the KiVa anti-bullying program: A comparison of two approaches. *Journal of Abnormal Child Psychology*, *42*, 981–991. https://doi.org/10.1007/s10802-014-9861-1.

Garbacz, A., Godfrey, E., Rowe, D. A., & Kittelman, A. (2022). Increasing parent collaboration in the implementation of effective practices. *Teaching Exceptional Children*, *54*(5), 324–327. https://doi.org/10.1177/00400599221096.

Grassetti, S. N., Hubbard, J. A., Smith, M. A., Bookhout, M. K., Swift, L. E., & Gawrysiak, M. J. (2018). Caregivers' advice and children's bystander behaviors during bullying incidents. *Journal of Clinical Child & Adolescent Psychology*, *47*(sup1), S329–S340. http://doi.org/10.1080/15374416.2017.1295381.

Gusfre, K. S., Støen, J., & Fandrem, H. (2023). Bullying by teachers towards students—A scoping review. *International Journal of Bullying Prevention*, *5*, 331–347. https://doi.org/10.1007/s42380-022-00131-z.

Hinduja, S., & Patchin, J. W. (2023). *What to do when your child is cyberbullied: Top ten tips for parents*. Cyberbullying Research Center. https://cyberbullying.org/tips-for-parents-when-your-child-is-cyberbullied.pdf.

Jensen Ex Rel. CJ v. Reeves, 45 F. Supp. 2d 1265 (D. Utah 1999).
Kolbert, J. B., Schultz, D., & Crothers, L. M. (2014). Bullying prevention and the parent involvement model. *Journal of School Counseling, 12*(7), n7. https://eric.ed.gov/?id=EJ1034733.
Lambe, L. J., Cioppa, V. D., Hong, I. K., & Craig, W. M. (2019). Standing up to bullying: A social ecological review of peer defending in offline and online contexts. *Aggression and Violent Behavior, 45*, 51–74. https://doi.org/10.1016/j.avb.2018.05.007.
Lenhart, A., Smith, A., Anderson, M., Duggan, M., & Perrin, A., (2015). *Teens, technology and friendships*. Pew Research Center. http://www.pewinternet.org/2015/08/06/teens-technology-and-friendships/.
Lindstrom Johnson, S., Waasdorp, T. E., Gaias, L. M., & Bradshaw, C. P. (2019). Parental responses to bullying: Understanding the role of school policies and practices. *Journal of Educational Psychology, 111*(3), 475–487. https://doi.org/10.1037/edu0000295.
Liu, T. L., Chen, Y. L., Hsiao, R. C., Ni, H. C., Liang, S. H. Y., Lin, C. F., Chan, H. L., Hsieh, Y. H., Wang, L. J., Lee, M. J., Chou, W.J., & Yen, C. F. (2023). Adolescent–caregiver agreement regarding the school bullying and cyberbullying involvement experiences of adolescents with Autism Spectrum Disorder. *International Journal of Environmental Research and Public Health, 20*(4), 3733. https://doi.org/10.3390/ijerph20043733.
Mental Health America. (2024). *Finding therapy*. https://www.mhanational.org/finding-therapy.
Mishna, F., Pepler, D., & Wiener, J. (2006). Factors associated with perceptions and responses to bullying situations by children, parents, teachers, and principals. *Victims and Offenders, 1*(3), 255–288. https://doi.org/10.1080/15564880600626163.
New England Association of Schools and Colleges. (2024). *School health and safety*. https://www.neasc.org/school-health-and-safety-independent.
New York Center for School Safety. (2024). *Dignity Act frequently asked questions for parents and guardians*. https://www.nyscfss.org/dasa-faqs-for-parents.
Nguyên, T. T. T., & Mark, L. K. (2014). Cyberbullying, sexting, and online sharing: A comparison of parent and school faculty perspectives. *International Journal of Cyber Behavior, Psychology and Learning (IJCBPL), 4*(1), 76–86. http://doi.org/10.4018/978-1-5225-8900-6.ch005.
Nickerson, A. B., Manges, M. E., Casella, J., Huang, Y., Bellavia, G. M., Livingston, J., Jenkins, L. N., & Feeley, T. H. (2024). Bystander

intervention in bullying and sexual harassment training: Mixed-method evaluation. *Journal of Prevention and Health Promotion, 5*(1), 6–34. https://doi.org/10.1177/26320770231200230.

Nickerson, A. B., Mele, D., & Princiotta, D. (2008). Attachment and empathy as predictors of roles as defenders or outsiders in bullying interactions. *Journal of School Psychology, 46*(6), 687–703. https://doi.org/10.1016/j.jsp.2008.06.002.

PACER National Bullying Prevention Center. (n.d.). *When "friends" are the ones doing the bullying.*

PACER's National Bullying Prevention Center. (2019). *What parents should know about bullying: Working with the school.* https://www.pacer.org/bullying/parents/working-with-school.asp.

PACER's National Bullying Prevention Center. (2020). *Five reasons youth don't report cyberbullying – and what parents can do about it.* https://www.fosi.org/good-digital-parenting/5-reasons-youth-dont-report-cyberbullying-and-what-parents-can-do-about-it.

PACER Teens Against Bullying. (2018). *Reasons teens don't tell.* https://pacerteensagainstbullying.org/advocacy-for-self/reasons-teens-dont-tell/.

Pimm, C. (2012). The perspectives of parents, carers and families. In C. McLaughlin, R. Byers, & C. Oliver (Eds.), *Perspectives on bullying and difference supporting young people with special educational needs and/or disabilities in school* (1st ed., pp. 54–65). National Children's Bureau.

Pozzoli, T., & Gini, G. (2013). Why do bystanders of bullying help or not? A multidimensional model. *The Journal of Early Adolescence, 33*(3), 315–340. https://doi.org/10.1177/0272431612440172.

Rapp, H. (2023). *An exploratory mixed methods study considering parents of adolescents with developmental disabilities as secondary victims of bullying abuse.* [Doctoral dissertation, the University of Wisconsin-Madison].

Rosenkrantz, H. (2021, December 13). *Bullying in private schools versus public schools.* U.S. News and World Report. https://www.usnews.com/education/k12/articles/bullying-in-private-schools-versus-public-schools.

Sheridan, S. M., Smith, T. E., Kim, E. M., Beretvas, S. N., & Park, S. (2019). A meta-analysis of family-school interventions and children's social-emotional functioning: Child and community influences and components of efficacy. *Review of Educational Research, 89*(2), 296–332. https://doi.org/10.1007/s10648-019-09509-w.

Stopbullying.gov. (2023). *Common components in state anti-bullying laws, policies, and regulations.* https://www.stopbullying.gov/resources/laws/key-components.

Stuart, J., Scott, R., Smith, C., & Speechley, M. (2022). Parents' anticipated responses to children's cyberbullying experiences: Action, education and emotion. *Children and Youth Services Review, 136,* 106398. https://doi.org/10.1016/j.childyouth.2022.106398.

Su, Y. W., Doty, J., Polley, B. R., Cakmakci, H., Swank, J., & Sickels, A. (2021). Collaborating with families to address cyberbullying: Exploring school counselors' lived experiences. *Professional School Counseling, 25*(1), 2156759X211053825. https://doi.org/10.1177/2156759X211053.

Tang, J. T., Saadi, A., Dunn, E. C., & Choi, K. (2024). Concordance in child-parent reporting of social victimization experiences in the Adolescent Brain Cognitive Development (ABCD) Study. *Academic Pediatrics.* Online first publication. https://doi.org/10.1016/j.acap.2024.02.001.

Ttofi, M. M., & Farrington, D. P. (2011). Effectiveness of school-based programs to reduce bullying: A systematic and meta-analytic review. *Journal of Experimental Criminology, 7,* 27–56. https://doi.org/10.1007/s11292-010-9109-1.

U.S. Department of Education. (n.d.). *Civil rights laws.* https://www.ed.gov/laws-and-policy/civil-rights-laws.

U.S. Department of Education. (n.d.). *Protecting student privacy: Frequently asked questions.* https://studentprivacy.ed.gov/frequently-asked-questions.

U.S. Department of Education. (2010). *How to file a discrimination complaint with the office for civil rights.* https://www2.ed.gov/about/offices/list/ocr/docs/howto.pdf.

Wahyuningrum, E., Suryanto, S., & Suminar, D. R. (2020). Parenting in digital era: A systematic literature review. *Journal of Educational, Health and Community Psychology, 30*(3), 226–258. https://doi.org/10.1080/23279095.2021.1943397.

Witte, A., Singleton, F., Smith, T., & Hershfeldt, P. (2021). *Enhancing family school collaboration with diverse families.* Center on Positive Behavioral Interventions and Supports, University of Oregon. www.pbis.org.

9

Legal Implications: Problematic Online Behavior and the Law

It is important for adults, including parents or caregivers, educators, and other adults who work with youth, to be familiar with potential legal implications for online behaviors such as cyberbullying. In order to understand the legal ramifications, it is important to be able to distinguish between online bullying and harassment, and to know when to involve police. This chapter will cover legal issues relevant to cyberbullying, sexting, and potential online predators (e.g., adults who may use the internet to contact youth with the intent to engage in harmful behavior). Both parents and schools should understand the legal responsibility of schools in these cases, especially in responding to cyberbullying and sexting. This chapter is just an overview of broad legal issues relevant to online behaviors, and parents and educators should consult legal advice for more serious specific issues.

Federal Laws for Harassment

There are no federal laws that specifically address bullying or cyberbullying. However, bullying may overlap with behaviors addressed under federal laws (e.g., harassment). When the bullying behavior targets a child or adolescent's identity, which is considered a protected class (e.g., race/ethnicity, color, national origin, sex [including sexual orientation and gender identity], disability, age, or religion) it changes from not only being considered cyberbullying behavior, but is also a form of harassment (www.stopbullying.gov/resources/laws). Although people often use the terms

---

Cyberbullying: Helping Children Navigate Digital Technology and Social Media, First Edition. Stephanie Fredrick, et al.
© 2025 John Wiley & Sons, Inc. Published 2025 by John Wiley & Sons, Inc.

bullying and harassment similarly, there are very important legal distinctions between them. It is easy to see why the terms are used interchangeably, especially because they both include the consequences of harming another person and often there is an imbalance of power.

The significant distinction that makes a bullying or cyberbullying incident harassment is when the harmful behavior toward the victim is based on a protected class. It may be challenging to determine this, so let us consider a couple of examples.

- Marcus is in 7th grade and has Down syndrome. He tells his parents that every day when he walks down a specific hallway to go to his class, there are a group of kids who call him "retarded" and make fun of him for going to his special education class. Marcus told the teachers at his school about the bullying, but they did not intervene and the bullying has continued.

   This would be a clear-cut example of a student being bullied based on the protected class of disability. In this example, the perpetrators are making derogatory comments and bullying Marcus because he has a disability.

- Every day when Marcus walks down the hallway, the group of kids trip him or knock his books out of his hand.

   In this situation, Marcus could be the target of bullying because he has a disability, but it is not as clear because the perpetrators are not making that clearly known. Finally, some youth are bullied for reasons that are not a protected class and those youth would, unfortunately, not have the same federal law protections such as youth experiencing harassment based on one or more protected classes.

The term harassment has a history in civil rights law and policy. Civil rights laws were developed to provide protection to individuals from various classes who are often susceptible to discrimination (Cornell & Limber, 2015). The important federal laws to know that are relevant to harassment of protected classes are:

- The Individuals with Disabilities Education Act (IDEA) protects individuals with disabilities from discrimination and ensures they receive a free and appropriate education (FAPE).
- Section 504 of the Rehabilitation Act of 1973 protects individuals with disabilities from discrimination.

- Titles II and III of the Americans with Disabilities Act protects individuals with disabilities from discrimination.
- Title IV and VI of the Civil Rights Act of 1964 provides protection from discrimination based on race, color, or national origin.
- Title IX of the Education Amendments of 1972 provides protection on the basis of sex, including sexual orientation and gender identity.

If a student is being harassed regarding a protected class, federally funded schools are required to address these behaviors. Thus, in the example about Marcus, the school is required to protect Marcus from bullying and harassment based on his disability. In 2010, the U.S. Department of Education and Office for Civil Rights provided a detailed "Dear Colleague" letter to schools detailing race, color, or national origin harassment; sexual harassment; gender-based harassment; and disability harassment. The letter reminds schools that although they should focus on reducing all bullying, they need to be aware that some bullying falls under the category of harassment. They note that school districts are in violation of the federal laws listed above if they allow harassment based on a protected class that is "sufficiently serious that it creates a hostile environment and such harassment is encouraged, tolerated, not adequately addressed, or ignored by school employees." The letter goes on to state that schools are responsible for addressing this harassment when they are aware it is occurring or even when they "reasonably should have known." The school must immediately complete a thorough investigation of the harassment and put a stop to any behavior that is determined to be harassment, including preventing it from recurring. To refer to the letter see this webpage: https://www.ed.gov/laws-and-policy/civil-rights-laws/harassment-bullying-and-retaliation/dear-colleague-letter-harassment-and-bullying-background-summary-and-fast-facts

State Laws and School District Policies for Cyberbullying

As previously mentioned, there are no federal laws regarding bullying, including cyberbullying, unless the behavior overlaps with harassment based on race, national origin, color, sex (including sexual orientation and gender identity), age, disability, or religion. We mentioned in

Chapter 8 that laws differ across states, so individuals should refer to their respective state laws. To learn about the specific laws in each state at the website, https://cyberbullying.org/bullying-laws, you can click on a state and read a detailed description of the state's respective bullying law. All states have criminal laws that might apply to bullying if the behavior includes a criminal act of harassment (e.g., threatening violence or actual physical violence). Forty-eight states include cyberbullying or online harassment in their laws (Patchin & Hinduja, 2023). Finally, all of the states have anti-bullying legislation that require schools to develop formal anti-bullying policies (Hinduja & Patchin, 2024).

School districts will each have their own unique policies regarding bullying and cyberbullying behaviors. The goal of the policies is to have procedures in place that will hopefully reduce bullying and cyberbullying. According to the U.S. Department of Health and Human Services (2019), the most common components of state anti-bullying laws and policies include:

1. A Statement of Purpose: This statement should note that bullying is unacceptable and describe the negative outcomes for youth who are bullied. They specifically mention that it should be stated that retaliation for reporting bullying should be prohibited, as well as behaviors that perpetuate bullying by spreading hurtful and demeaning information and materials (e.g., sharing a text or social media post).
2. Definition: It should include a definition of both bullying and cyberbullying that is easily understood by stakeholders (e.g., students, educators, families, and community members).
3. Scope: Defines the scope of behaviors that fall under the policy such as location where bullying occurs and that it causes a significant disruption to the school environment the school needs to respond. This is especially important for cyberbullying as the behaviors that occur off campus or outside of the school day still need to be managed by the school if they cause a significant disruption to the school environment.
4. Protected Groups: The policy acknowledges that some groups are more at risk for being bullied than others (e.g., LGBTQ+ youth) and those at-risk groups could be listed in the policy.
5. District Policies: Schools are required to develop and implement an anti-bullying policy with relevant stakeholders (e.g., teachers, parents, and students).

6. Reporting and Investigations: There should be procedures for individuals to report bullying incidents that include a way to report bullying anonymously with protection from negative retaliation. It also requires that reported incidents are promptly investigated and victims are protected from further bullying and retaliation.
7. Consequence: There should be a description of any consequences for those who bully others.
8. Communication of Policy: Students, families, and staff should be informed of the policy and know how to access the policy.
9. Safeguards and Supports: Safeguards should be in place for victims of bullying including referral to mental health services when needed, such as on-site school counselors or school support staff, or a list of referrals to community mental health resources.
10. Review and Update of Local Policies: There should be plans to periodically review and update the policy as necessary.
11. Preventative Education: School districts are encouraged to engage in preventive education for students, families, and staff (see Chapter 7 for more information on cyberbullying school preventative education, such as social emotional learning (SEL), positive behavioral interventions and support (PBIS), and digital citizenship).
12. Staff Training: Encourages the school district to provide training for all staff regarding bullying (such as what bullying looks like and how staff should intervene if they witness bullying in their classroom or hallway or if a student reports bullying or cyberbullying to them).
13. Parent Engagement: School districts are encouraged to involve parents in the bullying policies and prevention and intervention strategies. As discussed in Chapter 8, parents should also be notified when their child is involved in any bullying incident.

Civil Law Regarding Cyberbullying

A significant number of civil law cases relevant to bullying and cyberbullying behaviors can help parents and school personnel to determine the actions to be taken (Jenkins et al., 2022). We describe a few civil law cases below. For a detailed list of relevant civil law cases, see Hinduja and

Patchin's (2024) book, *Bullying Beyond the Schoolyard Preventing and Responding to Cyberbullying* (Chapter 4, Table 4.1).

Davis v. Monroe County Board of Education (1999)

In this case, LaShonda Davis, a 5th grader, reported that other students at school were sexually harassing her. LaShonda and her mother reported this harassment to the school; however, the school did not take action and this led to an abusive and hostile school environment that negatively affected her schoolwork and well-being. LaShonda's mother argued in the case that the school violated her protections from discrimination based on sex in Title IX of the Education Amendments of 1972. In this case, the U.S. Supreme Court ruled in favor of LaShonda Davis stating that the school was aware of the sexual harassment and these behaviors affected her access to education. This case not only focused on sexual harassment between students, but also made it clear that schools have a responsibility to intervene and end harassment from peers (Jenkins et al., 2022).

J.S. v. Bethlehem Area School District (2002)

In this case, an 8th grade student, J.S., created a website from his home computer writing negative things about his math teacher and school principal. He was expelled from school due to his creation of this website. J.S.'s parents appealed the expulsion, noting that J.S.'s First and Fourteenth Amendment rights were violated. However, the U.S. Supreme Court ruled in favor of the school on the basis that the website was disruptive to the school environment. This case demonstrates that if the cyberbullying behavior disrupts the educational environment, courts will support consequences imposed on those students by their schools (Jenkins et al., 2022).

Tinker v. Des Moines Independent School District (1969)

Students in a public school in Des Moines, IA, planned to wear black armbands to protest the Vietnam War. The school principal warned students they would be suspended if they wore the armbands to avoid any disruption to school. A few students still wore the armbands and the principal suspended those students. The parents of the suspended students sued the school for violation of their First Amendment rights to free speech. In this case, the initial decision in a district court supported the school that the armbands could disrupt learning; however, the decision was appealed and the U.S. Supreme Court eventually ruled in favor of the students, stating that the school could not assume wearing the armbands would disrupt the learning environment.

The decisions from the civil cases demonstrate several patterns: (a) schools are able to discipline a student if their bullying or cyberbullying behaviors, even if they happened online and off campus, causes a substantial disruption to the learning environment; (b) courts will often support free speech of students based on their first amendment rights unless there is a substantial disruption to the learning environment; and (c) students who are members of protected classes are protected from bullying, cyberbullying, and harassment due to harassment and discrimination laws (Jenkins et al., 2022).

When Should School Districts Intervene?

Intervening in cyberbullying for educators has been less clear because the behaviors do not always occur on the school grounds. School personnel may be reluctant to intervene in cyberbullying that happened away from the school premises and that did not happen on school-based technology. However, school administrators have a moral and sometimes legal obligation to take action when they become aware of the harassment (Hinduja & Patchin, 2024). Schools need to be careful about balancing the right to free speech, as seen in some of the sample cases above, when they investigate the incident and ascertain consequences. Schools have been sued and lost cases when they implemented consequences for bullying that have been determined to infringe on students' rights to free speech (Hinduja & Patchin, 2024). As noted earlier, court cases have often supported students in terms of their right to free speech. However, there are times when schools are able to intervene and discipline perpetrators without repercussions (Hinduja & Patchin, 2024), which can be found in Table 9.1.

Table 9.1 Situations where schools should intervene with cyberbullying.

Situation	Example
Cyberbullying substantially and negatively impacts learning	Many LBGTQ students in a school are being bullied online, and this information begins to spread throughout the school and the group of students are scared and anxious in their classes. Teachers are spending significant time handling these sensitive situations. Overall, the educational environment has been negatively impacted.
Cyberbullying occurs through school-owned technology	A student cyberbullied others utilizing their school-issued Chromebook. Even though the bullying happened when the device was at the student's home, the school may intervene because the behavior happened on technology the school owns.
Cyberbullying threatens others or infringes on the civil rights of others	A group of students creates a group chat to spread rumors about a particular student that are hurtful and derogatory. As a result, this student experiences emotional distress and stops coming to school. The cyberbullying behaviors have infringed on the targeted student's right to a safe and supportive educational environment.

Source: Adapted from Hinduja and Patchin (2024).

Criminal Cyberbullying Behaviors

Although there are no federal or state criminal laws regarding cyberbullying, when cyberbullying activities threaten or include criminal activity, they should be reported to the police (U.S. Department of Health and Human Services, 2024). These behaviors could be reported to school administration, school resource officers, and local police officers. The types of behaviors that may be considered a crime include:

- Threatening violence toward an individual
   An example of this criminal behavior may be an online post where a peer threatens violence toward another student, such as beating someone up or bringing a weapon to school to harm them.

- Taking a photo or video of a child in a location where they would expect privacy

    An example of this could be a student taking a picture of another student in the bathroom or locker room. The target student would expect privacy in both of these locations.
- Stalking

    An example of stalking could include a peer who becomes infatuated with another student and continually comments on the target student's social media and makes comments about them online. In addition, the behavior is very intrusive and the target student starts to feel uncomfortable.
- Hate crime

    A hate crime could include a peer targeting another student based on a protected class, such as race, and then creating a website about this student that contains hateful statements about this person using racial slurs.
- Child pornography or sending sexually explicit images or texts

    An example of this could be sending a sexually explicit image, which a student obtained consensually from the target student, to a large group chat to make fun of the target student.

More on sexually explicit images will be covered next regarding behaviors. It is especially important to get law enforcement involved when you need to assist with investigation of a potentially criminal activity.

Sexting

An additional concern about online behaviors that has legal ramifications is sexting, which includes both sending and receiving sexually explicit images or texts within online communications (Lee & Darcy, 2021; Strasburger, Jordan, & Donnerstein, 2012). A large meta-analysis of rates of sexting between 2016 and 2022 found that 19% of youth report sending and 35% report receiving sext messages (Mori et al., 2022). Before discussing legal issues relevant to sexting, it should be acknowledged that many experts consider sexting as a more modern form of sexual exploration and engagement between romantic partners (King & Rings, 2022; Strasburger, Jordan, & Donnerstein, 2012). Some experts propose a "sex-positive" approach that does not overly emphasize punishment for those who engage in it in a consensual manner (Woodley et al., 2024). Of course, along with consensual sexting that may be considered part of normal sexual development comes the misuse of shared photos and content. Strasburger, Jordan, and Donnerstein (2012) break sexting down into several helpful categories that distinguish between consensual and nonconsensual sexting. The first group of behaviors falls under consensual sexting:

(1) Purely consensual teen sexting between two consenting adolescents. This is considered normative adolescent sexual development; and
(2) Consensual but coerced sexting with one teen pressuring the other to engage in the behavior.

The second group of behaviors falls under nonconsensual sexting and includes:

(3) Disseminating sexts that were shared without one of the partner's consent;
(4) Sextortion, which is threatening that you will disseminate a sexual image to gain something (e.g., sex, money, etc.); and
(5) Teen sexts requested or obtained by adults. This behavior usually fits within the definition of child pornography.

Research demonstrates that most youth realize the potential social repercussions that could occur when sexting. In other words – youth know that the photos could eventually be shared without consent, and they report their biggest fear regarding sexting is the photos being shared with others (Daniels et al., 2024). They also report they are afraid of being rejected after sexting and/or being laughed at by others. Additionally, they know that these risks could affect their mental health and social standing in school; however, they are less likely to be aware of legal consequences. Thus, education on the potential legal implications are important discussions for parents and educators to have with adolescents.

Legal Implications of Sexting

The U.S. laws have not kept up with the changing digital technologies, including adolescent sexting, and most of the current laws were implemented to protect minors from sexual exploitation and pornography (King & Rings, 2022). Sometimes sexting incidents fall under federal child pornography laws, especially when the images cross state lines including email and social media apps because the images are shared through the internet (King & Rings, 2022; Strasburger, Jordan, & Donnerstein, 2012). These federal laws are very serious offenses and a first-time offender who "created, possessed, received, or distributed sexually suggestive or explicit images of a minor could face substantial monetary fines and anywhere between 15 to 30 years in prison" (King & Rings, 2022, p. 473).

State laws that could be related to sexting vary in definitions and consequences. States are starting to develop laws that are specific to teen sexting. Researchers have been advocating for laws that specifically address sexting and protect adolescents from more harsh consequences.

Currently, 27 states have implemented laws that address sexting for minors; however, only nine actually mentioned the word sexting (Hinduja & Patchin, 2022a,b; King & Rings, 2022). These laws were put in place to create more updated laws and protect minors from the harsh consequences of being charged with felonies for child pornography (King & Rings, 2022). To learn about the specific sexting laws in your state, a helpful website to read about each state's laws can be found here: https://cyberbullying.org/sexting-laws

Responding to Sexting
Upon finding out that a student is involved in sexting, especially if it is being used for harm, adults should act quickly by reaching out to school resource officers or police officers to assist with investigating the incident (Hinduja & Patchin, 2010) to intervene to prevent or reduce the spread of the information and potentially the damage done if the image or text spreads widely. Hinduja and Pathchin (2024) from the Cyberbullying Research Center also caution that adults involved with the incident (parents and educators) should not copy, forward, or download any sexually explicit images of minors, as this could lead to criminal child pornography charges even when the adult is doing this in the best interest of the adolescents involved. Thus, this is a time to seek support from experts and legal authorities. When investigating the incident, it is important to address the situation in a supportive manner and make sure that the target whose photos were shared and their family have mental health support. The information shared is highly sensitive and can be traumatic for the youth involved. As mentioned in Chapter 5, The National Center for Missing & Exploited Children has a helpful website

that will assist with the removal of sexually explicit photos of minors at https://takeitdown.ncmec.org.

Online Predators

A worry for many parents about risky online behavior is that their child may be contacted by an online adult predator. As discussed in Chapter 3, preteens and teenagers are reporting that strangers are contacting them on social media platforms in ways that make them uncomfortable. Youth may be especially susceptible to being groomed or manipulated by adults online. Online grooming is a relationship between a minor and an adult that is developed on trust and uses technology to solicit and then exploit youth for sexual reasons (Schoeps et al., 2020). As with any online interaction, youth cannot know for sure whom they are interacting with, and adults may portray themselves as similar in age and develop a trusting relationship over time. Many adults are not familiar with the term online grooming, and more education is needed about these risks and how to protect children from predatory online behaviors (Dorasamy et al., 2021). Some important warning signs that your child may be interacting with an online predator include (https://internetsafety101.org/predatorwarningsigns):

(a) being secretive and obsessive regarding being online;
(b) being angry when they cannot be online;
(c) receiving phone calls or texts from people you do not know;
(d) receiving mail or packages from people you do not know;
(e) withdrawing from friends and family;
(f) hiding their devices or computer screens from you, and
(g) engaging with pornography online.

It is important to note that many of these warning signs overlap with warning signs of other problematic online behaviors (e.g., cyberbullying, problematic social media use), as discussed in Chapter 6. Further, many of the strategies to prevent your child from engaging with an online predator have been discussed in earlier chapters. These strategies include communicating and educating your child about online predators, teaching your child about privacy settings on the apps they utilize, encouraging youth to have a private account and not accept friend requests from people they do not know, helping them to think critically about the intentions of others reaching out to them on the internet, teaching them how to report and block individuals when necessary, and providing monitoring and supervision (Okpokwasili & Onwuatuegwu, 2023). The most important point is to have ongoing conversations with your child regarding all these issues and their experiences online. Without ongoing communication, you will not be aware of any potential issue concerning online interactions. Should you have a concern about experiences your child had online with potential online predators, this is a time to get law enforcement involved. There are also some important online safety resources for you and your child to be aware of including:

- Federal Bureau of Investigation (FBI)
https://www.fbi.gov/how-we-can-help-you/parents-and-caregivers-protecting-your-kids
- National Center for Missing & Exploited Children (NCMEC)
www.missingkids.org
- National Center for Missing & Exploited Children CyberTipline
https://report.cybertip.org/
- Take It Down
https://takeitdown.ncmec.org

The FBI website works in conjunction with the NCMEC to host a cyber tip line to report online child exploitation. It is a 24-hour hotline at 1-800-843-5678. The Take It Down service also works in conjunction with NCMEC and is a helpful resource should your child have a sexually explicit photo posted online. The service assists in helping sexually explicit minor photos removed from the internet. The individual asking for assistance can also stay anonymous and still receive assistance.

Summary

The legal issues surrounding online behaviors for youth are complex and continue to change and evolve. This chapter overviewed broad legal issues for cyberbullying, sexting, and online predators. However, individuals are encouraged to consult legal experts for specific incidents when necessary. It is important for parents or caregivers, educators, and other adults who work with youth to be familiar with potential legal implications for online behaviors, including students' protections under the law.

References

Cornell, D., & Limber, S. P. (2015). Law and policy on the concept of bullying at school. *American Psychologist, 70*(4), 333–343. https://doi.org/10.1037/a0038558.

Daniels, E. A., Dajches, L., Terán, L., Gahler, H., Choi, H. J., Speno, A., & Stevens Aubrey, J. (2024). The sexual landscape of youth: How adolescents from the U.S. make sense of sexting. *Journal of Adolescent Research.* https://doi.org/10.1177/07435584241231448.

Davis v. Monroe County Board of Education, 526 U.S. 629 (1999). https://supreme.justia.com/cases/federal/us/526/629/.

Dorasamy, M., Kaliannan, M., Jambulingam, M., Ramadhan, I., & Sivaji, A. (2021). Parents' awareness on online predators: Cyber grooming deterrence. *The Qualitative Report, 26*(11), 3685–3723. https://doi.org/10.46743/2160-3715/2021.4914.

Hinduja, S., & Patchin, J. W. (2010). *Sexting: A brief guide for educators and parents.* https://cyberbullying.org/Sexting-Fact-Sheet.pdf.

Hinduja, S., & Patchin, J. W. (2022a). *State sexting laws.* Cyberbullying Research Center. https://cyberbullying.org/sexting-laws.

Hinduja, S., & Patchin, J. W. (2022b). *Teen sexting: A brief guide for educations and parents.* Cyberbullying Research Center. https://cyberbullying.org/sexting-research-summary-2022.pdf.

Hinduja, S., & Patchin, J. W. (2024). *Bullying beyond the schoolyard: Preventing and responding to cyberbullying* (3rd ed.). Corwin.

Jenkins, L. N., Demaray, M. K., Eldridge, M., & Kaminski, S. (2022). Bullying and the law. In *Psychology in the Real World.* Routledge. https://doi.org/10.4324/9780367198459-REPRW193-1.

J.S v. Bethlehem Area School District, 807 A.2d 847 (Pa. 2002). https://law.justia.com/cases/pennsylvania/commonwealth-court/2002/179cd01-2-15-02.html.

King, C. K., & Rings, J. A. (2022). Adolescent sexting: Ethical and legal implications for psychologists. *Ethics & Behavior, 32*(6), 1–11. https://doi.org/10.1080/10508422.2021.1983818.

Lee, J. R., & Darcy, K. M. (2021). Sexting: What's law got to do with it? *Archives of Sexual Behavior, 50*, 563–573. https://doi.org/10.1007/s10508-020-01727-6.

Mori, C., Park, J., Temple, J. R., & Madigan, S. (2022). Are youth sexting rates still on the rise? A meta-analytic update. *Journal of Adolescent Health, 70*(4), 531–539. https://doi.org/10.1016/j.jadohealth.2021.10.026.

Okpokwasili, O. A., & Onwuatuegwu, I. N. (2023). Online predators: Protecting teenagers from internet sexual exploitation. *International Journal of Modern Science and Research Technology, 1*(4), 41–51.

Patchin, J. W., & Hinduja, S. (2023). *Bullying laws across America.* Cyberbullying Research Center. https://cyberbullying.org/bullying-laws.

Schoeps, K., Mónaco, E., Cotolí, A., & Montoya-Castilla, I. (2020). The impact of peer attachment on prosocial behavior, emotional difficulties and conduct problems in adolescence: The mediating role of empathy. *PLoS One, 15*(1), 1–18. https://doi.org/10.1371/journal.pone.0227627.

Strasburger, V. C., Jordan, A. B., & Donnerstein, E. (2012). Children, adolescents, and the media: Health effects. *Pediatric Clinics of North America, 59*(3), 533–587. https://doi.org/10.1016/j.pcl.2012.03.025.

Tinker et al. v. Des Moines Independent Community School District, 393 U.S. 503 (1969). https://supreme.justia.com/cases/federal/us/393/503/.

U.S. Department of Education, Office for Civil Rights. (2010, October). *Dear Colleague Letter: Harassment and bullying—Background, summary, and fast facts.* https://www.ed.gov/sites/ed/files/about/offices/list/ocr/docs/dcl-factsheet-201010.pdf.

U.S. Department of Health and Human Services. (2019, September 24). *Key components in state anti-bullying laws, policies and regulations.* StopBullying.gov. https://www.stopbullying.gov/resources/laws/key-components.

U.S. Department of Health and Human Services. (2024). *Report cyberbullying.* StopBullying.gov. https://www.stopbullying.gov/cyberbullying/how-to-report.

Woodley, G. N., Green, L., & Jacques, C. (2024). "Send nudes?": Teens' perspectives of education around sexting, an argument for a balanced approach. *Sexualities.* https://doi.org/10.1177/13634607241237675.

10

International Efforts to Address Cyberbullying and Other Forms of Cyber Aggression

Cyberbullying and related behavior are recognized as concerns around the world. Throughout the book, we have focused on parenting involvement, strategies, and school responses to cyberbullying in the United States. This chapter discusses how parents can help prepare children to navigate the digital world as global citizens safely. We first provide an overview of the global trends of cyberbullying and its impact on youth. We then give an extended overview of the different parenting styles and strategies revolving around digital media use across North America, Europe, Asia, and countries in the global south. Information about some widely applied and effective digital citizenship education (DCE) initiatives and resources across different countries is shared.

Global Trends of Cyberbullying

Cyberbullying is a global issue, affecting youth in every region, though its prevalence and impact vary. As mentioned previously, nearly 46% of teenagers in the United States have reported experiencing cyberbullying, with platforms such as Instagram and TikTok being common sites for such incidents (Vogels, 2022). Europe faces a similar challenge, with the UK reporting that over 51% of children have been victims of online abuse, including trolling and cyberstalking (Dixon, 2022). In Poland, high rates of name-calling and reputational damage are also prevalent (Sas, 2024).

Cyberbullying: Helping Children Navigate Digital Technology and Social Media, First Edition. Stephanie Fredrick, et al.
© 2025 John Wiley & Sons, Inc. Published 2025 by John Wiley & Sons, Inc.

In Asia, cyberbullying is equally alarming. In India, approximately 65% of children have encountered cyberbullying, often on platforms like Facebook, where the scale of bullying can be overwhelming (Ranjith et al., 2023). Japanese schools have seen a continuous increase in cyberbullying incidents, particularly among middle school students (Statista Research Department, 2023). South Korea reports significant rates of cyberbullying, with about 41.6% of teenagers experiencing online harassment (Korea Communications Commission, 2023). Additionally, over 40% of Chinese internet users experience victimization (Feng, 2023).

The Global South is not immune to this trend. In countries like Brazil and South Africa, the prevalence of cyberbullying is also high. Brazil is among the top three countries where parents report the highest incidence of cyberbullying (Rovenstine, 2024). In South Africa, a study found that approximately 46.8% of teenagers have experienced some form of cyberbullying, reflecting a significant challenge in managing online safety for youth (Burton & Mutongwizo, 2009).

In previous chapters, we discussed awareness, understanding, and knowing what to do if your child is involved in cyberbullying. In this chapter, we "zoom out" to discuss the concepts and practical implications of digital citizenship from a global perspective. Digital citizenship is not limited to local norms or individual experiences; it encompasses a wide range of cultural, social, and ethical considerations that vary across countries (Choi, 2016). Understanding these global dynamics is crucial for parents to help their children navigate the internet safely and responsibly, given the diverse digital landscapes they interact with daily.

International Digital Citizenship and Parenting Practices

As the internet transcends geographical boundaries, children are exposed to a wide range of cultural norms, values, and practices online. These cultural differences can significantly influence a child's worldview, behavior, and digital interactions. For parents, recognizing and respecting these diverse perspectives is essential to guide their children effectively in navigating the digital landscape. By fostering an awareness of cultural and cross-country diversity, parents can help their children develop empathy, tolerance, and a more nuanced understanding of the world, which are critical skills for thriving in a globalized society. Here we provide a brief review of the main characteristics of digital citizenship and parenting styles and strategies in some major regions across the globe.

In North America, we see more active monitoring and use of parental control software. Around 50% of U.S. parents check their children's social media profiles and browsing histories regularly, although many feel underprepared to address online risks comprehensively (Kaspersky, 2021). This approach highlights a culture of vigilance where parents take a hands-on role in safeguarding their children's digital interactions. It is also important to recognize the various cultural backgrounds that influence values, beliefs, and methods of supervising children online. For example, some parents may come from cultures that emphasize collective family decision-making and strict monitoring of their children's online activities to uphold family honor, while others might value individual autonomy and take a more hands-off approach (Lansford, 2022). Additionally, differences in access to technology and levels of digital literacy among cultural groups can impact how parents engage with their children's online experiences – some may rely more on technology-based controls, while others might focus on open dialogue and trust (Mesch, 2009). These diverse approaches reflect the rich cultural fabric of North America and underscore the importance of culturally sensitive resources and strategies to help parents guide their children safely through the digital world.

In Europe, there is also considerable variation in parenting strategies and digital citizenship. For instance, in the UK, about 70% of parents utilize parental control software to restrict access to certain websites, showcasing a proactive stance in managing internet use (Ofcom, 2022). In contrast, in countries like Poland, there is a stronger emphasis on communication and trust between parents and children rather than relying solely on technical controls (Sas, 2024).

Children in Nordic countries tend to have greater digital skills, which is linked to the open and supportive parenting styles prevalent in those regions (Livingstone & Helsper, 2008). These findings reflect a cultural preference for open dialogue and mutual understanding as key components of internet safety. In contrast, parents in Southern European countries are more likely to adopt stricter internet parenting practices. Central Europe presents a more integrated approach; for instance, in Turkey, research by Özgür (2016) categorizes internet parenting into four types: permissive, tolerant, authoritative, and authoritarian. The study revealed that Turkish children are at higher risk of internet misuse due to parents' limited digital knowledge and traditional family attitudes. As children grow older, Turkish parents often shift from an authoritarian to a more tolerant approach, but there remains a need for improved parental education on internet safety to create a better online environment for children.

It is important to recognize that distinct parenting styles revolving around digital media use may be due to cultural differences between Eastern and Western societies. The Eastern cultures in Asia emphasize collectivism and social harmony and often favor more authoritative approaches. For example, parents' strong control over their children's internet use may vary in effectiveness depending on the type of control use. Zhu et al. (2023) found that behavioral control in China, such as monitoring activities, protects against adolescent internet addiction. In contrast, psychological control, such as guilt induction, increases risk by undermining emotional well-being. In Japan, parents also tend to use strict rules and close monitoring to shield their children from online dangers (Yoshida & Bussey, 2011). Japanese parents are increasingly aware of the risks of cyberbullying and implement stringent rules on internet use, including limiting screen time and closely monitoring social media interactions (Murakawa, 2022). South Korean parents emphasize education, with schools and government programs playing a significant role in teaching children about the dangers of the internet (Lee, 2016). On the other hand, in Singapore, parents generally adopt a more open and communicative parenting style with regard to digital technology. According to Chng et al. (2015), this approach helps children develop healthy internet habits and effectively prevents cyberbullying. While the authoritative styles in China and Japan provide short-term protection, the open and guided approach seen in Singapore may be more beneficial for fostering independence and positive well-being in the long term. These practices reflect a broader cultural focus on discipline and education as tools for ensuring children's online safety.

In the Global South, parenting strategies may be heavily influenced by economic development and internet infrastructure. In many regions, limited access to technology and the internet influences how parents manage online activities. For example, Cummings and O'Neil (2015) note that in areas with underdeveloped internet infrastructure, parents often take an overly lenient or restrictive approach to internet parenting due to limited knowledge of the online environment. Similarly, van Deursen and van Dijk (2014) discuss how the digital divide in these regions leads to varying parenting styles, with parents' digital literacy directly impacting their ability to manage their children's online behaviors. For parents in these regions, enhancing their understanding of the internet is crucial for creating a safer online environment for their children. However, where internet use is more widespread, parents often rely on community norms and collective parenting approaches rather than individual monitoring. For example, in parts of Latin America and Africa, extended families and community networks play a significant role in guiding children's online behavior, reflecting a communal approach to internet safety (Robb et al., 2019).

Laws and Policies on Internet and Device Use Across the Globe

Laws and policies concerning children's safety also vary worldwide. In the United States, laws around children's online safety are less stringent than in other countries, as federal regulations have developed slower (Kelly, 2024). The United States relies heavily on outdated federal laws that limit tech companies' liability, unlike European regulations that hold companies accountable. The European Union has passed the Digital Services Act, which prohibits personalized advertising to children, leading the way in regulatory trends (Kelly, 2024). The UK has also implemented the Age-Appropriate Design Code (Children's Code), which imposes strict requirements for digital platforms to protect children's privacy and safety online (UK Information Commissioner's Office, 2022). Additionally, countries like China and India have enacted laws to enhance children's online safety, while Brazil has put specific protections in place for children's data (Kelly, 2024). These varying approaches reflect different levels of urgency and commitment to protecting children's online experiences globally.

DCE Across the Globe

As parents, the importance of education, especially in teaching global and digital citizenship, cannot be overstated. In today's digital world, it is essential to equip our children with the skills they need to navigate the internet safely and responsibly. DCE helps them learn how to access, critically engage with, create, use, and share information on various platforms, including social media. It also involves guiding children on online etiquette, critical thinking, and empathy, which are key to understanding and managing online interactions. According to the International Society for Technology in Education (ISTE, n.d.), these skills help children navigate their digital lives safely and positively. However, the concept of digital citizenship can look different depending on where you are in the world. In Chapter 7, we provided information about the widely used framework and practical resources of digital citizenship programs implemented in the United States. Here, we provide a review of DCE frameworks, initiatives, and practical resources in Europe, Asia, and the global south. Understanding the current state of DCE in Asia and the Global South is crucial for parents who want to effectively support their children in navigating the digital world. Awareness of the gaps and advancements in DCE enables parents to take proactive steps in teaching their children about online safety and responsible internet use, regardless of their region's current educational landscape.

DCE in Europe

DCE initiatives in Europe are generally well developed, reflecting a broad commitment to integrating digital literacy and online safety into educational frameworks across the continent. European countries have adopted various approaches to equip students with the skills needed to navigate the digital world responsibly. In Northern Europe, countries like Finland and Sweden are at the forefront of integrating digital citizenship into their educational systems. Finland's comprehensive educational reforms include digital skills as a core component, with an emphasis on critical thinking and online safety (Kumpulainen et al., 2022). Similarly, Sweden's curriculum incorporates digital literacy, focusing on fostering safe and responsible online behavior from a young age (Eurydice, 2018). In Western Europe, the UK has developed several national initiatives aimed at promoting digital citizenship. The UK's education policies emphasize the importance of digital literacy and online safety, supported by resources like the "Internet Matters" platform, which offers guidance and tools for parents and educators

(Internet Matters, 2023). In Germany, the Federal Ministry of Education and Research supports DCE through various programs aimed at enhancing students' digital competencies and online safety (European Commission, 2024). Southern and Eastern Europe show more variability in the adoption and implementation of digital citizenship. For example, in Italy and Spain, there is growing recognition of the need for DCE, but implementation varies by region and school (Frau-Meigs et al., 2017). In Eastern European countries such as Poland and Hungary, efforts are underway to integrate digital skills into the curriculum, but these initiatives often face challenges related to resource availability and educational infrastructure (European Commission/EACEA/Eurydice, 2019). Across the European countries, the Council of Europe has created a helpful framework through its Digital Citizenship Education Handbook (2019a). This framework breaks down digital citizenship into 10 key areas across three main domains, offering clear guidance on what children need to learn. These key areas and domains are presented in Table 10.1. To make these ideas easy to understand, especially for younger children, the Council produced a fun video series called *The Digi-Nauts* (Richardson & Samara, 2023a). These videos, along with an accompanying Activity Book, help children, parents, and educators explore what it means to be a good digital citizen, reinforcing important lessons through engaging activities. Moreover, the Council of Europe provides practical tips specifically for parents (Richardson & Samara, 2023b). These resources are designed to help parents guide their children in behaving responsibly and respectfully online. They offer practical recommendations (see examples in Table 10.1) on how to protect your kids from online dangers, such as cyberbullying and social exclusion, ensuring they can enjoy a safe and positive experience both online and offline.

For parents, it is not always easy to know what their children are up to and if their digital citizenship competencies are meeting the challenge. To address this need, the Council of Europe (2019b) has also developed a checklist for parents to take concrete and easy steps to spot where their children could need extra help for developing the broader areas of digital citizen competencies and to help them master what it takes to act responsibly and respectfully online. The questions on this checklist could also serve as a conversation starter for parents to talk with their children about their digital activities (See Table 10.2 for the checklist).

Table 10.1 Practical recommendations for parents to promote digital citizenship competencies and prevent cyberbullying and exclusion online and offline.[1]

Digital citizenship competencies domains	Implications for cyberbullying and online and offline exclusion	Practical recommendations for parents
Domain 1: Being online		
Access and inclusion	No child should ever feel excluded off- or online.	With your children, imagine a world in black and white, where we can see no color. Explain that differences in the way people look, think, and act bring color to our world if only we are open to exploring them.
Being online learning and creativity	Children learn better and less bullying occurs in a relaxed, friendly environment where they can express themselves freely and know that their ideas and creations will be respected.	• Explain to your children that not everyone is interested in or good at the same things. • Build their confidence in recognizing and promoting their talents and skills to help them cope with teasing.
Media and information literacy	The internet is an open space where we may often encounter hate speech and hurtful content. Children need to know why and how to report and block anything offensive.	Explain to your children how it is to be influenced by online opinions and trends. Encourage them to think critically about what other people write, say, and do.

[1]Checklist extracted from Richardson, W., & Samara, A. (2023). *Easy steps for educators.* Council of Europe. https://rm.coe.int/prems-119723-dce-leaflet-easy-steps-for-educators-eng/1680ace5c0

Digital citizenship competencies domains	Implications for cyberbullying and online and offline exclusion	Practical recommendations for parents
Domain 2: Well-being online		
Ethics and empathy	Bullying can be prevented if we all make an effort to understand and respect the feelings and perspectives of others.	Choose some examples of your own to show your children how things they say or do can easily be misinterpreted, especially online. Let them think about why something "funny" for one person can be hurtful for another.
Health and well-being	It is important for your children to grow up in a home and school environment where they feel safe and protected.	Children need to develop resilience to stand up to bullying and disappointment in life. You can help them by providing positive role models and encouraging their self-esteem.
e-Presence and communications	Knowing how to communicate respectfully is an essential part of being a digital citizen.	Remind your children that everything they do online can shape their online reputation permanently. It is best to think hard before being mean online or posting nasty comments.
Domain 3: Rights online		
Active participation	Bullying has permanent lifelong consequences in terms of health, social, and economic well-being, for bullies as well as those who are frequently bullied.	Talk about bullying with your children and use your own life experience to show them how and why they should take action when they, or anyone else, are being bullied.

(Continued)

Table 10.1 (Continued)

Digital citizenship competencies domains	Implications for cyberbullying and online and offline exclusion	Practical recommendations for parents
Rights and responsibilities	Everyone has the right to be respected and the responsibility to treat others as they would like to be treated themselves.	• Ask your children to show you how to report or block a person or a post on their favorite social media platforms. • Explain that, as a parent, you have a right to know when they see something scary or feel uncomfortable online and a responsibility to help them handle it
Privacy and security	Behaving recklessly online and publishing personal data without thinking about the possible consequences can lead to bullying.	• Use examples to make sure your children understand what personal data is. • Show them which bits of their data they can safely share or should not share. What types of information, if shared, could lead to bullying?
Consumer awareness	Children are big advertising targets and families should be made aware of this. Giving in to their every request regarding the latest trends or gadgets can lead them to feel more special than others and less empathetic toward others.	• Ask your children why they always want to have the same sneakers, backpacks, etc., as their friends. • Build their empathy by getting them to think about how it must feel for children who cannot follow these trends because of budget or culture.

Source: Information adapted from Richardson and Samara (2023b).

DCE in Asia and the Global South

DCE initiatives in Asia and the Global South are progressing but face distinct challenges and opportunities depending on regional contexts. In technologically advanced Asian countries like Japan and South

Table 10.2 Checklist for supporting children in building their digital citizenship competencies.[1]

Access

Do you know what sort of activities your children do online?

Does your family have technology downtime, switching off technology at mealtime or after a certain time at night?

Do your children show a healthy balance between face-to-face, physical, and online activities?

Do you surf online with your children and discuss with them how to use the internet responsibly and ethically?

Do your children discuss with you things that bother them online or unpleasant content they have seen?

Participation

- How many of your children's online and offline friends do you know?
- Do you know how many online groups they are part of, and what points of interest bring these groups together?
- After they create and share their content, do they spend more time communicating with friends, playing online, or watching videos?
- Are they good listeners and observers, able to understand the other person's point of view?
- Do they take an interest in talking about what they believe is wrong in the digital world and ways they could try to make things better?

Lifelong Learning

- What percentage of the time online do your children spend doing projects, homework, or exploring new things (for example, visiting an online museum)?
- Are they able to use search engines effectively and compare the results they get?
- Which are their favorite information sources, and do they have any favorite news channels?
- Are they able to judge which online information is reliable and which is false or fake?
- Do they use digital technology at school, and what sort of things do they do with it?

---

[1]The checklist for supporting children in building their digital citizenship competencies was directly extracted from the Council of Europe. (2019). *Digital citizenship and your child: What every parent needs to know and do.* Council of Europe. https://edoc.coe.int/en/human-rights-democratic-citizenship-and-intercultu ralism/7865-digital-citizenship-and-your-child-what-every-parent-needs-to-know-and-do.html

Korea, digital citizenship is actively integrated into educational systems. These countries emphasize comprehensive digital citizenship programs that promote online safety, responsible behavior, and digital skills from an early age (UNESCO Office Bangkok and Regional Bureau for Education in Asia and the Pacific, 2023). However, in regions such as India and Southeast Asia, DCE is less developed, with significant variability in program implementation and resource availability (Singh, 2021). Efforts are underway to enhance digital literacy, but challenges such as limited infrastructure and educational resources hinder the widespread adoption of effective DCE programs. Some widely recognized digital citizenship initiatives in Asian countries are presented in Table 10.3.

In addition to localized digital citizenship initiatives in different countries, UNESCO has been implementing the "Enhancing National Capacity to Foster Digital Citizenship in Asia-Pacific" project to support the development of evidence-based policies for fostering children's digital citizenship and promoting safe, effective, and responsible information and communication technologies use. Building from the emerging data and insights of the project, UNESCO (2023) published a milestone publication, "Digital Citizenship in Asia-Pacific: Translating Competencies for Teacher Innovation and Student Resilience," to provide insights into what constitutes "requisite competencies" if teachers and students are to become responsible digital citizens, and it offers guidance on how to integrate these competencies into educational policies and practices.

In the Global South, many countries need more digital infrastructure and educational resources, which impacts the effectiveness of DCE initiatives. For example, in parts of Sub-Saharan Africa, the lack of access to technology and the internet contributes to a digital divide that affects the implementation of digital citizenship programs (van Deursen & van Dijk, 2014). Despite these challenges, there are ongoing efforts supported by international organizations and local governments to improve digital literacy and online safety education. Initiatives focus on expanding access to technology and providing training for educators and parents to support digital citizenship (Cummings & O'Neil, 2015). Examples of digital citizenship initiatives in the Global South are provided in Table 10.4.

Table 10.3 Examples of digital citizenship initiatives in Asia.

Initiatives	Parental resources
Japan – MEXT Cyberbullying Prevention Resources (MEXT, 2017)	The Ministry of Education, Culture, Sports, Science, and Technology (MEXT) in Japan offers resources to help parents prevent and address cyberbullying. The materials include guidelines for recognizing signs of cyberbullying, how to intervene effectively, and ways to support children who may be victims. Website: https://www.mext.go.jp/en/policy/education/elsec/title02/detail02/1373868.html
South Korea – National Center for Youth Internet Addiction Treatment (2020)	The Internet Dream Village, under the Ministry of Gender Equality and Family, offers onsite, Wi-Fi-free rehabilitation programs for youth with internet addiction. Although no online resources are currently available through government-affiliated institutions, parents can register their children for programs designed to help them disconnect from excessive internet use and promote healthier digital habits. Website: https://nyit.or.kr/user/index.asp
Malaysia – Digi CyberSAFE Program (CyberSAFE Malaysia 2024)	The Digi CyberSAFE Program in Malaysia, run by the Digi telecommunications company in partnership with the Malaysian Communications and Multimedia Commission (MCMC), offers resources aimed at preventing cyberbullying. They provide workshops, parent guides, and online resources to help parents address cyberbullying and promote a positive digital environment. Website: https://www.cybersafe.my/en/
Philippines – CyberSafePH (Department of Information and Communications Technology, n.d.)	CyberSafePH is an initiative by the Philippines' Department of Education and UNICEF, which provides resources to help parents combat cyberbullying. They offer educational materials, campaigns, and tools to raise awareness about cyberbullying and how to prevent it. Website: https://dict.gov.ph/#
Digital Thumbprint Program (Globe Telecom, n.d.)	The Digital Thumbprint Program was integrated by the Department of Education in the Philippines to increase students' knowledge of digital citizenship and cybersafety by taking a critical look at their online behavior and helping them develop insights into the influences of the online world and the choices they are making. Website: https://www.globe.com.ph/about-us/sustainability/learning/digital-thumbprint#gref

(Continued)

Table 10.3 (Continued)

Initiatives	Parental resources
Thailand – ThaiSafeNet (2024) (in Thai and English language)	ThaiSafeNet is an initiative in Thailand aimed at providing parents with the tools and knowledge to help their children navigate the internet safely. They offer resources that cover various aspects of digital citizenship, including online safety, privacy, and respectful communication. Website: https://thaisafe.net
Singapore – Media Literacy Council (2024)	The Media Literacy Council organizes and plans outreach events, such as youth forums and parent workshops to provide parents with resources on managing children's internet use and promoting healthy digital habits. Website: https://www.mlc.sg/programmes/

Table 10.4 Examples of digital citizenship initiatives in the Global South.

Initiatives	Parental resources provided by the initiatives
Brazil – SaferNet Brasil (n.d.)	SaferNet Brasil provides a range of resources for parents to address online safety and digital citizenship. Their platform offers information on preventing cyberbullying, protecting privacy, and fostering responsible online behavior. Website: https://new.safernet.org.br
India – eRaksha Portal (2023)	The eRaksha initiative by the National Commission for Protection of Child Rights provides resources for parents to help children use the internet safely. It covers topics like cyberbullying, online privacy, and digital responsibility. Website: https://www.eraksha.net
Nigeria – Safer Internet Nigeria by Paradigm Initiative (n.d.)	This initiative focuses on educating young people and their parents about online safety, digital rights, and responsible internet use through workshops and campaigns. Website: https://paradigmhq.org/
South Africa – Be in Ctrl Campaign by the Department of Basic Education and Google South Africa (Department of Basic Education, 2021)	Be in Ctrl Campaign by the Department of Basic Education in partnership with Google South Africa offers educational content, workshops, and resources focusing on online safety, digital citizenship, and responsible digital engagement for schools and parents. Website: https://www.education.gov.za/ArchivedDocuments/ArchivedArticles/DBE-Google-partnership-to-fight-cybercrimes-0624.aspx

Summary

Effective digital parenting and fostering strong digital citizenship are crucial for helping your child navigate the online world safely and preventing cyberbullying. This chapter has highlighted the widespread issue of cyberbullying among young people, emphasizing the need for thoughtful and proactive parenting strategies. By exploring various internet parenting styles and DCE approaches from around the world, including North America, Europe, Asia, and the Global South, we have shown how different approaches can be adapted to fit your family's needs. The chapter also provides examples of widely applied digital citizenship programs and resources that can guide you in supporting your child's journey as a responsible and respectful digital citizen. As technology continues to evolve, staying informed with an international perspective will empower you to help your child thrive in a safe and positive online environment as a global citizen.

References

Burton, P., & Mutongwizo, T. (2009). Inescapable violence: Cyber bullying and electronic violence against young people in South Africa. *Centre for Justice and Crime Prevention, 8*, 1–12. https://www.researchgate.net/profile/Tariro-Mutongwizo/publication/317226235_Inescapable_violence_Cyber_bullying_and_electronic_violence_against_young_people_in_South_Africa/links/592cab61a6fdcc84da8da313/Inescapable-violence-Cyber-bullying-and-electronic-violence-against-young-people-in-South-Africa.pdf.

Cheng, A. W., Rizkallah, S., & Narizhnaya, M. (2020). Individualism vs. collectivism. In B. J. Carducci, C. S. Nave, J. S. Mio, & R. E. Riggio (Eds.), *The Wiley encyclopedia of personality and individual differences: Clinical, applied, and cross-cultural research* (pp. 287–297). John Wiley & Sons, Inc.

Chng, G. S., Li, D., Liau, A. K., & Khoo, A. (2015). Parental influences on cyberbullying in Singapore: A longitudinal study. *Journal of Interpersonal Violence, 30*(16), 2831–2857. https://doi.org/10.1177/0886260514554295.

Choi, M. (2016). A concept analysis of digital citizenship for democratic citizenship education in the internet age. *Theory & Research in Social Education, 44*(4), 565–607. https://doi.org/10.1080/00933104.2016.1210549.

Council of Europe. (2019a). *Digital citizenship education handbook*. Council of Europe.

Council of Europe. (2019b). *Digital citizenship and your child: What every parent needs to know and do*. Council of Europe. https://edoc.coe.int/en/human-rights-democratic-citizenship-and-interculturalism/7865-digital-citizenship-and-your-child-what-every-parent-needs-to-know-and-do.html.

Cummings, C., & O'Neil, T. (2015). *Do digital information and communications technologies increase the voice and influence of women and girls. A rapid review of the evidence*. Overseas Development Institute. https://assets.publishing.service.gov.uk/media/57a08971e5274a31e00000ac/Rapid_Review_March_2015.pdf.

CyberSecurity Malaysia. (2024). *CyberSAFE Malaysia*. https://www.cybersafe.my/en/.

Department of Basic Education. (2021). *DBE and Google enter into partnership to fight cybercrimes targeted at school-going children*. https://www.education.gov.za/ArchivedDocuments/ArchivedArticles/DBE-Google-partnership-to-fight-cybercrimes-0624.aspx.

Department of Education, Republic of the Philippines. (n.d.). *#BeCyberSafe project*. https://www.deped.gov.ph/alternative-learning-system/resources/downloads/becybersafe/.

Department of Information and Communications Technology. (n.d.). *Department of Information and Communications Technology*. https://dict.gov.ph.

Dixon, S. J. (2022, July 13). *UK: Harassment experienced online 2022*. Statista. https://www.statista.com/statistics/1319815/uk-online-abuse-experienced/.

eRaksha Portal. (2023). *eRaksha portal*. https://www.eraksha.net.

European Commission. (2024). *6.8 Media literacy and safe use of new media—Germany*. National Policies Platform. https://national-policies.eacea.ec.europa.eu/youthwiki/chapters/germany/68-media-literacy-and-safe-use-of-new-media.

European Commission/EACEA/Eurydice. (2019). *Digital education at school in Europe*. Publications Office of the European Union. https://op.europa.eu/en/publication-detail/-/publication/7c527b6b-6876-11ea-b735-01aa75ed71a1/language-en.

Eurydice. (2018, September 5). *Digital skills enter into Sweden schools*. European Commission. https://eurydice.eacea.ec.europa.eu/news/digital-skills-enter-sweden-schools.

References | 211

Feng, J. (2023, March 29). *Cyberbullying in China finds victims in all corners.* The China Project. https://thechinaproject.com/2023/03/29/cyberbullying-in-china-finds-victims-in-all-corners/.

Frau-Meigs, D., O'Neill, B., Soriani, A., & Tomé, V. (2017). *Digital citizenship education: Overview and new perspectives.* Council of Europe. https://www.coe.int/en/web/digital-citizenship-education/newsroom/-/asset_publisher/BeRMYvLEwEdD/content/digital-citizenship-education-overview-and-new-perspectives.

Globe Telecom. (n.d.). *Digital Thumbprint Program: Creating a safer online environment.* https://www.globe.com.ph/about-us/sustainability/learning/digital-thumbprint#gref.

Information Commissioner's Office. (2022). *Age appropriate design: A code of practice for online services.* https://ico.org.uk/media/for-organisations/uk-gdpr-guidance-and-resources/childrens-information/childrens-code-guidance-and-resources/age-appropriate-design-a-code-of-practice-for-online-services-2-1.pdf.

International Society for Technology in Education. (n.d.). *ISTE.* https://iste.org.

Internet Matters. (2023, July). *Impact report 2022-23.* https://www.internetmatters.org/wp-content/uploads/2023/07/Internet-Matters-Impact-Report-2022-23-July-2023.pdf.

Kaspersky. (2021, December 2). *Study finds 50% of parents use parental control apps.* https://usa.kaspersky.com/about/press-releases/study-finds-50-of-parents-use-parental-control-apps.

Kelly, S. M. (2024, February 13). *Outside the US, teens' social media experiences are more tightly controlled.* CNN. https://www.cnn.com/2024/02/13/tech/social-media-regulation-outside-us/index.html.

Korea Communications Commission. (2023, April 7). *Four out of 10 teenagers have experienced cyberbullying, one more person than last year.* https://www.kcc.go.kr/user.do?mode=view&page=E04010000&dc=E04010000&boardId=1058&cp=5&searchKey=ALL&searchVal=wi&boardSeq=54874.

Kumpulainen, K., Kajamaa, A., Erstad, O., Mäkitalo, Å., Drotner, K., & Jakobsdóttir, S. (2022). *Nordic childhoods in the digital age: Insights into contemporary research on communication, learning and education* (p. 243). Taylor & Francis.

Lansford, J. E. (2022). Annual research review: Cross-cultural similarities and differences in parenting. *Journal of Child Psychology and Psychiatry, and Allied Disciplines, 63*(4), 466–479. https://doi.org/10.1111/jcpp.13539.

Lee, S. H. (2016). Cyberbullying in Eastern countries: Focusing on South Korea and other Eastern cultures. In R. Navarro, S. Yubero, & E. Larrañaga (Eds.), *Cyberbullying across the globe: Gender, family, and mental health* (pp. 149–167). https://link.springer.com/chapter/10.1007/978-3-319-25552-1_8.

Livingstone, S., & Helsper, E. J. (2008). Parental mediation of children's internet use. *Journal of Broadcasting & Electronic Media, 52*(4), 581–599. https://doi.org/10.1080/08838150802437396.

Media Literacy Council. (2024). *Media Literacy Council.* https://www.mlc.sg/programmes/.

Mesch, G. S. (2009). Parental mediation, online activities, and cyberbullying. *Cyberpsychology & Behavior, 12*(4), 387–393. https://doi.org/10.1089/cpb.2009.0068.

Ministry of Education, Culture, Sports, Science and Technology. (2017, March). *Guidelines for investigations on serious situations of bullying.* https://www.mext.go.jp/en/policy/education/elsec/title02/detail02/__icsFiles/afieldfile/2020/06/05/20200605-mxt_kouhou02-02.pdf.

Murakawa, M. (2022, October 8). *FOCUS: Japanese parents urged to set boundaries on kids' internet usage.* Kyodo News. https://english.kyodonews.net/news/2022/10/b231a448b84e-focus-japanese-parents-urged-to-set-boundaries-on-kids-internet-usage.html.

National Center for Youth Internet Addiction Treatment. (2020). *Program overview.* https://nyit.or.kr/user/index.asp.

Ofcom. (2022). *Children and parents: Media use and attitudes report 2022.* https://www.ofcom.org.uk/siteassets/resources/documents/research-and-data/media-literacy-research/children/childrens-media-use-and-attitudes-2022/childrens-media-use-and-attitudes-report-2022.pdf.

Özgür, H. (2016). The relationship between Internet parenting styles and Internet usage of children and adolescents. *Computers in Human Behavior, 60,* 411–424. https://doi.org/10.1016/j.chb.2016.02.081.

Paradigm Initiative. (n.d.). *Connecting African youth: Digital opportunities and digital rights for all.* https://paradigmhq.org.

Ranjith, P. J., Vranda, M. N., & Kishore, M. T. (2023). Predictors, prevalence, and patterns of cyberbullying among school-going children and adolescents. *Indian Journal of Psychiatry, 65*(7), 720–728. https://doi.org/10.4103/indianjpsychiatry.indianjpsychiatry_313_23.

References | 213

Richardson, J., & Samara, V. (2023a, December). *Digi-nauts teachers' guide.* Council of Europe. https://rm.coe.int/digi-nauts-teachers-guide-eng/1680aeca00.

Richardson, W., & Samara, A. (2023b, October). *Easy steps for educators.* Council of Europe. https://rm.coe.int/prems-119723-dce-leaflet-easy-steps-for-educators-eng/1680ace5c0.

Robb, M. B., Bay, W., & Vennegaard, T. (2019). *The new normal: Parents, teens, and mobile devices in Mexico.* San Francisco, CA: Common Sense. https://assets.uscannenberg.org/docs/new-normal/new-normal-full-report-mexico-english-2019.pdf.

Rovenstine, R. (2024, January 24). *Cyberbullying statistics 2024.* The Checkup by SingleCare. https://www.singlecare.com/blog/news/cyberbullying-statistics/.

Safernet. (n.d.). *Safernet Brazil.* https://new.safernet.org.br.

Sas, A. (2024, June 4). *Parental control over children using the internet in Poland 2022.* Statista. https://www.statista.com/statistics/1027696/poland-parental-control-over-internet-use/.

Sas, A. (2024, March 13). *Types of cyberbullying experienced by children in Poland 2020–2021.* Statista. https://www.statista.com/statistics/1274276/poland-cyberbullying-experienced-by-children/.

Singh, H. (2021). Building effective blended learning programs. In *Challenges and opportunities for the global implementation of e-learning frameworks* (pp. 15–23). IGI Global.

Statista Research Department. (2023, November 2). *Number of cyberbullying incidents among students reported by schools in Japan in fiscal year 2022, by school level.* Statista. https://www.statista.com/statistics/1303058/japan-number-reported-cyberbullying-cases-schools-by-school-level/.

ThaiSafe. (n.d.). *ThaiSafe.* https://thaisafe.net.

UNESCO Office Bangkok and Regional Bureau for Education in Asia and the Pacific. (2023). *Digital citizenship in Asia-Pacific: Translating competencies for teacher innovation and student resilience.* UNESCO. https://doi.org/10.54675/NNVF6123.

Van Deursen, A. J., & Van Dijk, J. A. (2014). The digital divide shifts to differences in usage. *New Media & Society, 16*(3), 507–526. https://doi.org/10.1177/1461444813487959.

Vogels, E. A. (2022, December 15). *Teens and cyberbullying 2022*. Pew Research Center. https://www.pewresearch.org/internet/2022/12/15/teens-and-cyberbullying-2022/.

Yoshida, R., & Bussey, K. (2011). Mother–child and father–child interactions in Japanese families. *Parenting: Science and Practice*, *11*(2–3), 201–220. https://doi.org/10.1080/15295192.2011.585564.

Zhu, X., Deng, C., & Bai, W. (2023). Parental control and adolescent internet addiction: the moderating effect of parent–child relationships. *Frontiers in Public Health*, *11*, 1190534. https://doi.org/10.3389/fpubh.2023.1190534.

Subject Index

Note: Page numbers in *italics* and **bold** refers to figures and tables respectively

a
accessibility, **9**
active co-viewing, **37**
active mediation, 39, **103**, 109
active social media use, 10, 47
addiction-like tendencies, 52
addictive phone use, 56, 117
adolescence
    addicted to gaming, 122
    effects of social media use on adolescent mental health, 50
    older adolescents, 51
    peer relationships in, 5–7
adverse childhood experiences (ACEs), 152
advertisements, negative content through, 30
American Academy of Child and Adolescent Psychiatry (AACAP), 31
American Academy of Pediatrics (AAP), 31, 117
    Family Media Plan, 110–111
American Psychological Association (APA), 99, 121, 167
Americans with Disabilities Act, 181
anonymity, **9**, **77**
anti-bullying laws, 160
asynchronicity, **9**, 10, **77**
attachment style, 1–2
Attention-Deficit/Hyperactivity Disorder (ADHD), 122
authoritarian parents, 96, 97, 198
authoritative parents, 96–97, 98
Autism Spectrum Disorder (ASD), 122

b
Bark company, 111
body mass index (BMI), 55
body scan meditation, 150

Cyberbullying: Helping Children Navigate Digital Technology and Social Media, First Edition. Stephanie Fredrick, et al.
© 2025 John Wiley & Sons, Inc. Published 2025 by John Wiley & Sons, Inc.

breathing exercise, 150
bullying
   characteristics of, 68
   experiencing bullying by teacher, 161
   forms of, 1, **13**, 68
   peer relationships and, 11–14
   traditional, 67
bystander intervention strategies
   child in, 168–169
   for cyberbullying, **105**
   support youth to engaging in, 104–105

C

Centers for Disease Control and Prevention (CDC), 73
child/childhood/children
   building positive peer relationships, 95–99
   bystander of cyberbullying, 168–169
   child development, digital media use effects on, 34–36
   cyberbullying others, 167–168
   digital media use, 28–32
   in Nordic countries, 197
   parental engagement in active mediation, 102–104
   parent monitoring digital media use, 109–110
   peer relationships in, 4–5
   pornography, 187
   promoting healthy online use, 100–109
   promoting safe media use, 99
   supporting social-emotional competencies, 95–99
   well-being, 167
Childrenandscreens.org, 111
Children's Online Privacy Protection Act of 1998 (COPPA), 107
civil law regarding cyberbullying, 183–185
Civil Rights Act of 1964, 181
classroom-wide mindfulness programs, 150–151
Cognitive Behavioral Intervention for Trauma in Schools (CBITS), 152
cognitive behavior therapy (CBT), 128
cognitive behavior therapy internet addiction (CBT-IA), 129
Common Sense Education, 141
Common Sense Media, 28–30, 46, 48, 52–53, 111
comprehensive digital citizenship education, 136
co-playing, 37, **37**
co-rumination, 6
co-use media, 101
co-using, 37, **37**
co-viewing, 37
criminal cyberbullying behaviors, 186–191
cross-sectional studies, 32, **33**
cyberbullying, **13**, 67, 68, 73–75
   characteristics of, 68
   civil law regarding, 183–185
   digital self-harm, 85–88
   factors impact youth development, *80*
   features of online disinhibition and associations with, **77–78**

Subject Index | 217

forms of, 70, **71–72**
global trends of, 195–199
laws and policies on internet and device use, 199
peer relationships and, 11–14
practical recommendations for parents, **202–204**
risk and protective factors, 79–86
state laws and school district policies for, 181–183
youth engagement in, 75–79
Cyberbullying Research Center, 70, 73, 111–112, 189
cyberflashing, **72**
cyberstalking, **71**

d

denigration, **71**
Diagnostic and Statistical Manual of Mental Disorders (DSM-5-TR), 121
dialectical behavior therapy (DBT), 129
Differential Susceptibility to Media Effects Model (DSMM), 52
digital citizenship, 81, 84, 183
digital citizenship education (DCE), 195, **205**
across Globe, 199–200
in Asia, 204–208, 206–207
in Europe, 200–201
in Global South, 204–208, **208**
Digital Citizenship Programs (DCPs), 135, 140
digital media, 10, 24–28, **25**
benefits of, 58
effects on child development, 34–36
media multi-tasking, 46
negative effects of, 28
parent media practices and joint media engagement, 36–39
recommendations by age, **31**
research methods and terminology, 32, **33–34**
use during childhood, 23
and youth, 50–58
digital self-harm, **72**, 85–88, **87**, 122–123, 130
digital technology, 24
evolution of, 23, 24–28
resources for parents and educators, 110–112
role in peer relationships, 8–11
setting rules about, 107–109, **108**
disinhibition, 68, 75
dose-response effect, 74

e

Ecological Systems Theory, 80
Education Amendments of 1972, 181, 184
educators
partner with families, 169–173
resources for, 110–112
Entertainment Software Rating Board, 26
E-reading, **25**
exclusion, **71**
experimental study, 32, **33**

f

Facebook, 23, 27, 47, 60, 196
Family Educational Rights and Privacy Act of 1974, 171
fear of missing out (FOMO), 55

Federal Bureau of Investigation (FBI), 191
federal laws for harassment, 179–181
Fictitious Online Victimization (FOV), 122
Fizz app, 70
flaming, **72**
Florida Department of Education (FDOE), 163
free and appropriate education (FAPE), 180

g
gaming
    affects youth academic performance, 56
    responding to problematic social media use and, 126–128
    youth addiction to, 55, 121–122
gap hypothesis, 57
Goldilocks Hypothesis, 51–52

h
Happyfeed app, 102
happy slapping, **72**
harassment, federal laws for, 179–181
hate crime, 187

i
impersonation/identity theft, **71**
indirect bullying. *see* relational bullying
Individuals with Disabilities Education Act (IDEA), 180
infancy
    digital media use, 28–32
    peer relationships, 2–4

information and communication technologies (ICT), 68
Instagram, 8, 27, 45, 53, 59
instant message (IM), 26
international digital citizenship and parenting practices, 196–199
Internet Gaming Disorder (IGD), 121, 128
Internetmatters.org, 112
internet parenting, 197, 198
invisibility, **77**

j
joint attention, 2
joint media engagement, 36–39, *37*, *38*

l
LGBTQ+ adolescents, social media and, 11, 53, 58, 87
longitudinal studies, 32, **33**

m
Maryland Age-Appropriate Design Code Act, 49
Mental Health America, 167
meta-analyses, 32, 34, 35
mindfulness, 150–151
Minecraft, 30
minimization of authority, **78**
Ministry of Education, Culture, Sports, Science, and Technology (MEXT), **206**
mobile media, 25
Multi-Tiered System of Support (MTSS), 137–138
MySpace, 26–27

n

National Bullying Prevention Center, 166
National Center for Missing & Exploited Children (NCMEC), 191
negative parenting practices, 98
negative social media-related behaviors, 52
Netflix, 29, 102
Netsmartz, 112

o

online communication
   adolescents in, 8
   features and activity, 9
   sexting and, 187
online disinhibition, 75–76, **77–78**
online gaming, 1, 10, 45, 177
online grooming, 190
online harassment, **71**
online predators, 179, 190–191
online videos, **25**

p

parent(ing)
   encouraging children's self-esteem, 7
   guidance by grade level, **142–146**
   important in children skills development, 3
   media practices, 36–39
   phubbing, 99
   resources for, 110–112
   role in preventing cyberbullying, 136–137
   styles, 96–97, 198–199
   supervision tools, 104
parent–child relationship, attachment style based on, 1–2
parent–teacher association (PTA), 153
passive co-viewing, **37**
passive social media use, 47
peer relationships, 2
   in adolescence, 5–7
   bullying and cyberbullying, 11–14
   digital technology role in, 8–11
   in early childhood, 2–4
   in infancy, 2–4
   in late childhood, 4–5
   in middle childhood, 4–5
   positive, 95–99
   in toddlerhood, 2–4
permanence, **9**
permissive parent, 96, 97
personally identifiable information (PII), 171
Pew Research Center, 31, 46, 73
photoshopping, **71**
physical bullying, **13**
positive behavior intervention support (PBIS), 135, 147–149, 183
positive parenting strategies, 98
posttraumatic stress disorder (PTSD), 152
preteen, 45
   digital media use among, 45–47
   effects of digital media use, 49–50
   smartphone use, 48–49
problematic internet use (PIU), 117, 129
problematic online behavior, 118, 128–130, 179–191
psychopharmacology, 129

r

randomized control trials (RCTs), 32
Rehabilitation Act of 1973, 180
relational bullying, **13**
relationship skills in digital world, **145**, 146–147
responsible decision-making in digital world, **144**
restorative justice approaches, 135, 151–152
Roblox, 30, 39

s

school
  in cyberbullying prevention, 136–137
  district policies for cyberbullying, 181–183
  districts intervening, 185, **186**
  in preventing cyberbullying and online aggressive behavior, 135
  school-based bullying prevention, 149
  school-wide digital citizenship programs, 138–147, **142**
  school-wide mindfulness programs, 150–151
  using positive behavior intervention support, 147–149
school–family partnership
  child is bystander of cyberbullying, 168–169
  child is cyberbullying others, 167–168
  communicating with school, 159
  educators partnering with families, 169–173
  experience bullying after reporting, 165–167
  knowledge about sharing information, 161–163
  parent's expectations from school, 163–165
  reporting bullying at school, 160–161
Second Step Middle School Program, 139
self-absorption, **78**
self-awareness in digital world, 141, **142**
self-management in digital world, 141, **143**
sensitivity, 3
sexting, 187–190
sextortion, 188
sexual relationships, 7
shared decision-making, 171–173
Sidechat app, 70
sleep displacement theory, 54
sleep disruption, 54
smartphone
  deciding to giving child, 106–107
  problematic content access, 53
  setting limits for using, 105
  use among preteens and teens, 48–49
Snapchat, 8, 27, 30, 45, 46, 53
social and emotional learning (SEL), 135, 138–147, 183
social awareness in digital world, **146**, 147
social bullying. *see* relational bullying

Subject Index | 221

social-emotional competence, 95–99
social-emotional skills, 23, 81
social media, 25
   addiction, 117
   cyberbullying and, 69, 70
   model responsible behavior on, 99
   problematic, 52
   responding to problematic, 126–128
stalking, 187
Stop Addictive Feeds Exploitation (SAFE) For Kids Act, 49
stop–walk–talk strategies, 148, 149
systematic reviews, 32, **34**

t

tagging, **71**
Take It Down service, 191
teenage/teens, 45
   affects of online communication, 8
   benefits of digital media use for, 58–59
   bullying and, 5
   effects of digital media use, 45–47, 49–58
   online gaming and, 10
   smartphone use, 48–49
   TikTok commonly used by, 54
television, **25**
TikTok, 8, 27, 30, 45, 46, 48, 53, 58, 59, 107
time displacement, 57
toxic disinhibition, 75–76
traditional bullying, 67–68
traditional media, 24, 54. *see also* digital media
trauma-informed programs, 135, 152–153
trickery/outing, **72**
trolling, **72**
Twitter, 27

u

University of North Carolina (UNC), 70

v

verbal bullying, **13**
video games, **25**, 26

w

"Wait Until 8th" movement, 106, 112
warning signs, 190, 118–123
Whisper app, 70

y

Yik Yak app, 70
youth
   academic performance, digital media use and, 56–58
   addiction to gaming, 121–122
   engagement in cyberbullying, 75–79
   engaging in bystander intervention, 104–105
   experiencing cyberbullying, 74
   mental health, digital media use and, 50–54
   physical health, digital media use and, 54–56
   with social anxiety, 10
YouTube, 30, 45, 46